WHAT COLOR
IS YOUR
PARACHUTE?

"I DON'T HAVE A PARACHUTE OF ANY COLOR."

RICHARD N. BOLLES

WHAT COLOR IS YOUR PARACHUTE?

2020

A PRACTICAL MANUAL FOR JOB-HUNTERS AND CAREER-CHANGERS

TEN SPEED PRESS
California | New York

PUBLISHER'S NOTE
This publication is designed to provide accurate and authoritative information in regard to the subject matter covered. It is sold with the understanding that the publisher is not engaged in rendering professional career services. If expert assistance is required, the service of the appropriate professional should be sought.

Published in the United States by Ten Speed Press, an imprint of Random House, a division of Penguin Random House LLC, New York.
www.tenspeed.com

Ten Speed Press and the Ten Speed Press colophon are registered trademarks of Penguin Random House LLC.

The drawings on pages 63, 73, and 211 are by Steven M. Johnson, author of *What the World Needs Now*. Meeting icon on pages 41 and 45 by Björn Andersson, Workspace icon on pages 41 and 56 by Universal Icons, Help icon on pages 41 and 60 by Luis Prado, Dawn icon (slightly altered) on pages 41 and 82 by Stephen Plaster, Brain icon on pages 41, 84, and 88 by Wes Breazell, Personal finance icon on pages 41 and 98 by Gregor Črešnar, Hand icon on page 62 by Chameleon Design, Stopwatch icon on page 62 by Nick Holroyd, Guitar icon on page 84 by Hum, Stethoscope icon on page 84 by Ralf Schmitzer, Lightbulb icon on page 84 by AB, Scale icon on page 84 by Edward Boatman, Heart icon on page 84 by Maria Maldonado, Singing icon on page 84 by Creative Stall, Earth icon on page 84 by João Proença, Praying icon on page 84 by Cristiano Zoucas, Restroom icon on page 84 by lipi, from thenounproject.com. Illustration on page 138 by Beverly Anderson.

Trade Paperback ISBN: 978-1-9848-5656-2
Hardcover ISBN: 978-1-9848-5657-9
eBook ISBN: 978-1-9848-5658-6
ISSN: 8755-4658

Printed in the United States of America

Cover design by Leona Legarte

10 9 8 7 6 5 4 3 2 1

Revised Edition

The wonderful actress Anne Bancroft (1931–2005)
was once loosely quoted as saying about
her husband, Mel Brooks,

My heart flutters whenever I hear his key
turning in the door, and I think to myself,
Oh goody, the party is about to begin.

That is exactly how I feel about my wife,
Marci Garcia Mendoza Bolles, God's angel
from the Philippines, with whom I fell deeply
in love, and married on August 22, 2004. What
an enchanted marriage this turned out to be!

Contents

The Orange Pages

Further resources to use in your journey, set in a different
color for easy access.

It was the best of times,
It was the worst of times,
It was the age of wisdom,
It was the age of foolishness,
It was the epoch of belief,
It was the epoch of incredulity,
It was the season of light,
It was the season of darkness,
It was the spring of hope,
It was the winter of despair,
We had everything before us,
We had nothing before us,
We were all going direct to heaven,
We were all going direct the other way . . .

— *Charles Dickens*

CHAPTER 1

It's a Whole New World for Job-Hunters

If you are trying to understand yourself better, and what you have to offer to the world, this book is for you.

If you are out of work, and want some practical help, this book is for you.

If you are trying to understand how the world, and particularly the world of work, really works these days, this book is for you.

If you've been out of work a long time, and think you're now permanently unemployable, this book is for you.

If you're on the edge of poverty these days, this book is for you.

If you've got some disability, this book is for you.

If you're trying to figure out a new career or your first career, this book is for you.

If you're going to college and you can't figure out what to major in, this book is for you.

If you are trying to figure out what you want to do next, with your life, this book is for you.

If you're just graduating from college and have to live with your parents 'cause you can't find any work, this book is for you.

If you're trying to figure out how to start your own business, this book is for you.

If you're a returning vet, this book is for you.

If you're facing retirement, and want to know what to do to support yourself, this book is for you.

A Two-Minute Crash Course on How Much Has Changed in the World of Work

Charles Dickens put it well: For some people, a lot of people, this is the best of times. But for others of us, this is the worst of times. The rules of the game have changed. Without notice. And without warning. Especially for the job-hunt, or for those trying to make a career-change.

The job-hunt is behaving differently now, than it used to. Things have changed. Dramatically.

The tipping point was 2008. We all know what happened then: *the so-called Great Recession*, the worst financial disaster since the Great Depression in 1929. We have recovered, but the landscape has been fundamentally altered, long term. What used to work, doesn't work anymore. What used to be easy, is now difficult or seemingly impossible. Our lament: *Out of work. Made up a resume. Sent it to all the places I'm s'posed to. Went to all the Internet "job-boards" and looked for vacancies in my field. Day after day. Week after week. Month after month. All of this worked the last time I went job-hunting. But now? Strikeout! Nothing!*

There are things we can do about this. Believe me, there are. That's what this book is all about. But before we change our strategies, we must know what we are up against. So, let's tick off—in rapid order—what's different since 2008:

1. Employers Changed, Job-Hunters Didn't

Year in and year out, when we are job-hunting, we tend to hunt in the same way we have for decades, regardless of whether the times are good or bad. Our hunt always depends on *resumes* (digital or printed), *agencies* (private or federal/state), and *ads* (online or off).

Employers don't. They don't stay the same. In good times they hunt one way. In bad times, they hunt another way. They adapt to the times.

What this means is that when times are good, employers often have difficulty filling their vacancies, so *they will typically cater to the job-hunters' preferences* in such a season. *We* like resumes, so *they* will take the trouble to solicit, look at, and read our resumes. *We* like job-postings, so *they* will post their vacancies where we can find them: on their own site or on job-boards, typically.

What we are not prepared for, is that when the economy turns tough (for us), and employers are finding it easier to fill a vacancy because there are many more unemployed to choose from, many—though not all—employers change their tactics. They will stop reading our resumes and stop posting their vacancies. So we can search *the old way* until we're blue in the face. But . . . *nothing*! Everything that used to work, doesn't work anymore. And we are baffled. It is like turning the key in our faithful car, but for the first time in five years the motor won't start.

We assume, of course, that the reason why nothing is working is that there are no jobs. It never occurs to us that there are indeed jobs—more than ten million of them a month, as we'll see in chapter 2—but that employers have changed *their* behavior when hunting for employees, and we have not caught up with, nor adapted to, employers' new behavior.

2. The Length of the Average Job-Hunt Has Increased Dramatically

From 1994 through 2008, roughly half of all unemployed job-seekers found jobs within five weeks. Only 10 percent of them were spending more than a year looking for work. After 2008, a far greater proportion—from 17 percent to 30 percent of all unemployed persons in the US—are spending more than a year looking for work. (According to a recent study, 30.1 percent are taking one to three months to find work; 13.9 percent are taking three to six months; and 20.8 percent are taking six months or longer.[1])

The chattering classes are speculating that this is creating a permanent underclass of The People Who Will Never Work Again—witness such headlines as *"The Long-Term Unemployed Are Doomed."* It ain't necessarily so, but certainly it can become true for *some* people. A lot depends on an individual's job-hunting skills. Are your job-hunting skills left over from the 1990s, or are they 2020's? In the workplace of today, that can be a matter of life or death.

---

1. Bureau of Labor Statistics, US Department of Labor, Table A-12, "Unemployed Persons by Duration of Unemployment," November 2018.

One thing we know for sure. A lot of people just don't want to be in the labor force, for the time being. They either are discouraged about the job market (that's 453,000 people) or may be outside the labor force for other reasons (1,225,000 people), such as school or family responsibilities, ill health, or transportation problems.[2]

3. The Length of Time the Average Job Lasts Has Decreased Dramatically

Of jobs that workers found between the time they were eighteen and twenty-four years old, 69 percent of those jobs lasted less than a year, and 93 percent lasted less than five years. *Ah, youth,* we think to ourselves. No, even at jobs that workers found between the time they were thirty-five and forty-four years old, 36 percent of those jobs lasted less than a year, and 75 percent lasted less than five years.[3]

The job market has changed, dramatically, since 2008. Full-time jobs (*usually defined as "working more than thirty-five hours a week"*) are getting harder and harder to find. The number of people with part-time jobs who really want to work full-time totals 5,060,000 currently.

So, a lot of job-hunters have redefined what they're looking for. Some *seek* shorter-lasting jobs, often just for the length of a project, or whatever.

There has been a dramatic increase in the number of temp or part-time jobs since 2008—a category that includes people who really only want short-term jobs, such as independent contractors, consultants, freelancers, and contract workers. This trend was first made famous by Daniel Pink in his 2001 book, *Free Agent Nation: How America's New Independent Workers Are Transforming the Way We Live.*[4] Currently, part-time workers in the US total 27,551,000 (that's 17.2 percent of all those employed, right now). It is predicted that in 2020, the number

---

2. Bureau of Labor Statistics, US Department of Labor, Table A-16, "Persons Not in the Labor Force and Multiple Jobholders by Sex, Not Seasonally Adjusted," November 2018.
3. Bureau of Labor Statistics, US Department of Labor, Economic News Release, "Number of Jobs Held, Labor Market Activity, and Earnings Growth Among the Youngest Baby Boomers: Results from a Longitudinal Survey Summary," March 31, 2017, www.bls.gov/news.release/nlsoy.nr0.htm.
4. Contract workers and "temp" workers are *legally* not the same category. An employer *can* prescribe what a temp worker does and how they do it. The very definition of independent contractor means the employer cannot. The two categories are alike only in the relative shortness of employment.

of part-timers, temp workers, free agents, freelancers—or whatever you want to call them—will number 60,000,000, or 40 percent of the US workforce. There are already 57 million freelancers in the US, as of this writing.[5]

The reason for this current rise in temporary hiring, as you've probably guessed, is employers' desire to keep their costs down—in the face of the global economy and online competition, hiring only when they need help, and letting the employee go as soon as they don't need that help, has become a budget-friendly strategy for employers across the country; and, indeed, across the world.[6] Not to mention that part-timers don't have to be paid any benefits, or granted paid vacation time. Indeed, 20 to 30 percent of those employed by the Fortune 100 now have short-term jobs, either as independent contractors or as temp workers, and this figure is predicted to rise to 50 percent during the next six years. Employers in the IT industry, in particular, are increasingly hiring someone just until a project is completed, rather than permanently hiring that person. Even in industries where people are hired allegedly for longer periods, employers are much more ready to cut the size of their workforce just as soon as things even begin to look bad. You thought you were being hired for a number of years, they said that, they meant that, but then fortunes change and suddenly you're back out on the street, job-hunting once again.

4. The Way Jobs Are Done Is Changing Dramatically

"Almost two-thirds of American households earn less money today than they did in 2002." That was the scary opening to an article in the *Washington Post* on March 6, 2015.[7] You want the worst-paying jobs these days? Oh, there are lots of lists. They include such jobs as food service workers, farm workers, cashiers, maids and housekeepers,

5. TJ McCue, "57 Million US Workers Are Part of the Gig Economy," Forbes.com, August 31, 2018, www.forbes.com/sites/tjmccue/2018/08/31/57-million-u-s-workers-are-part-of-the-gig-economy/#6920e72e7118.
6. And no, this is not due to the Affordable Care Act. See www.advisorperspectives.com/dshort/commentaries/Full-Time-vs-Part-Time-Employment.php.
7. Jim Tankersley, "The 21st Century Has Been Terrible for Working Americans," *Washington Post*, March 6, 2015, www.washingtonpost.com/blogs/wonkblog/wp/2015/03/06/the-21st-century-has-been-terrible-for-working-americans.

nannies and child-care workers, nursing home and psychiatric ward workers, textile and laundry workers, parking lot attendants, etc.

Let's dig deeper. Economists say that a decent middle-class job these days should be a stable, dependable job that pays between $40,000 and $80,000, annually. The jobs that used to pay *that* were manufacturing jobs. Now the fields that do are finance (as in Wall Street), corporate jobs, sales, and, above all else, health care. (It is expected the health sector will offer 21.8 million jobs by 2024. Why? Well, one reason is more and more people are living longer and dealing with the maladies of *aging*.)

Of greater importance is not that certain jobs are vanishing, while some jobs are flourishing, but that *all jobs are being reimagined.* The ability of each of us to survive in this new world depends on our understanding *how* the world, especially the world of work, is being reimagined. Things that never used to be connected are increasingly being reimagined as connected. This reimagining of our world as hyperconnected is not going to be implemented . . . some day, down the road. It is being implemented now. In fact, this has given rise to a whole new field called "the Internet of Things" or IoT for short—a term first coined in 1999 by Kevin Ashton. To quote one expert, the premise of the Internet of Things is that "all things, including every physical object, can be connected—making those objects intelligent, programmable, and capable of interacting with humans."[8] Experts predict 62 billion devices will be connected by the year 2024. That's less than four years away.

As the world reimagines itself without our consent, we are told—by raving futurists—that in the not-too-distant future, robots are going to take away all our work, thus making humans unnecessary to the future of this planet. Many believe that all jobs are going to be eliminated by technology. But when you press the experts—as I have—as to what percentage of jobs they think will be completely replaced by technology, they predict that only 5 percent, or at worse 19 percent, of current jobs in the US will be replaced by robotics, technology, and computer programs.

Alternatively, a Pew Research Center report on robotics in the future offers hope in that technology often creates new jobs while reducing

---

8. "Internet of Things Community," IEEE, www.ieee.org/membership-catalog/productdetail/ showProductDetailPage.html?product=CMYIOT736&N=&tcType=#.

old jobs. And technology can reduce the drudgery of many jobs, open-ing the opportunity for more interesting and innovative jobs.[9]

What robots and related technology will do is not eliminate all jobs, but rather tackle certain tasks within jobs. This means that most jobs are going to become a partnership—a partnership between Humans and Machines.

By "Machines" I mean all our inventions, such as computer pro-grams, Wi-Fi, the Internet, digital electronics, mobile computers (smart-phones), AI (artificial intelligence), integrated circuits and sensors, robots that learn and share that knowledge with other robots, tran-sistors, wearables, 3-D printers, a new generation of computer chips, processors, algorithms, actuators, voice and image recognition, soft-ware that analyzes facial expressions, as well as things—machines—that are able to talk to each other directly or through a centralized computer platform or hub. And so on. . . . In a nutshell, by "Machines" I intend to mean "anything we've invented." MIT scientists call this partnership "human-machine symbiosis." *Yikes!*

What happened to our jobs? you ask. Well, as we have seen, they are being reimagined as a partnership between People and Machines. Large parts of the world of work will not see or feel this reimagination until some years down the road; other parts are already seeing it, or will see it tomorrow. We must begin—now—to reimagine our own lives in the world of work, and get comfortable with the idea of future jobs as a partnership between People and Machines (loosely defined as I have).

So, we are going to have to learn new skills to survive in this reimagined world. We must begin by knowing ourselves better. Imagine you are hiking in a wilderness and find a strong running stream suddenly swirling around your feet; your first instinct would be to find something solid to stand on, before you get swept off your feet. In similar fashion, taking an inventory of yourself will give you that "something solid to stand on" in the midst of all this reimagining that is swirling around you. A good self-inventory can be found in this book, in chapters 4 and 5. Knowing who you are, what you like and do best,

9. Aaron Smith and Janna Anderson, "AI, Robotics, and the Future of Jobs," Pew Research Center, August 6, 2014, www.pewinternet.org/2014/08/06/future-of-jobs.

what kindles your brain, and what enables you to do your best work, has never been more important than in this reimagined workplace that is coming and is already here. Don't ignore this step.

Then we must ask ourselves, How will I fit in, in this reimagined world where jobs are increasingly becoming partnerships between People and Machines? We will have to reimagine our attitude toward robots, and start thinking of Machines (and particularly robots) as our friends, come to help us with certain tasks, not as an enemy come to steal our jobs away.

Once you've done the self-inventory I mentioned previously, you may well have thought of a field you would really like to be in, or a job you might really like to do. If so, get permission to "shadow" a worker for a day or two, to see what that job or field actually involves, in this reimagined world. Above all, become familiar with the basic actors on this stage, people and technology. These principal actors are going to be around for a long time.

5. Job-Hunting Is Increasingly Becoming a Repetitive Activity in the Lives of Many of Us

This is obviously because jobs don't last as long as they used to. So, even when we find a job now, we may be job-hunting again, sooner than we think. How often? In a study, released August 24, 2017, by the US Department of Labor, it was revealed that the average person in the US born between 1957 and 1964 held 11.9 jobs from when they were eighteen years old until they were fifty.[10] Job-hunting is no longer an optional exercise. It is a survival skill. This means the one thing in our life that we must get really skilled at, and become masters of, is the *new* job-hunt.

---

10. Bureau of Labor Statistics, US Department of Labor, Economic News Release, "Number of Jobs Held, Labor Market Activity, and Earnings Growth Among the Youngest Baby Boomers: Results from a Longitudinal Survey Summary," August 24, 2017, www.bls.gov/news.release/nlsoy.nr0.htm.

6. Job-Hunting Has Moved
More and More Online

From the earliest days of the Internet there have been employment websites, commonly called "job-boards," places where employers post vacancies that they are trying to fill. Thousands of job-boards now exist, including Indeed, Glassdoor, and LinkedIn.

Job-boards can be broken down into the following categories:

1. Mega job-boards and search engines that hunt for job vacancies— they scrub job-boards, companies, newspapers, or wherever, to find these. *Indeed* is the most famous (www.indeed.com). Proven.com provides a list of one hundred mega job-boards for a variety of industries (https://blog.proven.com/100-best-job-boards-to-find-niche-talent).

2. Niche job-boards, for job vacancies in particular fields or industries. If you want one hundred of them, try: www.good.co/blog /list-of-100-niche-job-boards.

3. Company job-boards, that run right on a company's website. Handy, if you know what companies you are particularly interested in. Information on how to research companies can be found at livecareer.com/career/advice/jobs/researching-companies-guide.

4. Job-boards for particular ages. Let us say you are a teen. There are job-boards just for you, such as http://readyjob.org/companies-hire-teens. Or say you are over fifty. There are sites such as www.seniorjobbank.org.

Job-boards, of course, aren't the only online sites useful to job-hunters or career-changers. As social media and other sites have become more and more popular—email, LinkedIn, Facebook, Twitter, Instagram, Pinterest, WhatsApp, Skype, YouTube, etc.—job-hunters and employers alike have figured out how to use them in the job-hunt. Now, ever-larger portions of the job-hunt can be done online. And on all kinds of devices. From computers to laptops to tablets to smartphones to wearables such as watches. It's all going increasingly mobile.

7. Increasingly Job-Hunters and Employers Speak Two Different Languages

What has gotten worse since 2008 is the fact that employers and job-hunters speak two entirely different languages, though often using the same words. Take the word *skills*. When we're job-hunting, you get turned down because—some employers say—"You don't have the skills we're looking for." You think they're referring to such things as *analyzing, researching, communicating,* etc. No, they really mean "experience," though they use the word *skills*. Sample employer memo: "We're looking for someone who has had five years of experience marketing software products to a demographic that is between the ages of twenty-four and thirty."

You should assume that the employers' world is like a foreign country; you must learn their language, and their customs, before you visit.

This is an idea from the authors of a book called *No One Is Unemployable.*[11] They suggested that when you approach the world of business for the first time, you should think of it as going to visit a foreign country; you know you're going to have to learn a whole new language, culture, and customs there. Same with the job market. When we are out of work we must now start to think like an employer, learn how employers prefer to look for employees, and figure out how to change our own job-hunting strategies so as to conform to theirs. In other words, *adapt to the employers' preferences.*

So, let's take a look at that world of the employer. Don't kid yourself, employers don't have all the power in the hiring game, but they do have an impressive amount. This explains why parts of the whole job-hunting system in this country will drive you nuts. It wasn't built for you or me. It was built by and for *them*. And they live in a world different from yours and mine, inside their head. (That's why I said *foreign* country!) This results in the following six contrasts:

You want the job market to be a hiring game. But the employer regards it as an elimination game—until the very last phase. Larger companies or organizations are looking at that huge stack of resumes

---

11. By Debra Angel MacDougall and Elisabeth Harney Sanders-Park. The book was published by Worknet Training Services in 1997. A more recent book of theirs is titled *The 6 Reasons You'll Get the Job: What Employers Look for—Whether They Know It or Not,* published in 2010 by Prentice Hall.

on their desks, with a view—first of all—to finding out who they can eliminate. Eventually, they want to get it down to the "last person standing." On average, a vacancy receives between 118 and 250 responses or resumes. On average, employers want to interview only 5.4 candidates. Getting that stack of 118 to 250 down to 5.4 is the employer's first preoccupation.

You want the employer to be taking lots of initiative toward finding you, and when they are desperate they will (*especially if you have applied math skills!*). Some HR departments will spend hours and days combing the Internet looking for the right person. But generally speaking, the employer prefers that it be you who takes the initiative, toward finding them.

In being considered for a job, you want your solid past performance (summarized on your written resume) to be all that gets weighed, but the employer weighs your whole behavior, including your social media behavior as they glimpse it from their first interaction with you.

You want the employer to acknowledge receipt of your resume— particularly if you post it right on their website, but the employer generally feels too swamped with other things to have time to do that, so only 45 percent do. A majority of employers, 55 percent, for legal and other reasons, do not. Now that you know this, don't take it personally.

You want employers to save your job-hunt by increasing their hiring, and you want the government to give them incentives to do so. Unhappily, employers tend to wait to hire until they see an increased demand for their products or services. In the meantime, most do not much care for government incentives to hire, because they know such incentives always have a time limit, and once they expire, that employer will be on the hook to continue the subsidy out of their own pocket.

You want the employer to hunt for you the same way you are hunting for them. Actually, the ways you hunt for each other are not just different; *they are exactly the opposite*, as you can see in the diagram on page 12.

Why are these strategies so contrary to each other? Values. Job-hunters and employers have completely different values, during their search.

Employers' main value/concern is risk.

Job-hunters' main value/concern is time.

MANY IF NOT MOST EMPLOYERS HUNT FOR JOB-HUNTERS IN THE EXACT OPPOSITE WAY FROM HOW MOST JOB-HUNTERS HUNT FOR THEM

The Way a Typical Employer Prefers to Fill a Vacancy (*in blue*)

1 / 6 From Within: Promotion of a full-time employee, or promotion of a present part-time employee, or hiring a former consultant for in-house or contract work, or hiring a former "temp" full-time. Employer's thoughts: *"I want to hire someone whose work I have already seen."* (A low-risk strategy for the employer.)

Implication for Job-Hunters: See if you can get hired as a temp, contract worker, or consultant at an organization you have chosen—aiming at a full-time position only later (or not at all).

2 / 5 Using Proof: Hiring an unknown job-hunter who brings proof of what he or she can do, with regard to the skills needed.

Implication for Job-Hunters: If you are a programmer, bring a program you have done—with its code; if you are a photographer, bring photos; if you are a counselor, bring a case study with you; etc.

3 / 4 Using a Best Friend or Business Colleague: Hiring someone whose work a trusted friend of yours has seen (perhaps they worked for him or her).

Implication for Job-Hunters: Find someone who knows the person-who-has-the-power-to-hire at your target organization, who also knows your work and will introduce you two.

4 / 3 Using an Agency They Trust: This may be a recruiter or search firm the employer has hired or a private employment agency—both of which have checked you out, on behalf of the employer.

5 / 2 Using an Ad They Have Placed (online or in newspapers, etc.).

6 / 1 Using a Resume: Even if the resume was unsolicited (*if the employer is desperate*).

The Way a Typical Job-Hunter Prefers to Fill a Vacancy (*in black*)

Let me explain.

We who are job-hunters want strategies that will enable us to cover as much of the job market as possible, in the least amount of time. So, our value is *time*. Our chosen vehicle is a resume. We want to write it, or have it written for us, then be able to spread it across a vast landscape, with a click of the mouse.

The employer's chief value, on the other hand, concerns **risk**. The employer wants to hire with the lowest possible risk. I mean *the risk that this hire won't work out*. Twenty-seven percent of US employers surveyed said that a bad hire cost their company more than $50,000.[12] The cost isn't only financial. A bad hire can hurt employee morale, threaten teamwork and productivity, and even damage an organization's reputation.[13] To avoid this, their chosen vehicle is hiring from within, or as close to *within* as possible, people whose work ethic and performance they—or someone they trust—have already observed, and tested, as explained in the chart on the facing page.

The Remedy

No, it's not all bad news. Think of these, instead, as *challenges*.

Sure, the workplace has changed dramatically since 2008.

And consequently, the job-hunt has changed dramatically since 2008.

Still, there is Hope. It's not that there are no jobs (see chapter 2). It's just that the old way you used to hunt for them doesn't work very well anymore.

In today's world, he or she who gets hired is not necessarily the one who can do that job best; but, the one who knows the most about how to get hired.

If you learn new advanced job-hunting skills, you can not only survive. You can thrive. The rest of this book is devoted to showing you exactly how to do just that.

---

12. Rachel Gillett, "Infographic: How Much a Bad Hire Will Actually Cost You," *Fast Company*, April 8, 2014, www.fastcompany.com/3028628/work-smart/infographic-how-much-a-bad-hire-will-actually-cost-you (http://tinyurl.com/ks4sbzf).
13. Brett McIntyre, "How Much Does a Bad Hire Really Cost?" Business 2 Community, August 21, 2018, www.business2community.com/human-resources/how-much-does-a-bad-hire-really-cost-02108605.

I am not lucky. You know what I am?
I am smart, I am talented, I take advantage
of the opportunities that come my way,
and I work really, really hard. Don't call me lucky.
Call me a badass.

—*Shonda Rhimes*

CHAPTER 2

There Are More Than Ten Million Vacancies Available Each Month

The Job-Hunt Hasn't Changed in Its Essence Since 2008

Yes, I know this contradicts what I said in the first chapter. But there you have it. Both things are true: the job-hunt has changed dramatically since 2008, yet the job-hunt hasn't really changed at all since 2008.

How can they both be true? The answer lies in the distinction between essence and surface behavior or form.

The *surface behavior* or *form* of the job-hunt is always changing, often dramatically, as we saw in the first chapter. This, because job-hunt *behavior* at any given time is determined by the current technology. And when a new technology arises—think *computers*, think *Internet*, think *smartphone*, think *digital* resumes, think *the Internet of Things*—job-hunting alters. On the surface.

But beneath all surface change, the *essence* of the job-hunt never really changes. Job-hunting is all about human nature, and in its essence is most like the human activity that we call *dating*. Both shake down to: "Do you like me?" *and* "Do I like you?" If the answer to both is "Yes," then it's "Do you want to try goin' steady?" In dating. In job-hunting. So, if you focus on essence rather than form, the job-hunt remains essentially constant year after year.

First question: *"Do you like me?"* In the job-interview that means "Hey employer, you are looking for someone who can do this thing that you want done, and can get along with you and the other people here. So, given that, do you like me?"

Second question: *"Do I like you?"* In the job-interview that means "Are you going to give me a work environment that will enable me to be at my most productive and most effective level, where I feel useful and appreciated, and can make a difference?"

Both questions are equally important, and permissible to ask. But that second question needs to be emphasized, underlined, and written in large letters because when we are job-hunting we are so prone to think all power belongs to employers. They have every right to ask their question. We have no right to ask ours—or so street wisdom claims.

But wait a minute. Meditate on why we have the word *quit* in our vocabulary, as in *"I quit,"* and you will realize that the job-hunt *and job* are always a matter of the job-hunter or worker asking themselves, "Do I like you?" And if you conclude, "No I don't really like you," or "I really hate it here," then eventually you quit.

Your big decision is, Do I wait three years to find out the answer to my question, or do I try to find it out now, during the job-hunt in general, during the job-interview in particular?

The job-hunt is a conversation—a two-way conversation—wherein your opinion matters as much as the employer's. That always has been true. Always will be.

There Are Always
Jobs Out There

If you're currently out of work, and looking for a job, you have every reason in the world to think you are up against overwhelming forces and the situation you face is rather hopeless. You may have struck out, again and again. The media is always filled with bad news about the unemployed. But the situation you face is not hopeless.

You are not powerless during the job-hunt. Maybe the employer has an overwhelming amount of power in the whole job-hunt. But the employer does not hold all the cards.

That is what never changes.

Of course, you will object, "Well, that may be true during normal times, but these ain't normal times. Even this long after the 2008 recession, good-paying jobs are still scarce. I cannot afford to be picky. *There are very few vacancies out there.*"

Where did we ever get *that* idea? From the media, that's where. Two reports come out each month in the US, about the state of the job market. One of those reports is usually hopeful. One of them is usually depressing. Both of them are put out by the federal government, in fact, by the same branch of the US government (the Bureau of Labor Statistics). The media invariably choose to publish, analyze, and lament only one of those two reports—the depressing one.

That report comes out on the first Friday of each month, with rare exceptions. It is typically called "news about the unemployment rate," though it is more accurate to think of it as "news of the *net change* in the size of the workforce in the US." Its technical name is the Current Population Survey (www.bls.gov/cps). Let's take a typical month, say, November 2018. It said only 155,000 jobs were added to the economy. With some 8,106,000 people wanting work that month—5,975,000 fully unemployed, and the rest, marginally attached, discouraged, or involuntary part-timers wanting full-time jobs—that was not good news.

But, there was that other report from the same department of the government. It comes out two months later. It's called JOLTS, which stands for Job Openings and Labor Turnover Survey (www.bls.gov/jlt). It said that during that same month of November 2018, 5,500,000 people found work, and even so, 6,052,000 vacancies remained unfilled at the end of that month.

You do the math. (*Okay, then, I will.*) That was more than 11,552,000 jobs available in the US during the month of November 2018. And this is typical, in the US, month in and month out.

What's going on here? Why such a difference between the two reports? Well, let me give you a parallel situation, on a much smaller scale.

Suppose I own a dress shop. You come in to visit me, and for fun you count the number of dresses I have in the shop. It turns out I have 100. You leave that day, and you don't return for a whole month. Upon your return, you count, again for fun, how many dresses I have in the shop now—one month later. It turns out I have 95. So you say to me, "Oh, I see you only sold 5 dresses this month. Poor you."

"No," I smile, "I added to the inventory during the month." "How many?" you ask. "50," I say.

You stop, and calculate: $100 + 50 - 95$. "Oh, so you actually sold 55 dresses this past month."

I say, "Right." 5 vs. 55. You get the first figure, if what you're looking for is *the net change* in the size of the inventory in my shop, with visits a month apart. You get quite a different figure if what you're looking for is *the actual change* in my inventory day by day throughout the entire month.

It's the same with the two US government reports. Not 5 vs. 55, but 313,000 vs. more than 11,552,000.

Of course, the question for us when we're out of work is, "If there are typically eleven million jobs available each month, why didn't I get one of them?" That's the subject of the rest of this book.

"Go and get your things," he said.
"Dreams mean work."
—*Paulo Coelho*

CHAPTER 3

The Best and Worst Ways to Look for Jobs

The Two Very Different Strategies for Finding a Job

There are two very different ways you can go about the job-hunt or a career-change. There's the way everyone tells us we should hunt for work. Because that's the way we've always done it. Because that's the only way we know. This strategy has a name. It's called *the Traditional Approach*. Most of us know how to do this, or can quickly learn. It doesn't demand much time. You begin with the so-called job market. You look at the ad postings by employers, online and off. You approach those companies that look the least bit interesting to you. Wait to see if you get any responses. At the same time, you slap together a resume. Post it. Or send out bushel baskets of resumes to mailing lists. If that doesn't turn up any job offer, send out another ton of resumes. Post your resume everywhere.

If this all works for you, great! (*But then, if it did, you probably wouldn't be reading this chapter, would you?*)

But, if it doesn't work (for you), the good news is that there is a radically different second way to hunt for work or a career-change. Let's call it *the Parachute Approach*.

Here you begin, not with the job market but with yourself. You figure out who you are, and among all your gifts which ones you most love to use. Then (and only then) you go looking for organizations

21

that match *You*. And you do not wait until they announce they have a vacancy. You approach them anyway, not through a resume but through *a person*, specifically a *bridge-person*—someone who knows *you* and also knows *them*, and therefore is a bridge between you two.

The opposite page has a detailed comparison of these two radically different strategies.

If you've tried as hard as you can to find a job, and nothing is working, stop looking for explanations. The remedy is staring you in the face: you need to *switch approaches.*[1] If you've been depending solely on *the Traditional Approach*—and it just isn't working this time—then you need to try using *the Parachute Approach*—as outlined in the right-hand column of the chart.

Sure, it's harder to use this approach.

Sure, it requires more of you. It's more work.

Sure, it asks you to do some hard thinking and reflect on who you are, and where you're going with your life.

But that is precisely its value. It's not just about jobs. It forces you to step back, and first think about your whole life. And what you want out of life. It begins with Who (are you) before considering What (shall I do).

Who precedes *What.*

These, then, are the two basic job-hunting or career-changing strategies that are at your command. *But the first strategy—the Traditional Approach—can be broken down further, into ten subcategories.*

Here are some comparative statistics for those ten. We'll start with the worst, and work our way up: from the ones with the poorest track record, to the ones with the best. (*Just remember, the figures here are not*

---

1. Here is a letter from a job-hunter who had great success:
   Before I read this book, I was depressed and lost in the futile job-hunt using Want Ads only. I did not receive even one phone call from any ad I answered, over a total of four months. I felt that I was the most useless person on earth. I am female, with a two-and-a-half-year-old daughter, a former professor in China, with no working experience at all in the US. We came here seven months ago because my husband had a job offer here.
      Then, on June 11 of last year, I saw your book in a local bookstore. Subsequently, I spent three weeks, ten hours a day except Sunday, reading every single word of your book and doing all of the flower petals in the Flower Exercise. After getting to know myself much better, I felt I was ready to try the job-hunt again. I used Parachute throughout as my guide, from the very beginning to the very end, namely, salary negotiation.
      In just two weeks I secured (you guessed it) two job offers, one of which I am taking, as it is an excellent job, with very good pay. It is (you guessed it again) a small company, with twenty or so employees. It is also a career-change: I was a professor of English; now I am to be a controller! I am so glad I believed your advice: there are jobs out there, and there are two types of employers out there, and truly there are! I hope you will be happy to hear my story.

	The Traditional Approach	The *Parachute* Approach
What you are looking for	A job.	A "dream job": one that uses your favorite skills and favorite fields or knowledges.
How you see yourself	As a "job-beggar."[2] You will be lucky to get them.	As a "resource." They will be lucky to get you.
Your basic plan	Look at job-boards for what is available.	Determine what job would interest and motivate you, before you start looking.
Your preparation	Do research to find out what the job market wants and what the "hot jobs" are. Your best weapon is your ability to "fit in."	Do homework on yourself, to figure out what you do best, AND most love to do. Your best weapon is your enthusiasm!
How you figure out which employers to approach	You wait for them to identify they have a vacancy.	Doing "informational interviews," you figure out which organizations most interest you—in light of your homework—even if they do not have an advertised vacancy at the time.
How you contact them	Through your resume.	Through a "bridge-person" (someone who knows you and also knows them).[3] Use LinkedIn to find them.
What the purpose of your resume is	To sell them on why you should be hired there.	To get a first interview with them.
What your main goal is if you get an interview	To sell them on why you should be hired there.	To get another interview there.
What you talk about in the interview	Yourself, your assets, your experience.	*Their* interests and needs; 50 percent of the time you let them ask the questions; 50 percent of the time you ask them the things *you* want to know about the place, and the job there, and how you can help.
What you're trying to find out	Do they want me?	Do I want them? (as well as "Do they want me?") Can I do the work I most love to do, here, and at the same time help them?
How you end the final interview there	You ask them: "When may I hope to hear from you?" (*You are leaving things hanging.*)	Determine the best way to convey your enthusiasm and ask about the hiring process. Could an offer be made that day? (You are seeking closure.)
What to do after getting the job, but before you start	Send a thank-you note. Then, "it's over." Rest, relax, and savor the successful end to your job-hunt.	Send a thank-you note. Then, keep on quietly looking. (Their offer may still fall through before you start, due to unforeseen developments there.)

2. I'm indebted to Daniel Porot for this term.
3. See page 136 for an explanation of this term.

exactly scientific. It's a mash *of actual studies I once saw, plus, where no stud-ies have ever been done, my own impressions over the past forty-five years of working with job-hunters or career-changers.*)

The Ten Best and Worst Traditional Approaches to Looking for a Job

1. Looking for employers' job-postings on the Internet. This method apparently works on average just **4 percent** of the time.[4] Yeah, it works for just four out of every one hundred who try it. You're somewhere between surprised and shocked at this finding? I was too.

   It *is* strange. If you're out of work, *everyone* will tell you the best way to look for a job is to look for employers' *job-postings* (vacancies)—either on the employer's own website (if the job-hunter or career-changer has a particular organization in mind); or on websites such as Monster, CareerBuilder, Indeed, Glassdoor, US.jobs, CareerArc, LinkedIn, Twitter, or Facebook; or even on non-job-sites such as the hugely popular Craigslist. The Internet is the place to look, they will tell you.

   The question is, are they right?

   The answer is: *well, that depends, because this is just part of the search process.*

   The anecdotal evidence is sometimes impressive. You will hear stories of job-hunters who have been tremendously success-ful in using the Internet to find a job. Examples:

   A job-seeker, a systems administrator in Taos, New Mexico, who wanted to move to San Francisco, posted his resume at 10 p.m. on a Monday night, on a San Francisco online site (it

---

4. The statistics I allude to, throughout this chapter, fluctuate somewhat, from year to year, from geographical region to region, from one field to another, from one city, town, or rural area to another. Their best value is how they compare to other job-hunting methods. That ratio tends to remain fairly constant, and predictable, year after year.

happened to be www.craigslist.org). By Wednesday morning he had more than seventy responses from employers.

Again, a marketing professional developed her resume following guidance she found on the Internet, posted it to two advertised positions she found there, and within seventy-two hours of posting her electronic resume, both firms contacted her, and she is now working for one of them.

And again: "Thanks to the Internet, I found what I believe to be the ideal job in [just] eight weeks—a great job with a great company and great opportunities."

The question is, are these stories just flukes, or is this a universal experience?

Sadly, it turns out that this job-search method actually doesn't work for very many who try it. Exception to this: If you are seeking a technical or computer-related job, an IT job, or a job in engineering, finances, or health care, the success rate rises, to around 10 percent. But for the other 12,741 job-titles that are in the *Dictionary of Occupational Titles*, at www.occupationalinfo.org, the success rate reportedly remains at just 4 percent.

2. Posting or mailing out your resume to employers. As you may have guessed from your own experience, this works at getting you a job (or, more accurately, at getting you an *interview* that leads to a job) only **7 percent** of the time, apparently. And that's assuming you're not just randomly sending your resume to any employer.

This comes as a shock to most job-hunters.

When you're unemployed, and job-hunting, or trying to change careers, *everyone* will tell you: a good resume will get you a job. It's virtually an article of faith among the unemployed (and their well-meaning helpers).

Why does everyone keep telling us this, when resumes in fact have such a miserable track record? Oh, you tell me. Why did   · everyone entrust their money to Bernie Madoff? Or why did so many people buy those incredibly risky financial instruments or mortgages that led to the Great Recession back in 2008? I don't know. I guess if you hear something often enough, and from enough different sources, you start to think it *must* be true.

Anyway, there it stands. Indisputable. The success rate of resumes is clearly no more than 7 percent. And I'm being generous with that estimate. One study suggested that only 1 out of 1,470 resumes actually resulted in a job. Another study found the figure to be even worse: 1 job offer for every 1,700 resumes floating around out there. Resumes are often a necessary part of the process, but randomly sending them out won't help.

By the way, once you post your resume on the Internet, it gets copied quickly by "spiders" from other sites, and you can never remove it completely from the Internet. There are reportedly now at least 40,000,000 resumes floating around out there in the ether, like lost ships on the Sargasso Sea. Yours among them. That can come back to haunt you if you ever fibbed (lied?) about anything, once a would-be employer Googles you, even years later.

3. Going to private employment agencies or search firms for help. This method apparently works somewhere between **5 percent** of the time, on up to **28 percent** (at best). These firms, also known as staffing agencies, talent agencies, and recruiting firms, used to place just office workers; now it's hard to think of a category of jobs they don't try to place, especially in large metropolitan areas. You can find these firms by Googling "employment agencies" with your location or employment field, such as "employment agencies in Austin, TX" or "employment agencies marketing careers." The wide variation in success rate (5 to 28 percent) is due to the fact that these agencies vary greatly in their staffing (ranging from *extremely competent* on down to *inept, or running a scam*). *But, at their best, agencies are four times more effective than just depending on your resume.* You can always check the agency through the Better Business Bureau (www.bbb.org) to see if any complaints have been filed.

4. Answering ads in professional or trade journals, appropriate to your field. This method apparently works only **7 percent** of the time. The method consists of looking at professional organizations in your profession or field, and answering any ads there that intrigue you. Some job-boards will be limited to members only, but the websites often contain articles about the job-search

for the profession. A directory of these associations and their journals can be found at www.directoryofassociations.com.

5. **Job-search support groups.** Job-search support groups can be found in virtually every community. While their job-hunting success rate is usually around **10 percent**, they can be valuable in providing emotional support and reducing your feelings of isolation.

Most support groups meet only once a week, and then for only one, two, or three hours, at best. Even so, they provide a community for the otherwise lonely job-hunter. This is a great gift. *No one should ever have to job-hunt all by themselves, if they can possibly avoid it.* We all need encouragement and support, along the way. And done well, as in the Rotary Club's Job-Search Support Group, in Cupertino, CA, they can enjoy a higher success rate than merely 10 percent. (Cupertino's is 50 percent, year after year, using this book as their guide.)

6. **Going to the state or federal employment office.** This method works **14 percent** of the time. You go to your local federal/ state unemployment service office (www.dol.gov/dol/location .htm) or to their nationwide CareerOneStop business centers (www.careeronestop.org) to get instructions on how to better job-hunt, and find job-leads. They are also a great resource for jobs in government: local, state, and federal.

7. **Going to places where employers pick up workers.** If you're a union member, particularly in the trades or construction, and you have access to a union hiring hall, this method will find you work, up to **22 percent** of the time.

What is not stated, however, is how long it may take to get a job at the hall, and how short-lived such a job may be. In the trades, it's often just a few days. Moreover, this is not a job-hunting method that is open to a very large percentage of job-hunters, at all. Only 6.4 percent of private sector employees are union members these days. (For employees in the public sector the comparable figure is 34.4 percent.[5])

---

5. Bureau of Labor Statistics, US Department of Labor, Economic News Release, "Union Members Summary," January 19, 2018, www.bls.gov/news.release/union2.nr0.htm.

If you're not a union member, there's something similar to union halls. That is, employers may pick up workers (called *day-laborers*) early in the morning on well-known street corners in your town or city (ask around). It's called *pickup work*, it's usually short term, usually yard work, or work that requires you to use your hands, usually paid to you in cash *that day*, and definitely *temp* work. But if you're not finding full-time work, as yet, this may be a stopgap approach that at least can bring in a little money.

8. **Participating in the gig economy/freelance work.** The modern-day version of "pickup work" is the so-called *gig economy, sharing economy,* or *access economy.* You can explore using your *home* (www.airbnb.com) or your 2005+ four-door *car* (either www.uber.com or www.lyft.com) or other things, even your driveway (www.justpark.com), to make some extra money. Other sites include dogvacay.com, taskrabbit.com, zaaarly.com, poshmark .com, and etsy.com. There are numerous articles about this *economy.* See a US article (http://time.com/3687305/testing-the-sharing-economy) and a British one (www.spectator.co.uk/2015/03/get-your-share-of-the-sharing-economy) if you want to explore this kind of work. While these opportunities represent short-term, stopgap ideas, it's always possible you'll meet someone who can help you find a better opportunity.

9. **Asking for job-leads.** This method works **33 percent** of the time. With this method you ask family members, friends, and people you know in the community (or on LinkedIn) if they know of any place where someone with your talents and background is being sought. It is a simple question: Do you know of any job vacancies at the place where you work—or elsewhere? *Using this method, you have an almost five times better chance of finding a job, than if you had just sent out your resume.*

10. **Knocking on the door of any employer, office, or manufacturing plant.** This method works **47 percent** of the time. It works best with *small* employers (twenty-five or fewer employees) as you might have guessed. Sometimes you blunder into a place where a vacancy has just developed. One job-hunter knocked on the door

of an architectural office at 11 a.m. His predecessor (for he did get hired there) had just quit at 10 a.m. that morning. If you try this method and nothing turns up, you broaden your definition of *small employer* to those with fifty or fewer employees. *With this method you have an almost seven times better chance of finding a job than if you had just depended on your resume.*

Well, that's it. That's *the Traditional Approach*, split up into its ten parts. These job-hunting methods were not created equal. Some methods, as we have seen, have a pretty good track record, and therefore will repay you for time spent pursuing them. But other methods have a really terrible track record, and are a waste of your time, and energy. Each of these methods can be useful, they just don't generally produce strong outcomes alone. They must be integrated into a larger process; so if you limit yourself to only a few methods, you are not as likely to be successful. It's all about *conservation of energy.* And wisdom would say conserve your energy. Invest it well.

So, we turn now—in the next chapters—to the other approach to job-hunting or career-changing: *the Parachute Approach.* It begins, not with examining the job market, but with examining yourself.

A Final Note

Job-hunting is, or should be, a full-time job. If your job-hunt isn't working, you must increase the amount of time you're devoting to your job-hunt. If you want to devote as little time to your job-hunt as possible, then fine; try it. But if that doesn't lead to a job, then you are going to have to devote more time to it. By the way, there is an app for your iPhone or Android that helps you stay on track by nudging you about your job-hunting activities *each* day. Its author is Marshall J. Karp, and it's free: www.jobsearchpowermeter.com. Its display *may* show only one column, but there are actually three columns; swipe left or right to see the other two. The left column is the one you most want. Your object: to get into "the green" part of the Meter each day, by doing the activities it suggests. Nice app!

You do get to a certain point in life
Where you have to realistically, I think,
Understand that the days are getting shorter.
And you can't put things off,
Thinking you'll get to them someday.
If you really want to do them,
You better do them. . . .
So I'm very much a believer in knowing
What it is that you love doing
So that you can do a great deal of it.

   —Nora Ephron

CHAPTER 4

Self-Inventory, Part 1

Make no mistake. This isn't just a matter of staring at your navel. This is a job-hunting method—the most effective one, at that. This method, faithfully followed, step by step, works **86 percent** of the time. That means that out of every 100 job-hunters or career-changers who faithfully execute this job-hunting method, 86 will get lucky and find a job thereby; 14 job-hunters out of the 100 will not—if they use only this method. *Note well: You have a twelve times better chance of finding work using this method, than if you had just sent out your resume.* Not just work, but work you really want to do. What we sometimes refer to as "our dream job."

Why a SELF-Inventory

Why does an inventory of who you are work so well in helping you find work, after traditional job-hunting methods have failed? That's important to know, because the answer will keep you motivated to finish this inventory, when otherwise you might say, *OMG, this is just too much work!* And just give up.

Okay, here are eight answers as to why this works so well:

1. **By doing this homework on yourself, you learn to describe yourself in at least six different ways, and therefore you can approach multiple job markets.** Retraining, as it is commonly practiced in Western culture, prepares you for only one market. Thus someone decides that out-of-work construction workers should be retrained, let us say, to be computer-repair people.

Hence, their job-hunt approaches only one market. And if no jobs can be found in that market, once they are trained? *Retraining wasted.* This is why retraining programs sometimes acquire such a bad reputation.

But with an inventory of who you are, you stop identifying yourself by only one job-title. You can now think of yourself as not just "a computer-repair person," or "a construction worker" or "accountant" or "engineer" or "minister" or "ex-military" or whatever. *You are a person who* has these *multiple* skills and experiences. If, say, teaching and writing and growing things are your favorite skills, then you can approach either the job market of teaching, or that of writing, or that of gardening. Multiple job markets open up to you, not just one.

2. Doing this exercise will bring mindfulness to the process, which has been shown to improve decision making. You are taking the time to focus on yourself and what is most important in your life now, leading to smarter choices, and keeping yourself open to possibilities.

3. By doing this homework on yourself, you can describe in detail exactly what you are looking for. This greatly enables your friends, LinkedIn contacts, and family, to better help you. You approach them not with, *"Uh, I'm out of work; let me know if you hear of anything,"* but with a much more exact description of what kind of "anything," and in what work setting. This greatly helps them to focus down, and look for something very specific, thus increasing their helpfulness to you, and your ability to find jobs you would otherwise never find.

4. By ending up with a picture of a job that would really excite you, and not just any old job, you will inevitably pour much more time, energy, and determination into your job-search. *This is really worth looking for.* So, you will redouble your efforts, your dedication, and your determination when otherwise you might try but soon give up. Persistence is the essence of a successful job-hunt, and persistence becomes your middle name, once you've identified a prize worth fighting for.

5. By doing this homework, you will no longer have to wait to approach companies until they say they have a vacancy. Armed with the knowledge you've gained, you can choose places that match who you are, and then approach them (*through a contact, or what I like to call a "bridge-person" because they know both you and them, and thus serve as a bridge between you*)—knowing confidently that you will be an asset there, whether they turn out to have a job opening or decide to create one for you.

    Create one for you? No, I'm not kidding. This happens more often than you would ever think, to the prepared job-hunter or career-changer. Wrote one job-hunter to me recently:

    > *In my mind I knew where I wanted to work: a company I had had a couple of meetings with about an imperfect job about two years ago and fell in love with. I found the CEO on LinkedIn, asked him if he remembered me and would he be up for a short meeting if I promised it would be fun. He said he would love to meet and I pitched the idea of setting up a training academy for them. About a month later, I had an email to say they definitely want to go ahead with providing training as I had pitched it. The job did not exist, they had not conceived of the job, and it meets all my criteria because I thought of it. [From]* Parachute *to dream job in six months is not bad is it?*

6. When you are facing, let us say, nineteen other competitors for the job you want—equally experienced, equally skilled—you will stand out above them all, because you can accurately describe to employers exactly what is unique about you, and what you bring to the table that the others do not. These will usually turn on adjectives or adverbs, what we normally call *traits*. More on that in the next chapter.

7. If you are contemplating a career-change, maybe—after you inventory yourself—you will see definitely what new career or direction you want for your life. Often you can put together a new career just using what you already know and what you already can do—with much less training or retraining than you thought you would have to do. I'm not talking about a dramatic change, like going from salesperson to doctor: for that,

you will need to start over. But most career-changes are not that dramatic, as I will show you in chapter 11.

It may turn out that the knowledge you need to pick up can be found in a vocational/technical school, or in a (one- or) two-year college. But first, please, please, inventory who you are and what you love to do.

And sometimes, *sometimes,* it can be found simply by doing enough *informational interviewing* (more about this in chapter 8). Example: A job-hunter named Bill had worked for a number of years in retail; now he was debating a career-change—working in the oil industry. But he knew virtually nothing about that industry. However, he went from person to person who worked at companies in that industry, just seeking information about the industry. The more of these "informational interviews" he conducted, the more he knew. In fact, coming down the home stretch, just before he got hired in the place of his dreams, he found he now knew more than the people he was visiting, about their competitors and some aspects of the industry.

In other words, with certain kinds of career-change, there is more than one way to pick up the knowledge you need.

8. **Unemployment is an interruption, in most of our lives, but interruptions are opportunities, to pause, to think, to assess where we really want to go with our lives.** Martin Luther King Jr. had something to say about this:

> *The major problem of life is learning how to handle the costly inter-ruptions. The door that slams shut, the plan that got sidetracked, the marriage that failed. Or that lovely poem that didn't get written because someone knocked on the door.*

A self-inventory is just that type of thinking and assessing. The Parachute Approach, with its demand that you do an inven-tory of who you are and what you love to do, before you set out on your search for (meaningful) work, helps you take advantage of the opportunity that this interruption presents.

So there you have it: the eight reasons why this inventory of who you are works so much better as a method of job-hunting than all other methods.

Being out of work, or thinking about a new career, should speak to your heart. It should say something like this:

Use this opportunity. Make this not only a hunt for a job, but a hunt for a life. A deeper life, a victorious life, a life you're prouder of.

The world currently is filled with workers whose weeklong cry is, "When is the weekend going to be here?" And, then, "Thank God it's Friday!" Their work puts bread on the table but . . . they are bored out of their minds. They've never taken the time to think out what they uniquely can do, and what they uniquely have to offer to the world. The world doesn't need any more bored workers. Dream a little. Dream a lot.

One of the saddest pieces of advice in the world is, "Oh come now—be realistic." The best parts of this world were not fashioned by those who were "realistic." They were fashioned by those who dared to look hard at their wishes and then gave them horses to ride.

How to Do Your SELF-Inventory

These are the things you will need:

1. Mental Preparation

You begin by stripping yourself (in your mind) of any past job-titles. When you ask yourself, "Who am I?" you must drop the vocational answer that first springs to mind. Like: I'm an accountant, or I am a truck driver, or a lawyer, or a construction worker, or salesperson, or designer, or writer, or account executive. That kind of an answer locks you into the past. You must think instead: "*I am a person . . .*"

"*I am a person who* . . . has had these experiences."

"*I am a person who* . . . is skilled at . . . "

"*I am a person who* . . . knows a lot about . . . "

"*I am a person who* . . . is unique in this way or that."

Yes, this is how a useful self-inventory begins. You are a person, not a job.

2. One Sheet of Paper *(Digital or Physical)*

Brain researchers such as Barbara Brown of USC discovered that when you are trying to make any kind of decision about your life, the most effective strategy is to shrink down every significant thing you know about yourself onto one piece of paper.[1] At least at the end. Not a journal, or a bunch of Post-It Notes, or several pieces of paper. Just one. (Write small.)

In this book that one piece of paper that you end up with is called *the Flower Exercise,* or *Flower Diagram.*

3. A Number of Worksheets

As you are working your way toward summarizing everything important about yourself on just one piece of paper, along the way you are going to need a number of disposable blank pieces of paper—I call them *worksheets*—in order to do a particular exercise (or two) that I will show you, for each flower petal. I emphasize *disposable.* You will ultimately be copying the final results from these worksheets onto your Flower Diagram, after which you can recycle these worksheets.

4. Some Kind of a Graphic or Picture

Again, brain researchers discovered that it helps immensely in making a decision about your life, if you don't just put a flood of *words* on that one piece of paper, but add some kind of a graphic, picture, or diagram. Particularly when you're dealing with a lot of information (known as *cognitive load* in psychology), graphic organizers can help you more easily remember, understand, and address the information you're working with. They discovered that this encouraged the right side of your brain to spring into action—the part of your brain that can look at a whole bunch of apparently unrelated data and exclaim, *"Aha! I see what it all means."* Some like to call this your intuitive side, the opposite of your logical side.

In the workshops that I taught from 1970 to 2012, I encouraged my students to choose any graphic they wished. We needed a picture with seven parts to it, corresponding to the seven parts of you that are

---

1. Barbara B. Brown (1921–1999) was a research psychologist who created and popularized the word *biofeedback*.

important in finding matching work. Well, the favorite graphic turned out to be a picture or diagram of yourself as a flower, with a center and six other petals. Hence the title of our self-inventory: *the Flower Diagram* (or *Flower Exercise*).

5. A Prioritizing Instrument or Grid

It is easy to imagine that the purpose of a self-inventory is to gather a series of personal *lists*, to which you then try to match possible jobs or careers. For example, *"Here's a list of all the things I want in my place of work."* Or *"This is a list of all the skills I want to be able to use at my next job, or career."* But over the past forty years or so, we have discovered that lists are useless, unless and until the items on each list are put into order of priority or importance for you: *this item is most important to me, this is next most important, next, then next, etc.*

And why is this? Well, we live in an imperfect world, and—at least initially—you may not be able to find a match for all the items on your lists. You may only be able to find a match for *some* of the items. There will be only a partial overlap between "dream job" and "actual job," in which case it is important that the overlap be the items you care the most about, not the least. And how will you know that, unless you put the items on each list in order of importance to you?

Here is the problem visually summarized:

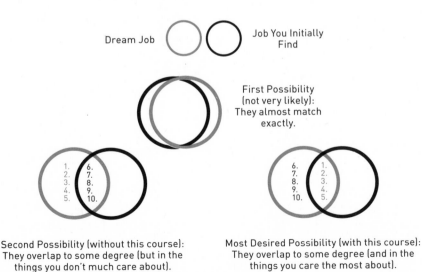

Dream Job — Job You Initially Find

First Possibility (not very likely): They almost match exactly.

Second Possibility (without this course): They overlap to some degree (but in the things you don't much care about).

Most Desired Possibility (with this course): They overlap to some degree (and in the things you care the most about).

Okay, so prioritizing is essential. How do you go about this? Having compiled a list of, say, ten items on one of the petals in your Flower Diagram, how will you decide which of the ten is absolutely the most important to you, which of the ten is next most important, etc.? It seems at first sight a bewildering challenge. Actually, it's easier than you think, *if . . .*

If . . . you compare just two items at a time, until you've compared all the possible pairs in that list of ten items. With all the pairs displayed in one diagram, this works out to be a grid. And the most popular form of that grid turns out to be my Prioritizing Grid, which I invented back in 1976. It can be for any number of items you choose, but the most common and simplest form of it is for ten items.

Where can you find blank copies of this Prioritizing Grid? Here are the three main places:

• In this book. A ten-item paper version (see page 55) appears throughout the next chapter. Plus, since some copy centers will not allow you to copy items out of a book without permission, tell them you have my permission to copy or reproduce that Grid as many times as you wish, *for your own private use* (not for inclusion in an e-book or another published work).

• In a workbook. Its title is *What Color Is Your Parachute? Job-Hunter's Workbook.* $12.99 online or at bookstores; another paper version, but its advantage here is that the workbook pages are larger—8" x 10".

• Online. I have given my friend Beverly Ryle permission to produce a simple online version of my Prioritizing Grid that is automated and interactive. It is found at www.beverlyryle.com/prioritizing-grid and it is free. You can use my ten-item Grid there, or customize a Grid for any number (of items) you choose. Needless to say, you can use her website as many times as you wish, and print out the results each time for your own keeping. I'll provide instructions for filling out the grid later.

6. Conclusion: Prioritizing the Petals

Before you go on to fill in the petals in the next chapter, it is sometimes helpful to ask yourself, Which petals—which parts of a job—do you instinctively feel will be most important to you—at least for now—and in what order?

a. The salary?

b. The geographical location?

c. The people you work with?

d. The look and feel of your workplace?

e. The degree to which it gives you a sense of purpose for your life, or fits in with the purpose you want your life to serve?

f. The degree to which it lets you use your favorite skills, abilities, or talents?

g. The degree to which this job lands you in your favorite field or fields of knowledge and interest?

If you want to know which petals other people have most often picked as their first priority in the past, the answer varies. A lot depends on where you are in your life, and which issue you are most preoccupied with, on this chart:

If they're just trying to survive, their first choice is usually the Salary petal. If they're on in years, it's the Purpose petal. If they're anywhere in between, it's the petals dealing with abilities/talents/skills. But all seven petals are important to you; don't leave any of them out.

Where flowers bloom, so does hope.

—*Lady Bird Johnson*

CHAPTER 5

Self-Inventory, Part 2

The Flower Exercise

This self-inventory is a flower with *seven* petals (including the center). That's because there are seven sides to You, or seven ways of thinking about yourself, or seven ways of describing who you are—*using the language of the workplace*:

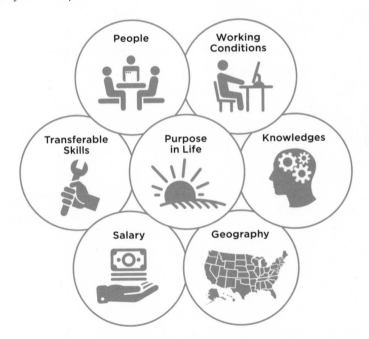

If you prefer a different metaphor, you are like a diamond, with seven facets to you, as we hold you up to the light.

1. *You and People.* You can describe *who you are* in terms of the kinds of people you most prefer to *work with or help*—age span, problems, physical or mental disabilities, education level, geographical location, etc.

2. *You and a Workplace.* Or you can describe *who you are* in terms of your favorite workplace, or working conditions—indoors/outdoors, small organization/large organization, windows/no windows, etc.—because they enable you to work at your top form, and greatest effectiveness.

3. *You and Skills.* Or you can describe *who you are* in terms of what you can do, and what your *favorite* functional/transferable skills are. For these are key to your being in top form, and at your greatest effectiveness.

4. *You and Your Purpose in Life.* Or you can describe *who you are* in terms of your goals or sense of mission and purpose for your life. Alternatively, or in addition, you can get even more particular and describe the goals or mission you want *the organization* to have, where you decide to work.

5. *You and the Knowledges You Already Have.* Or you can describe *who you are* in terms of what you already know—and what your *favorite* knowledges or interests are among all that stuff stored away in your head.

6. *You and Salary/Responsibility.* Or you can describe *who you are* in terms of your preferred salary and level of responsibility—working by yourself, or as a member of a team, or supervising others, or running the show—that you feel most fitted for, by experience, temperament, and appetite.

7. *You and Geography.* Or you can describe *who you are* in terms of your preferred surroundings—here or abroad, warm/cold, north/south, east/west, mountains/coast, urban/suburban/rural/rustic—where you'd be happiest, do your best work, and would most love to live, all year long, or part of the year, or vacation time, or sabbatical—either now, five years from now, or at retirement.

I Am a Person Who . . .
IS ALL THESE THINGS

You could choose just one, two, or three of these sides of yourself—let us say, "what you know," or "what you can do," or "your preferred salary"— as your guide to defining what kind of work you are looking for.

But what the Flower Diagram does is describe who you are in *all seven* ways, summarized on one page, in one graphic. After all, you are not just one of these things; you are *all* of these things. The Flower Diagram is a complete picture of *You*. All of you. In the language of the workplace.

And believe me, you want the complete picture. I'll tell you why. Let's say there is some job out there that matches just one petal, one side to yourself, one way of defining who you are. For example, let's say this job lets you use your favorite knowledges that you already have. But that's it.

That job doesn't let you use your favorite skills, nor does it have you working with the kinds of people you most want to, nor does it give you the surroundings where you can do your best work.

What would you call such a job? At the very least: *boring*. You would barely be able to wait for *Thank God it's Friday!* Some of us have already sung that song. A lot.

But now let us suppose you could instead find another kind of work that matches all seven sides of you. All seven petals. What would you call *that* work? Well, that's *your dream job*.

So, your complete Flower Diagram is a picture of who You most fully are. *And,* at the same time it is a picture of a job that would most completely match and fulfill all that you are. Where you would shine, because it uses the best of You.

Make it your goal to completely fill in your Flower. *And try to feel it as a joy rather than a duty.* Determine from the beginning that this is going to be fun. Because it sure can be. And should be.

Readers have asked for a list of all the places, or forms, where they can find this Flower. Here are the three main forms:

• **In this chapter.** Of course. *A paper version. Free, since you already have the book.*

• **In a workbook.** As I mentioned earlier, its title is *What Color Is Your Parachute? Job-Hunter's Workbook,* and its advantage is that the workbook pages are larger—8" x 10".

• **Online.** In response to many requests, we finally produced an online video course a few years ago, walking you through this Flower Exercise step-by-step, with me as your guide throughout. Requirements: a computer and a printer and paper (to print out the worksheets). It is available at a discounted price for readers of this book. The unique URL for ordering it is www.eParachute.com/para20. It can be used by individual readers or by a whole workshop. (*The course was put together by the principals at eParachute—myself as Content and Onscreen Host, Marci Bolles as Executive Producer, Gary Bolles as Producer, and Eric Barnett as Technical Consultant, on Udemy's platform.*) You can also access the course directly at www.udemy.com. Occasionally, like all Udemy courses, it will be on sale.

And, since you asked, there are other online resources on topics related to this Flower Exercise and this book. Dozens of videos may be found at www.youtube.com/user/TheParachuteGuy. And a bunch of articles can be found at www.jobhuntersbible.com. One word of caution: don't spend a lot of time on these side roads. Stay focused on your one main task: completing your Flower, in whatever form you choose. You can go roaming later.

Now, let's begin with the seven petals. Here is the first.

I Am a Person Who . . .

HAS THESE FAVORITE KINDS OF PEOPLE

First Petal

My Preferred Kinds of People to Work Beside or Serve

Goal in Filling Out This Petal: To identify the types of people who can either make the job delightful, or ruin your day, your week, your year.

What You Are Looking For: (1) A better picture in your mind of what kind of people surrounding you at work will enable you to operate at your highest and most effective level. (2) A better picture in your mind of what kind of people you would most like to serve or help: defined by age, problems, geography, and so forth.

Form of the Entries on Your Petal: They can be adjectives describing different kinds of people ("kind," "patient") or they can be types of people, as in the "Holland Code" or "Myers-Briggs" typologies (see pages 46–49 and 80, respectively).

Example of a Good Petal: Holland Code: IAS. (1) Kind, generous, understanding, fun, smart. (2) The unemployed, people struggling with their faith, worldwide, all ages.

Example of a Bad Petal: People in trouble, young, smart, in urban settings.

  Why Bad: Not much help. Too vague.

Petal One, Worksheet #1

A HEXAGON: THE PARTY GAME EXERCISE

Every job or career has a people-environment that is characteristic of that career. Tell us what career or job interests you, and we can tell you, in general terms, what kind of people you would prefer to work with (from among six possibilities). Or start at the other end: tell us what kinds of people you prefer to work with—in terms of those same six factors—and we can tell you what careers will give you *that*.

It was Dr. John L. Holland who came up with this theory, and with a system for applying the theory to yourself. Surveying the whole workplace, he said there are basically six people-environments that jobs can give you. Let's tick them off (the quotes are John's definitions).

1. The Realistic People-Environment: Filled with people who prefer activities involving "the explicit, ordered, or systematic manipulation of objects, tools, machines, and animals." ("Realistic," incidentally, refers to Plato's conception of "the real" as that which one can apprehend through the senses. "Knock on wood!")

   I summarize this as: R *= people who like nature, or plants, or animals, or athletics, or tools and machinery, or being outdoors.*

2. The Investigative People-Environment: Filled with people who prefer using their brains, specifically "the observation and symbolic, systematic, creative investigation of physical, biological, or cultural phenomena."

   I summarize this as: I *= people who are very curious, and like to investigate or analyze things, or people, or data.*

3. The Artistic People-Environment: Filled with people who prefer activities involving "ambiguous, free, unsystematized activities and competencies to create art forms or products."

   I summarize this as: A *= people who are very creative, artistic, imaginative, and innovative, and don't like time clocks.*[1]

---

1. Incidentally, there is a fascinating book about those whose primary code is "A." It's called *The Career Guide for Creative and Unconventional People*, Fourth Edition, by Carol Eikleberry with Carrie Pinsky.

4. The Social People-Environment: Filled with people who prefer activities involving "the manipulation of others to inform, train, develop, cure, or enlighten."

   I summarize this as: S = *people who are bent on trying to help, teach, or serve people.*

5. The Enterprising People-Environment: Filled with people who prefer activities involving "the manipulation of others to attain organizational or self-interest goals."

   I summarize this as: E = *people who like to start up projects or organizations, or sell things, or influence, or persuade, or lead people.*

6. The Conventional People-Environment: Filled with people who prefer activities involving "the explicit, ordered, systematic manipulation of data, such as keeping records, filing materials, reproducing materials, organizing written and numerical data according to a prescribed plan, operating business and data-processing machines." "Conventional," incidentally, refers to the "values" that people in this environment usually hold—representing the historic mainstream of our culture.

   I summarize this as: C = *people who like detailed work, and like to complete tasks or projects.*

According to John's theory, every one of us *could become skilled in all six*, if we were given enough time. Instead, in the limited time we have from childhood to adulthood, we tend to develop preferences and survival skills in just three of these people-environments, and this is determined by who we grew up with, who we admired, and what time we gave to practicing expertise in these people-environments, as we wended our way into adulthood. From among the six letters—RIASEC—you name your three preferred people-environments and this gives you what is called your "Holland Code," for example, SIA. Your question is, Which three?

I was friends with John for many years, and back in 1975 I invented a quick and easy way for you to find out your Code, based on John's Self-Directed Search (SDS). It turned out that it agrees with the results you would get from John's SDS 92 percent of the time (this made John laugh). So if you want a more certain answer, you can take the

O*NET Interest Profiler online, which will give you your three-letter code (www.mynextmove.org/explore/ip). You can also take John's SDS ($9.95 at www.self-directed-search.com). But when you're in a hurry, this is close. And doesn't require access to the Internet. I call it "The Party Exercise." Here is how the exercise goes (*do it, please*):

Below is an aerial view of a room in which a party is taking place. At this party, people with the same interests have (for some reason) all gathered in the same corner of the room. And that's true for all six corners.

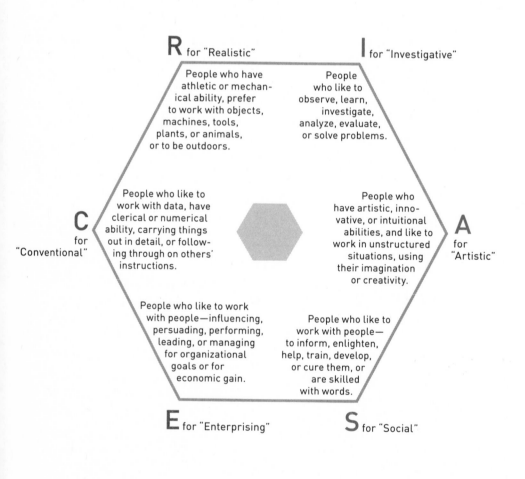

R for "Realistic"

I for "Investigative"

People who have athletic or mechanical ability, prefer to work with objects, machines, tools, plants, or animals, or to be outdoors.

People who like to observe, learn, investigate, analyze, evaluate, or solve problems.

C for "Conventional"

People who like to work with data, have clerical or numerical ability, carrying things out in detail, or following through on others' instructions.

People who have artistic, innovative, or intuitional abilities, and like to work in unstructured situations, using their imagination or creativity.

A for "Artistic"

People who like to work with people—influencing, persuading, performing, leading, or managing for organizational goals or for economic gain.

People who like to work with people— to inform, enlighten, help, train, develop, or cure them, or are skilled with words.

E for "Enterprising"

S for "Social"

1. Which corner of the room would you instinctively be drawn to, as the group of people you would most enjoy being with for the longest time? (Leave aside any question of shyness, or whether you would have to actually talk to them; you could just listen.)

   Write the letter for that corner here: ☐

2. After fifteen minutes, everyone in the corner you chose leaves for another party across town, except you. Of the groups that still remain now, which corner or group would you be drawn to the most, as the people you would most enjoy being with for the longest time?

   Write the letter for that corner here: ☐

3. After fifteen minutes, this group too leaves for another party, except you. Of the corners, and groups, which remain now, which one would you most enjoy being with for the longest time?

   Write the letter for that corner here: ☐

   The three letters you just chose are called your "Holland Code."[2]

   Put that code here: ☐ ☐ ☐

Now, copy that code onto Petal #1, My Preferred Kinds of People to Work With, found on pages 116–17. So far, so good.

---

2. Incidentally, John always encouraged people to write down somewhere all six versions (technically called *permutations*) of your code. Thus, if your code were, say, SIA, its permutations would be SIA, SAI, IAS, ISA, ASI, AIS. This is especially useful if you are ever going to look up careers that correspond to your code. Put "Holland Codes for careers" into your favorite search engine, and you will find such sites as www.vista-cards.com/occupations.

   Further, he and I worked together on this application of his system to daydreams: list all the things you've ever dreamed of doing. Then, to the right of each, try to *guess*—guess!—at what you think the three-letter Holland Code would be for each. When done, look at each code and assign a value of 3 to any letter in the first position; assign a value of 2 to any letter in the second position; and assign a value of 1 to any letter in the third position (e.g., in the case of IAS, you'd give 3 points to "I," 2 points to "A," and 1 point to "S"). Do this for every code you've written down, then total up all the points for each letter. How many points did "R" get, how many points did "I" get, etc. Choose the top three with the most points, in order, when you're done, and you have the Holland Code of your daydreams. As John said to me, "This is the most reliable way of determining someone's code, but who would believe it, except you and me?"

Petal One, Worksheet #2

A CHART: ENERGY DRAINERS VS. ENERGY CREATORS

Why do *the people you prefer* to be around matter at all—in the larger scheme of things? Because, the people we work with are either energy drainers or energy creators. They either drag us down and keep us from being our most effective, or they lift us up and help us to be at our best, and perform at our greatest effectiveness.

Here is an exercise to help you identify which is which, for you. You'll probably need to copy the chart below onto a larger piece of paper—8½" x 11"—before you start filling it in.

Column 1	Column 2	Column 3	Column 4
Places I Have Worked Thus Far in My Life	Kinds of People There Who Drove Me Nuts (from the first column) (No names, but describe what about them drove you nuts; e.g., bossy, always pestering me with their personal problems, always left early before the job was done. List these in any order; it doesn't matter—at least in this column . . .)	Kinds of People I'd Prefer Not to Have to Work With, in Order of Preference (This is now a ranking of the items in the second column, in exact order of: which is worse? next? etc. Use the Prioritizing Grid on page 55 to do this.) 1a. 2a. 3a. 4a. 5a.	Kinds of People I'd Most Like to Work With, in Order of Preference (The opposite of those qualities in the third column, in the same order) 1b. 2b. 3b. 4b. 5b.

Start, of course, by filling in the first column in the chart, and then the second. This will bring you to the third column, and here you're gonna need some help. How do you look back at that stuff in the second column, and prioritize it? Well, you use the Prioritizing Grid, in either paper or online form, of course. The following page shows an example, which illustrates how you use the ten-item Grid.

(I originally had more than ten items as a result of this exercise, but by guess and by gosh I narrowed them down to my top ten, and then worked just with them here.)

Section A. Here I put my list of ten items, in any order I choose. So, as you can see, the people I'd prefer not to have to work with are those who are *bossy, never thank anyone, are messy in dress or office space, claim too much, are uncompassionate, never tell the truth, are always late, are totally undependable, feel superior to others,* or *never have any ideas.* The order in which I list these items here in Section A doesn't matter at all.

Section B. Here are displayed all the possible pairs among those ten. Each pair is in a little box, or rather the *numbers* that represent each pair are in a little box. You ask each box a question. The framing of the question is crucial. The question you address to each box is *"Between these two items, which is more important to me?"* Or, since this is a Grid of dislikes, *"Which of these two do I dislike more?"* (Think of choosing between two hypothetical jobs.)

Let's see how this works. We'll start with the first little box at the top. The box has the numbers 1 and 2 in it. (#1 stands for *bossy*, while #2 stands for *never thanks anyone*). So, the question is *Which do you dislike more: #1 or #2?* You circle your preference—in that box. I circled #1—as you can see—because I dislike being around bossy people at work more than I dislike being around ungrateful people.

You go on now to the second box (down diagonally to the southeast) which has in it the second pairing, in this case, the numbers 2

(continued)

PRIORITIZING GRID FOR 10 ITEMS OR FEWER

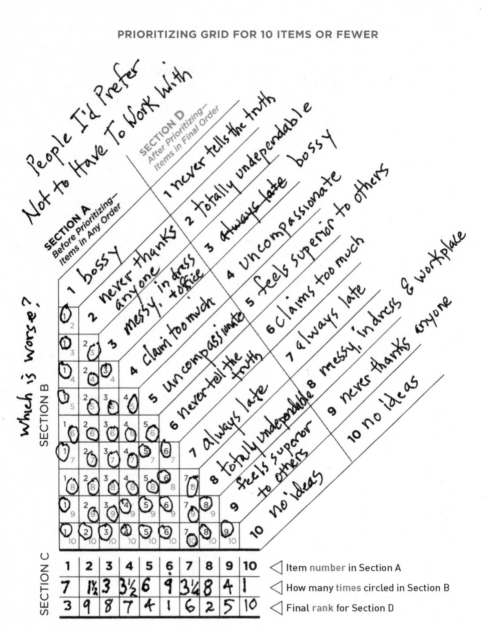

Which is worse?

People I'd Prefer Not to Have To Work With

SECTION A
Before Prioritizing—
Items in Any Order

SECTION D
After Prioritizing—
Items in Final Order

SECTION B

SECTION C

	1	2	3	4	5	6	7	8	9	10	
	7	1½	3	3½	6	9	3½	8	4	1	◁ How many times circled in Section B
	3	9	8	7	4	1	6	2	5	10	◁ Final rank for Section D

◁ Item number in Section A

1 bossy
2 never thanks anyone
3 messy, in dress & office
4 claim too much
5 uncompassionate
6 never tell the truth
7 always late
8 totally undependable
9 feels superior to others
10 no ideas

1 never tells the truth
2 totally undependable
3 always late
4 uncompassionate
5 feels superior to others
6 claims too much
7 always late
8 messy, in dress & workplace
9 never thanks anyone
10 no ideas

and 3. The question again: *Which do you dislike more?* I circled #3 in that box—as you can see—because I dislike being around messy people at work more than I dislike being around people who never thank anyone.

And so it goes, until you've circled one number in each little box in Section B.

Section C. Section C has three rows to it, at the bottom of the Grid, as you can see. The first row is just the ten numbers from Section A.

The second row is how many times each of those numbers just got circled in Section B. As you can see, item #1 got circled 7 times, item #2 got circled 1 time (as did item #10—a tie—so, to break the tie I look up in section B to find the little box that had both #2 and #10 in it, to see which I preferred at that time, and I see it was #2, so I give #2 an extra ½ point here, over #10). Item #3 I notice got circled three times, but so did item #4 and item #7—*a three-way tie!* How to break that tie? Well, here you'll just have to do some guessing. I guessed these were important to me in this order: #4, #7, and then #3. So, I added ½ point to #4 and ¼ point to #7; I left #3 as it was.

In the third and bottommost row of Section C, I put the ranking according to the number of circles in the second row. Item #6 had the most circles—9—so it is number 1 in ranking. Item #8 got the next most circles—8—so it is number 2 in ranking. And so it goes, until that whole bottom line is filled in. Now the only task remaining on this Grid is to copy the reorganized list onto Section D.

Section D. The aim here is to relist my ten items (from Section A) in the exact order of preference or priority, for me, using Section C as my guide. Item #6 got the most circles there, and it ranked number 1, so I copy the words for item #6 in the

(continued)

number 1 position in Section D. Item #8 ranked second, so I copy the words for item #8 into the second spot in Section D. Etc. Etc.[3] What I am left with, now, in Section D, is the ten items in the exact order of my preference and priority. *Nice!*

When you've completed the blank Grid on the opposite page for yourself, go back to the chart on page 50. Copy the first five factors from Section D of the Grid, into the third column of the chart. What you've got there, now, is a negative list of what you're trying to avoid. But what you want to end up with is a positive list of what you're trying to find.

So, look at the five negative items you just put in the third column of the chart, and in the fourth column write their opposite, or something near the opposite, directly beside each item. By "opposite" I don't necessarily mean "the exact opposite." If one of your complaints in the third column was "I was micromanaged, supervised every hour of my day," the opposite, in the fourth column, wouldn't necessarily be "No supervision." It might be "Limited supervision" or something like that. Your call.

Note that by first putting your negative list in exact order of what you most want to avoid (third column in the chart), your related positive list (fourth column) will have its factors in the exact order of what you most want to find in a future job.

Now copy the top five in column 4, onto Petal #1, My Preferred Kinds of People to Work With, on pages 116–17. And we are done (with that petal).

Time now to move on to another side of Who You Are.

---

3. Note that I made a mistake on line 3 in Section D. It never matters if you make a mistake. Just cross it out and jot down the correct information. It's okay not to be perfect.

PRIORITIZING GRID FOR 10 ITEMS OR FEWER

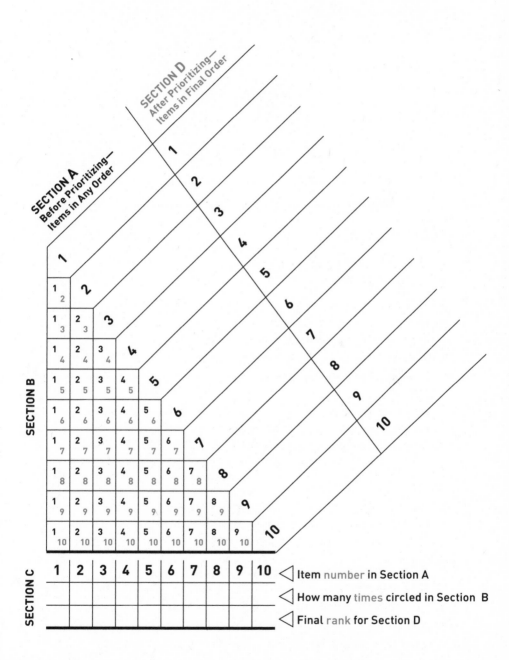

Item number in Section A

How many times circled in Section B

Final rank for Section D

I Am a Person Who . . .
HAS THESE FAVORITE WORKING CONDITIONS

Working Conditions

Second Petal

My Preferred Working Conditions

Goal in Filling Out This Petal: To state the working conditions and surroundings that would make you happiest, and therefore enable you to do your most effective work.

What You Are Looking For: Avoiding past bad experiences.

Form of the Entries on Your Petal: Descriptors of physical surroundings.

Example of a Good Petal: A workspace with lots of windows, nice view of greenery, relatively quiet, decent lunch period, flexibility about clocking in and clocking out, lots of shops nearby.

Example of a Bad Petal: Understanding boss, good colleagues, fun clients, etc.

> **Why Bad:** These all belong on the petal called Preferred Kinds of People to Work With, not this one, which is just about the physical surroundings at your work, not the "people surroundings." Of course, since this is your Flower Diagram, you can put any info you like on any petal you like. It's just that if you want your thinking to be clear, it's useful to preserve the difference between "What is my preferred physical setting?" and "What kinds of people do I prefer to work with?" or "What clients/customers with what kinds of problems would I most like to help or serve?"

Your physical setting where you work can cheer you up or drag you down. It's important to know this before you weigh whether to take a particular job offer, or not. The most useful way to do this has proved to be starting with working conditions that made you unhappy in the past and then flip them over into positives, just as we did in the previous exercise.

Plants that grow beautifully at sea level often perish if they're taken ten thousand feet up the mountain. Likewise, we do our best work under certain conditions, but not under others. Thus, the question "What are your favorite working conditions?" actually is a question about "Under what circumstances do you do your most effective work?"

Petal Two, Worksheet #1

A CHART: PHYSICAL ENVIRONMENTS WHERE I WOULD THRIVE

As I just mentioned, the best way to approach this is by trying to remember all the things you *disliked* about *any* previous job, using the chart on page 58 to list these. (*Copy this chart onto a larger piece of paper if you wish, before you begin filling it out.*) Column A may begin with such factors as "too noisy," "too much supervision," "no windows in my workplace," "having to be at work by 6 a.m.," etc.

As before, when you get to Column B, use a new ten-item Prioritizing Grid (on page 59).

This time, when you compare each two items, the frame you should put it in is, "If I were offered two jobs, and in the first job offer I would be rid of my distasteful working condition #1 but not #2; while in the second job offer I would be rid of my distasteful working condition #2, but not #1, which job offer would I take?"

DISTASTEFUL WORKING CONDITIONS CHART

	Column A — Distasteful Working Conditions	Column B — Distasteful Working Conditions Ranked	Column C + The Keys to My Effectiveness at Work
Places I Have Worked Thus Far in My Life	I Have Learned from the Past That My Effectiveness at Work Is Decreased When I Have to Work Under These Conditions	Among the Factors or Qualities Listed in Column A, These Are the Ones I Dislike Absolutely the Most (in order of decreasing dislike)	I Believe My Effectiveness Would Be at an Absolute Maximum If I Could Work Under These Conditions (the Opposite of the qualities in Column B, in the same order)
		1a.	1b.
		2a.	2b.
		3a.	3b.
		4a.	4b.
		5a.	5b.

After you've finished prioritizing, copy the first five items in Section D into Column B of your Distasteful Working Conditions Chart, above.

Once you have that list in Column B ranked—in terms of most distasteful down to least distasteful working conditions—turn to Column C in that chart and write *the opposite*, or something near *the opposite*, directly beside each item in Column B.

Copy the five items in Column C onto Petal #2, the Favorite Working Conditions petal of your Flower Diagram, pages 116–17.

Okay, on to another side of Who You Are.

PRIORITIZING GRID FOR 10 ITEMS OR FEWER

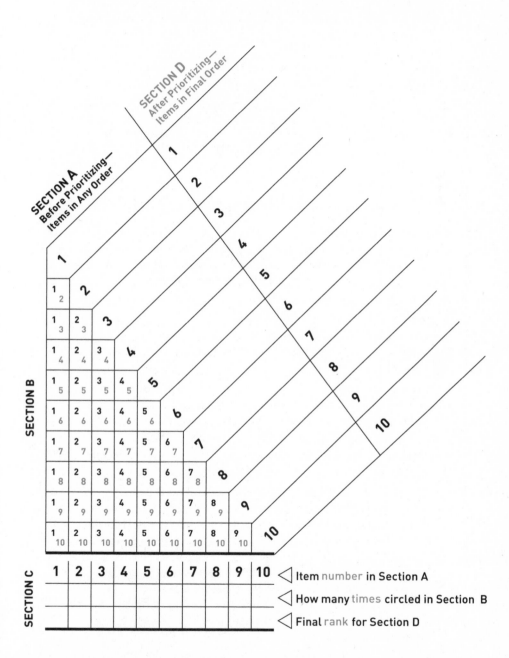

I Am a Person Who . . .
CAN DO THESE PARTICULAR THINGS

Transferable
Skills

Third Petal

My Favorite Transferable Skills

Goal in Filling Out This Petal: To discover what your *favorite* functional skills are, that can be transferred to any field of interest. They are things you probably were born knowing how to do, or at least you began with a natural gift and have honed and sharpened it since.

What You Are Looking For: Not just what you *can* do, but more particularly which of those you most *love* to use.

Form of the Entries on Your Petal: Verbs, usually in pure form (e.g., analyze) though they may sometimes be in gerund form (ending in -ing, e.g., analyzing).

Example of a Good Petal: (These stories show that I can) innovate, manipulate, analyze, classify, coach, negotiate; OR (to use the gerund form of these verbs), these stories show that I am good at innovating, manipulating, analyzing, classifying, coaching, negotiating.

Example of a Bad Petal: Adaptable, charismatic, reliable, perceptive, discreet, dynamic, persistent, versatile.

> **Why Bad:** These are all traits, or self-management skills; that is, they turn out to be the style with which you do your best, favorite, transferable skills. They are important, but they are not transferable skills. Incidentally, there is a new category floating around in the past ten years, called "soft skills." These are really just another way of speaking about your skills with people, and/or your self-management skills, because examples typically are things like "a good work ethic," "a positive attitude," "acting as a team player," "flexibility," "working well under pressure," and "ability to learn from criticism."

A CRASH COURSE ABOUT SKILLS, TALENTS, ABILITIES

Skills is one of the most misunderstood words in all the world of work. It begins with high school job-hunters: "I haven't really got any skills," they say. *Wrong!*

It continues with college students: "I've spent four years in college. I haven't had time to pick up any skills." *Wrong!*

And it lasts through the middle years, especially when a person is thinking of changing his or her career: "I'll have to go back to college, and get retrained, because otherwise I won't have any skills in my new field." Or: "Well, if I claim any skills, I'll have to start at a very entry kind of level." *Wrong!*

All of this confusion about the word *skills* stems from a total misunderstanding of what the word means. A misunderstanding that is shared, we might add, by altogether too many employers, and human resources departments, and other so-called vocational experts.

By understanding the word, you will automatically put yourself way ahead of most job-hunters. And, especially if you are weighing a change of career, you can save yourself much wasted time on the adult folly called, "I'll have to go back to school." I've said it before, and I'll say it again: *maybe* you need some further schooling, but very often it is possible to make a dramatic career-change without any retraining. It all depends. And you won't really *know* whether or not you need further schooling, until you have finished all the exercises in this self-inventory.

So, let's begin again. Simple. Precise. Clear. What are skills? According to "the father" of the *Dictionary of Occupational Titles,* industrial psychologist Sidney Fine, we all have three kinds of skills, abilities, talents, or whatever you want to call them.

SIDNEY FINE'S THREE KINDS OF SKILLS

Functional (Transferable) Skills	Special Knowledges	Self-Management Skills or Traits
WHAT YOU CAN DO and Love to Do with Data/Statistics, People, or Things	**WHAT YOU KNOW** and Love to Use	**HOW YOU CONDUCT YOURSELF** Alone or with Others
Usually These Are Verbs	Usually These Are Nouns	Usually These Are Adjectives or Adverbs
constructing	graphic design	adaptable
creating	physics	self-confident
researching	mathematics	cooperative
painting	warehouse procedures	dependable
analyzing	bookkeeping	enthusiastic
supervising	religion	disciplined
teaching	data analysis	flexible
illustrating	auto repair	innovative
organizing	Spanish	outgoing
counseling	music	supportive
repairing	principles of	persistent
healing	conference planning	resourceful
initiating		tactful

We will deal with the first kind of skills, *Functional Skills,* and the third, *Self-Management Skills,* during this Petal #3. We will save the second kind of skills, *Special Knowledges Skills,* for Petal #5. So, let's begin with the *Functional (Transferable) Skills.*

There is a trend these days toward breaking down your functional skills into categories such as *"action verbs,"* or *"communication or people skills,"* *"soft skills,"* *"technical skills,"* *"research and analytical skills,"* *"management, supervision, and leadership skills,"* *"clerical and administrative skills,"* *"problem-solving and development skills,"* *"financial skills,"* etc.

Maybe that's helpful to you. If so, use it. But for most of us I recommend breaking down transferable skills into just three simple categories:

Are they skills you use with information, data, and the like, or are they skills you use with people, or are they skills you use with things?

Here's how Sidney Fine further broke them down:

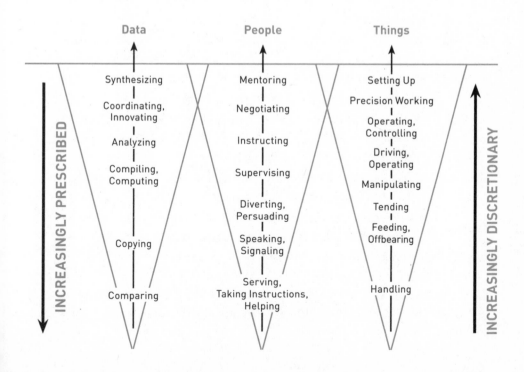

Data	People	Things
Synthesizing	Mentoring	Setting Up
Coordinating, Innovating	Negotiating	Precision Working
Analyzing	Instructing	Operating, Controlling
Compiling, Computing	Supervising	Driving, Operating
	Diverting, Persuading	Manipulating
Copying	Speaking, Signaling	Tending
		Feeding, Offbearing
Comparing	Serving, Taking Instructions, Helping	Handling

INCREASINGLY PRESCRIBED

INCREASINGLY DISCRETIONARY

It's an outdated list, but here are the main points he was trying to make with these inverted triangles (and these points are timeless):

1. Your transferable (functional) skills are the most basic unit—the atoms—of whatever job or career you may choose.

2. You should always claim the highest skills you legitimately can, as demonstrated by your past performance.

   As this diagram makes clear, within each family there are *simple* skills, and there are higher, or *more complex* skills above them; so these can be diagrammed as inverted pyramids, with the simpler skills at the bottom, and the more complex ones in order above them, for data or people or things.

   Incidentally, as a general rule—to which there are exceptions—each *higher* skill requires you to be able also to do all those skills listed below it. So of course you can claim *those*, as well. But you want to especially emphasize the highest skill you legitimately can, on each pyramid, demonstrated by yourself at work or at play in the past.

3. The higher your transferable skills, the more freedom you will have on the job.

   As you can see from the side arrows in the diagram, simpler skills can be, and usually are, heavily *prescribed* (by the employer), so if you claim *only* the simpler skills, you will have to *"fit in"*—following the instructions of your supervisor, and doing exactly what you are told to do. The *higher* the skills you can legitimately claim, the more you will be given discretion to carve out the job the way you want to—so that it truly fits *you*.

4. The higher your transferable skills, the less competition you will face for whatever job you are seeking.

   Not for you is the way of classified ads, resumes, and agencies. No, if you can legitimately claim higher skills, then to find such jobs you *should* follow the step-by-step process I will be describing in the next chapter.

   The essence of this approach to job-hunting or career-changing is that once you have identified your favorite transferable skills, and your favorite special knowledges, you may then approach any organization that interests you, whether they have a known vacancy or not. Naturally, whatever places you visit—and particularly those that have not advertised any vacancy—you will find far fewer job-hunters with whom you have to compete.

In fact, if the employers you visit happen to like you well enough, they may be willing to create for you a job that does not presently exist. *In which case, you will be competing with no one, since you will be the sole applicant for that newly created job.* While this doesn't happen all the time, it is astounding to me how many times it *does* happen. The *reason* it does is that the employers often have been *thinking* about creating a new job within their organization, for quite some time—but with this and that, they just have never gotten around to *doing* it. Until you walked in.

Then they decided they didn't want to let you get away, since *good employees are as hard to find as good employers.* And they suddenly remember that job they have been thinking about creating for many weeks or months now. So they dust off their *intention*, create the job on the spot, and offer it to you! And if that new job is not only what *they* need, but is exactly what *you* were looking for, then you have a dream job. Match-match. Win-win.

5. Don't confuse transferable skills with traits.

Functional/transferable skills are often confused with traits, temperaments, or type. We often think that transferable skills are such things as: *has lots of energy, gives attention to details, gets along well with people, shows determination, works well under pressure, is sympathetic, intuitive, persistent, dynamic, dependable,* etc. These are not functional/transferable skills, but *traits, self-management skills,* or *the style* with which you do your transferable skills.

For example, let's assume that one of your traits is *"gives attention to details."* And let's suppose that one of your *transferable skills* is *"conducting research."* In that case *"gives attention to details"* describes the manner or style with which you *conduct research.*

More about this, later in this petal.

Petal Three, Worksheet #1

A SKILLS CHART: ANALYZING SEVEN STORIES WHEN YOU WERE ENJOYING YOURSELF

Now that you know what transferable skills technically *are*, the problem that awaits you now, is figuring out your own. If you are one of the few lucky people who already knows what your transferable skills are, blessed are you. Write them down, and put them in the order of preference, for you, on the Flower Diagram (pages 116–17).

If, however, you don't know what your skills are (and 95 percent of all workers *don't*), then you will need some help. Fortunately, there is an exercise to help.

It involves the following steps.

1. Write One Story About Some Episode in Your Life (the First of Seven)

Yes, I know, I know. You can't do this exercise because you don't like to write. *Writers are a very rare breed.* That's what thousands of job-hunters have told me, over the years. And for years I kind of believed them—until "texting" came along. Let's face it: we human beings are "a writing people," and we only need a topic we have a real passion for, or interest in—such as your life—for the writing genie to spring forth from within each of us, pen or keyboard in hand.

So, call the *Seven Stories from your life* that you're about to write your personal *offline blog*, if you prefer. But start writing. Please. Okay, the next step is actually writing. Here is one person's first story:

> *Several years ago, our family adopted a mixed-breed puppy from a shelter. Based on her appearance, she seemed to be part Poodle, part Labrador, and maybe part Border Collie. We named her Ruffles. Not only was Ruffles adorable, she had the sweetest, gentlest nature and loved everyone. She was a hit at the local dog park and everywhere I took her. The only challenge was her high energy level: she jumped around and pulled on her leash; she got*

bored easily and chewed up the furniture, and anything else, if I didn't keep her busy. A friend suggested I get her obedience training so I enrolled her in Puppy Kindergarten at a local pet store. We failed miserably. She preferred socializing with the other dogs and people and had no interest in listening to me.

Something about this experience triggered my own stubborn nature, so I decided to train her myself. In fact, I had a secret goal: I would train her to be a therapy dog and take her to a local children's hospital. I started by getting some books from the library on dog training. I watched TV programs on the topic and started trying the various techniques to see which worked best. She was doing great at home, but I still had challenges with her in public. I looked up therapy dog training and discovered that the American Kennel Club has an AKC Good Citizen program for training dogs. The training I had done at home helped Ruffles quickly succeed in the group environment and she was able to complete the ten-step test (which included sitting politely for petting and ignoring distractions in her environment) and achieve her Good Citizen certificate.

After that, I checked with the local children's hospital and learned that Ruffles and I needed to go through another program to certify her as a therapy dog, so we enrolled in online training through a nonprofit organization. Once she was through the training process and attained her "novice" status, we started visiting the children's hospital.

I didn't realize what a commitment I had made when I set my first goal with Ruffles, but the experience was incredible. I met so many wonderful children and families who were going through a terrible time in their lives, and watching their faces light up when they saw Ruffles was the highlight of my week. As I look back, I think I benefited more than anyone from the experience.

As illustrated with this story, each story should have the following points:

a. Your goal/what you wanted to accomplish: "I wanted my dog to stop chewing up the furniture and I also wanted to find an outlet for her energy and friendly personality."

b. Some kind of hurdle, obstacle, or constraint you faced: "She and I failed miserably in Puppy Kindergarten. She was stubborn and too interested in other dogs and people. I couldn't control her, and I was sure I wouldn't be able to train her."

c. A description of what you did, step by step, to ultimately achieve your goal: "I read everything I could about training dogs. I watched TV shows, too, and I tried all the techniques. I kept taking her to the park and working on her socialization skills. I searched out local training programs for preparing her to be a therapy dog. I enrolled in several programs both in person and online. I then started taking her to the hospital to try out and improve her skills."

d. A description of the outcome or result: "Ruffles received the appropriate certificate and was able to volunteer at the local children's hospital."

e. Any measurable/quantifiable statement of that outcome: "I'd have to say that the outcome is more emotional than financial. I learned a lot about myself, particularly my tenacity and my patience. I also learned a lot about compassion and kindness, and the value of small experiences that can make someone's day. I think working with Ruffles made me a better person."

Now write *your* story, using the sample as a guide.

Don't pick a story where you achieved something *big*, like *"how I got my college degree over a period of ten years."* At least to begin with, write a story about some brief episode or task you accomplished, and you had fun!

Do not try to be *too* brief. This isn't Twitter.

THE PARACHUTE SKILLS GRID

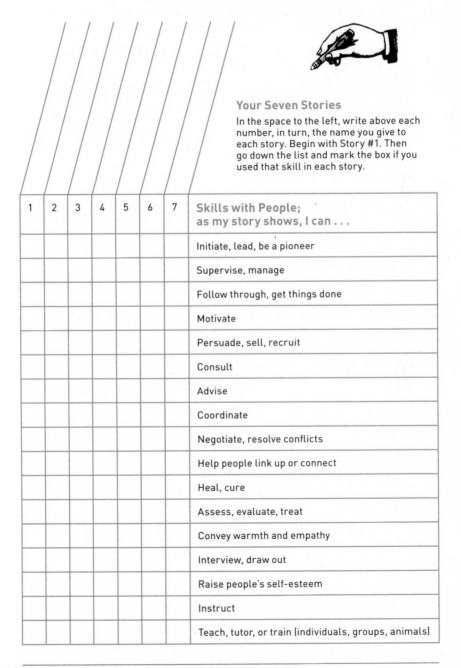

Your Seven Stories

In the space to the left, write above each number, in turn, the name you give to each story. Begin with Story #1. Then go down the list and mark the box if you used that skill in each story.

1	2	3	4	5	6	7	Skills with People; as my story shows, I can . . .
							Initiate, lead, be a pioneer
							Supervise, manage
							Follow through, get things done
							Motivate
							Persuade, sell, recruit
							Consult
							Advise
							Coordinate
							Negotiate, resolve conflicts
							Help people link up or connect
							Heal, cure
							Assess, evaluate, treat
							Convey warmth and empathy
							Interview, draw out
							Raise people's self-esteem
							Instruct
							Teach, tutor, or train (individuals, groups, animals)

1	2	3	4	5	6	7	Skills with People; as my story shows, I can . . . (continued)
							Speak
							Listen
							Counsel, guide, mentor
							Communicate well, in person
							Communicate well, in writing
							Divert, amuse, entertain, perform, act
							Play an instrument
							Interpret, speak, or read a foreign language
							Serve, care for, follow instructions faithfully
							Skills with Data, Ideas; as my story shows, I can . . .
							Use my intuition
							Create, innovate, invent
							Design, use artistic abilities, be original
							Visualize, including in three dimensions
							Imagine
							Use my brain
							Synthesize, combine parts into a whole
							Systematize, prioritize
							Organize, classify
							Perceive patterns
							Analyze, break down into parts
							Work with numbers, compute
							Remember people, or data, to unusual degree
							Develop, improve
							Solve problems

1	2	3	4	5	6	7	Skills with Data, Ideas; as my story shows, I can . . . (continued)
							Plan
							Program
							Research
							Examine, inspect, compare, see similarities and differences
							Use acute senses (hearing, smell, taste, sight)
							Study, observe
							Compile, keep records, file, retrieve
							Copy
							Skills with Things; as my story shows, I can . . .
							Control, expedite things
							Make, produce, manufacture
							Repair
							Finish, restore, preserve
							Construct
							Shape, model, sculpt
							Cut, carve, chisel
							Set up, assemble
							Handle, tend, feed
							Operate, drive
							Manipulate
							Use my body, hands, fingers, with unusual dexterity or strength

2. Analyze Your First Story, Using the Skills Grid, to See What Transferable Skills You Used

Above the number 1 on page 69, write a brief title for your first story. Then work your way down the column below that number 1, asking yourself in each case: "Did I use this skill in this story?"

If the answer is "Yes," color in the little square for that skill, in that column, with a red pen or whatever.

Work your way through the entire Parachute Skills Grid that way, with your first story.

3. Write Six Other Stories, and Analyze Them for Transferable Skills

Voilà! You are done with Story #1. However, "one swallow doth not a summer make," so the fact that you used certain skills in this first story doesn't tell you much. You have to keep writing stories—seven is the ideal, five is the minimum to be of any use—because what you are looking for is patterns—transferable skills that keep reappearing in story after story. They keep reappearing because they are your favorites (assuming you chose stories where you were *really* enjoying yourself).

So, write your Story #2, from any period in your life, analyze it using the skills grid, etc., etc. And keep this process up, until you have written, and analyzed, all your stories. A weekend should do it! In a weekend, you can inventory your *past* sufficiently so that you have a good picture of the *kind* of work you would love to be doing *in the future.* (*You can, of course, stretch the inventory over a number of weeks, maybe doing an hour or two one night a week, if you prefer. It's up to you as to how fast you do it.*)

4. Discover Patterns and Priorities

Okay, when you've finished this whole inventory, for all seven of your accomplishments/achievements/jobs/roles or whatever, you want to look down your completed skills grid to discover any PATTERNS or PRIORITIES.

a. Patterns, because it isn't a matter of whether you used a skill only once, but rather whether you used it again and again. "Once" proves nothing; "again and again" is very convincing.

b. Priorities (that is, which skills are most important to you), because as we saw earlier, the job you eventually choose may not be able to use all of your skills. You need to know *what you are willing to trade off, and what you are not.* This requires that you know which skills, or family of skills, are most important to you.

So, after finishing your seven stories (or if you're in a hurry, at least five), look through that Skills Grid, and now *guess* which *might* be your top ten favorite skills. These should be your best *guesses,* and they should be about *your favorite* skills—not the ones you think the job market will like the best, but the ones *you* enjoy using the most.

At this point, now that you've guessed your top ten, you want to be able to prioritize those ten *in exact order of priority.* Run your *guesses* through the Prioritizing Grid on the opposite page and when you're done with that grid's Section D, copy the top ten onto the building blocks diagram on page 78, as well as onto your Favorite Transferable Skills petal, on pages 116–17.

PRIORITIZING GRID FOR 10 ITEMS OR FEWER

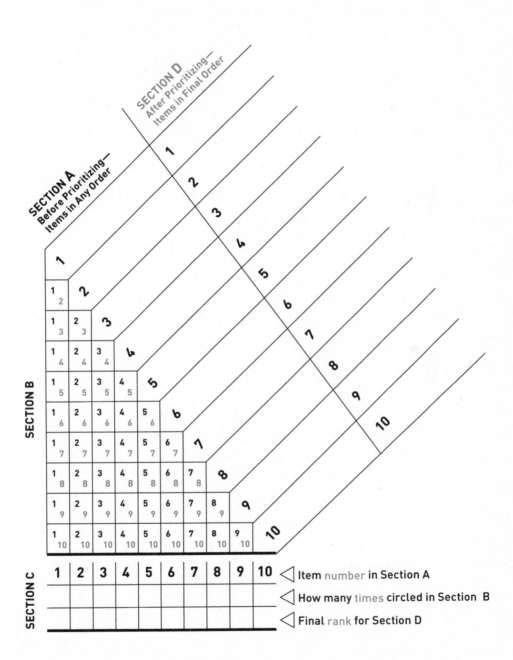

If you are finding it difficult to come up with seven stories, it may help you to know how others chose one or more of their stories.[4]

As I look back, I realize I chose a story that:

- ❏ Is somehow abnormal or inconsistent with the rest of my life
- ❏ Reveals my skills in a public way
- ❏ Is in a field (such as leisure, learning, etc.) far removed from my work
- ❏ I remembered through or because of its outcome
- ❏ Represented a challenge/gave me pride because it was something:
  - I previously could not do
  - My friends could not do
  - I was not supposed to be able to do
  - Only my father/mother could do, I thought
  - Only authorized/trained experts were supposed to be able to do
  - Somebody told me I could not do
  - My peers did not do/could not do
  - The best/brilliant/famous could or could not do
  - I did not have the right degree/training to do
  - People of the opposite sex usually do
- ❏ I would like to do again:
  - In a similar/different setting
  - With similar/different people
  - For free for a change/for money for a change
- ❏ Excited me because:
  - I never did it before
  - It was forbidden

---

4. This list is the brainchild of Daniel Porot (© 1994 Daniel Porot).

- I took a physical risk
- I was taking a financial risk
- No one had ever done it before
- It demanded a long and persistent (physical/mental) effort
- It made me even with someone

❑ I loved doing because:

- I kind of like this sort of thing
- The people involved were extremely nice
- It did not cost me anything

❑ Will support/justify the professional goals I have already chosen

Don't forget to look for skills that you use outside of work, such as those you use, or develop, playing video games (*strategic planning, navigating changing environments, active listening, communicating, collaborating, etc.*). Not only are these useful in various jobs and fields; but in and of themselves, video game skills can get you a scholarship to college—more than thirty colleges offer scholarships to study gaming, including NYU.

If you absolutely can't think of any experiences you've had where you enjoyed yourself, and accomplished something, then try this. Describe the seven most enjoyable jobs that you've had; or seven roles you've had so far in your life, such as wife, mother, cook, homemaker, volunteer in the community, citizen, dressmaker, student, etc. Tell us something you did or accomplished, in each role.

The Virtue of Depicting Your Transferable Skills in Terms of Building Blocks. Suppose it turned out that these were my top ten favorite skills: *analyze, teach, research, write, diagnose, synthesize, entertain, classify, lead, motivate.* (I might prefer to put these verbs in their gerund form, ending in –ing: *analyzing, teaching, researching, writing, diagnosing, synthesizing, entertaining, classifying, leading, motivating.*)

If I then enter these terms onto a diagram of Building Blocks in the order of my personal priority, the top one defines the kind of job or career I'm looking for. If I put "analyzing" in the top block, I might seek a job as an analyst. But, if instead I move "teaching" to the top block, then I might seek a job as a teacher. And so on, with "researching," "writing," "diagnosing," etc. I can choose among several goals.

5. Now Let's Turn to Your Self-Management Skills or Traits

A CHECKLIST OF MY STRONGEST TRAITS

I am very . . .

- ❑ Accurate
- ❑ Achievement-oriented
- ❑ Adaptable
- ❑ Adept
- ❑ Adept at having fun
- ❑ Adventuresome
- ❑ Alert
- ❑ Appreciative
- ❑ Assertive
- ❑ Astute
- ❑ Authoritative
- ❑ Calm
- ❑ Cautious
- ❑ Charismatic
- ❑ Competent
- ❑ Consistent
- ❑ Contagious in my enthusiasm
- ❑ Cooperative
- ❑ Courageous
- ❑ Creative
- ❑ Decisive
- ❑ Deliberate
- ❑ Dependable/have dependability
- ❑ Diligent
- ❑ Diplomatic
- ❑ Discreet
- ❑ Driving
- ❑ Dynamic
- ❑ Effective
- ❑ Energetic
- ❑ Enthusiastic
- ❑ Exceptional
- ❑ Exhaustive
- ❑ Experienced
- ❑ Expert
- ❑ Extremely economical
- ❑ Firm
- ❑ Flexible
- ❑ Human-oriented
- ❑ Impulsive
- ❑ Independent
- ❑ Innovative
- ❑ Knowledgeable
- ❑ Loyal
- ❑ Methodical
- ❑ Objective
- ❑ Open-minded
- ❑ Outgoing
- ❑ Outstanding
- ❑ Patient
- ❑ Penetrating
- ❑ Perceptive
- ❑ Persevering
- ❑ Persistent
- ❑ Pioneering
- ❑ Practical
- ❑ Professional
- ❑ Protective
- ❑ Punctual
- ❑ Quick/work quickly
- ❑ Rational
- ❑ Realistic
- ❑ Reliable
- ❑ Resourceful
- ❑ Responsible
- ❑ Responsive
- ❑ Safeguarding
- ❑ Self-motivated
- ❑ Self-reliant
- ❑ Sensitive
- ❑ Sophisticated
- ❑ Strong
- ❑ Supportive
- ❑ Tactful
- ❑ Thorough
- ❑ Unique
- ❑ Unusual
- ❑ Versatile
- ❑ Vigorous

Now, let's go a little deeper.

In general, your self-management skills describe:

How you deal with time and promptness.

How you deal with people and emotions.

How you deal with authority and being told what to do at your job.

How you deal with supervision and being told how to do your job.

How you deal with impulse vs. self-discipline, within yourself.

How you deal with initiative vs. response, within yourself.

How you deal with crises or problems.

If you want to know what your traits or self-management skills are, popular tests such as the MBTI (*the Myers-Briggs Type Indicator*) measure that sort of thing.

If you have access to the Internet, there are clues, at least, about your traits or "type." Here are three sites to check out:

Working Out Your Myers-Briggs Type
www.teamtechnology.co.uk/tt/t-articl/mb-simpl.htm
An informative article about the Myers-Briggs

The 16 Personality Types
www.personalitypage.com/high-level.html
A helpful site about Myers types

Myers-Briggs Foundation home page
www.myersbriggs.org
The official website of the foundation; lots of testing resources

Another excellent test to learn more about your values is the Values-in-Action (VIA) assessment, which you can take for free online at www.authentichappiness.sas.upenn.edu/testcenter. This site, developed by the Positive Psychology Center at the University of Pennsylvania, contains several interesting and helpful work-related assessments. Try experimenting; they are free, although you have to register.

You can use your self-management skills to flesh out each of your favorite transferable skills so that you are able to describe each of your talents or skills with more than just a one-word verb or gerund.

Let's take *organizing* as our example. You tell us proudly: "I'm good at organizing." That's a fine *start* at defining your skills, but unfortunately it doesn't yet tell us much. Organizing WHAT? People, as at a party? Nuts and bolts, as on a workbench? Or lots of information, as on a computer? These are three entirely different skills. The one word *organizing* doesn't tell us which one is yours.

So, please look at your favorite transferable skills, and ask yourself if you want to flesh out any of them with an object—some kind of Data/Information, or some kind of People, or some kind of Thing—plus a self-management skill, or trait or style (adverb or adjective).

Why is the trait important here? Well, "I'm good at organizing information painstakingly and logically" and "I'm good at organizing information in a flash, by intuition," are two entirely different skills. The difference between them is spelled out not in the verb, nor in the object, but in the adjectival or adverbial phrase there at the end. So, expand the definition of any of your ten favorite skills that you choose, in the fashion I have just described.

When you are face-to-face with a person-who-has-the-power-to-hire-you, you want to be able to explain what makes you different from nineteen other people who can basically do the same thing that you can do. It is often the self-management skill, the trait, the adjective or adverb that will save your life, during that explanation.

Now, on to the fourth side of Who You Are.

I Am a Person Who . . .
HAS A CERTAIN GOAL, PURPOSE, OR MISSION IN LIFE

Fourth Petal

My Purpose or Sense of Mission for My Life

Goal in Filling Out This Petal: To know the moral compass or spiritual values by which you want to guide your life. The most victorious life is one that is dedicated to some larger cause or mission.

What You Are Looking For: Some definition of the purpose and mission of your life. This may help you pick out the kinds of organizations or companies you'd like to work for, if you find ones that are serving the same mission as yours.

Form of the Entries on Your Petal: A description of what sphere of life you want to make better, with some attending details.

Example of a Good Petal: My purpose in life is to help the human spirit. I want there to be more faith, more compassion, more forgiveness, in families, because I have lived.

Example of a Bad Petal: More justice in the world.

> **Why Bad:** An admirable goal, but it is too vague. Doesn't give you any guidance as to what kind of justice to look for.

You need to dream about the broad outcome of your life, and not just this year's job-search. What kind of footprint do you want to leave on this Earth, after your journey here is done? Figure that out, and you're well on your way to defining your life as having purpose and a mission. As John L. Holland famously said, "We need to look further down the road than just headlight range at night." The road is the road of Life.

Petal Four, Worksheet #1

DIAGRAM: THE NINE SPHERES OF PURPOSE OR MISSION

Generally speaking, purpose breaks down into nine spheres—corresponding to our nature. As you look these over in the diagram on page 84, the question is, Which one appeals to *you* the most? Time for some hard thinking (ouch!). So, study this diagram *slowly.* Take time to ponder and think.

Now, let's look at these in more detail. Consider these as spheres, environments, or arenas in which you like to play.

1. The Sphere of the Senses. The question is: *When you have finished your life here on Earth, do you want there to be more beauty in the world, because you were here? If so, what kind of beauty entrances you? Is it art, music, flowers, photography, painting, staging, crafts, clothing, jewelry, or what?* If this is your main purpose in life, then write one paragraph about it.

2. The Sphere of the Body. The question is: *When you have finished your life here on Earth, do you want there to be more wholeness, fitness, or health in the world, more binding up of the body's wounds and strength, more feeding of the hungry, and clothing of the poor, because you were here? What issue in particular?* If this is your main purpose in life, then write one paragraph about it.

3. The Sphere of Our Possessions. The question is: *Is your major concern the often false love of possessions in this world? When you have finished your life here on Earth, do you want there to be better stewardship of what we possess—as individuals, as a community, as a nation—in the world, because you were here? Do you want to see simplicity, quality (rather than quantity), and a broader emphasis on the word "enough," rather than on the words "more, more"? If so, in what areas of human life in particular?* If this is your main purpose in life, then write one paragraph about it.

4. The Sphere of the Will or Conscience. The question is: *When you have finished your life here on Earth, do you want there to be more morality, more justice, more righteousness, more honesty in the world, because you were here? In what areas of human life or history, in particular? And in what geographical area?* If this is your main purpose in life, then write one paragraph about it.

THE PURPOSE FOR MY LIFE:
I WANT THERE TO BE MORE . . . *(CHOOSE)*

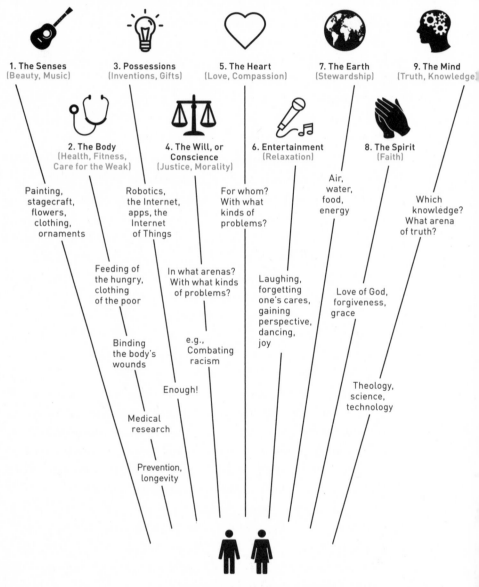

1. The Senses
(Beauty, Music)

3. Possessions
(Inventions, Gifts)

5. The Heart
(Love, Compassion)

7. The Earth
(Stewardship)

9. The Mind
(Truth, Knowledge)

2. The Body
(Health, Fitness,
Care for the Weak)

**4. The Will, or
Conscience**
(Justice, Morality)

6. Entertainment
(Relaxation)

8. The Spirit
(Faith)

Painting,
stagecraft,
flowers,
clothing,
ornaments

Robotics,
the Internet,
apps, the
Internet
of Things

For whom?
With what
kinds of
problems?

Air,
water,
food,
energy

Which
knowledge?
What arena
of truth?

Feeding of
the hungry,
clothing
of the poor

In what arenas?
With what kinds
of problems?

Laughing,
forgetting
one's cares,
gaining
perspective,
dancing,
joy

Love of God,
forgiveness,
grace

Binding
the body's
wounds

e.g.,
Combating
racism

Enough!

Theology,
science,
technology

Medical
research

Prevention,
longevity

. . . in the World Because I Was Here

You may pick more than
one. Write a one-page essay.
Summarize it on the Goal,
Purpose, or Mission in Life
petal, pages 116–17.

5. The Sphere of the Heart. The question is: *When you have finished your life here on Earth, do you want there to be more love and compassion in the world, because you were here? Love or compassion for whom? Or for what?* If this is your main purpose in life, then write one paragraph about it.

6. The Sphere of Entertainment. The question is: *When you have finished your life here on Earth, do you want there to be more lightening of people's loads, more giving them perspective, more helping them to forget their cares for a spell; do you want there to be more laughter in the world, and joy, because you were here? If so, what particular kind of entertainment do you want to contribute to the world?* If this is your main purpose in life, then write one paragraph about it.

7. The Sphere of the Earth. The question is: *Is the planet on which we stand, your major concern? When you have finished your life here on Earth, do you want there to be better protection of this fragile planet, more exploration of the world or the universe—exploration, not exploitation—more dealing with its problems and its energy, because you were here? If so, which problems or challenges in particular, draw your heart and soul?* If this is your main purpose in life, then write one paragraph about it.

8. The Sphere of the Spirit. The question is: *When you have finished your life here on Earth, do you want there to be more spirituality in the world, more faith, more compassion, more forgiveness, more love for God and the human family in all its diversity, because you were here? If so, with what ages, people, or with what parts of human life? If this is you, then your sense of purpose is pointing you toward the sphere of the spirit, or (if you prefer) the Kingdom of God.* If this is your main purpose in life, then write one paragraph about it.

9. The Sphere of the Mind. The question is: *When you have finished your life here on Earth, do you want there to be more knowledge, truth, or clarity in the world, because you were here? Knowledge, truth, or clarity concerning what in particular?* If this is your main purpose in life, then write one paragraph about it.

In sum, remember that all of these are worthwhile purposes and missions, all of these are necessary and needed, in this world. The question is, Which one in particular draws you to it, *the most?* Which one do you most want to lend your brain, your energies, your skills and gifts, your life, to serve, while you are here on this Earth?

When you are done, enter a summary paragraph or essay of what you have decided your purpose or mission is, on the Goal, Purpose, or Mission in Life petal, on pages 116–17.

Petal Four, Worksheet #2

ESSAY: YOUR PHILOSOPHY ABOUT LIFE

There are two challenges you may run into with this Petal.

First Challenge: You just come up empty on this exercise, despite hard thinking. No harm done. If you want an answer, just keep the question on the back burner of your mind; eventually, some insight is going to break through—tomorrow, next week, next month, or a year from now. Be patient with yourself.

Second Challenge: This subject doesn't grab you at all. Okay. Then instead of writing a statement of purpose or mission for your life, you can write instead a statement outlining what you think about *life*—why are we here, why are *you* here, and so on. This is often called "Your Philosophy of Life."

In writing a philosophy of life, it should be no more than two pages, single spaced, and can be less; it should address whichever of the elements listed here you think are most important; pick and choose. You do not have to write about all of them. In most cases, you will only need two or three sentences about each element you choose to comment on.

Beauty: what kind of beauty stirs you, what the function of beauty is in the world

Behavior: how you think we should behave in this world

Beliefs: what your strongest beliefs are

Celebration: how you like to play or celebrate, in life

Choice: what its nature and importance is

Community: what your concept is about belonging to each other; what you think our responsibility is to each other

Compassion: what you think about its importance and use

Confusion: how you live with it, and deal with it

Death: what you think about it and what you think happens after it

Events: what you think makes things happen, how you explain why they happen

Free will: whether we are "predetermined" or have free will

Happiness: what makes for the truest human happiness

Heroes and heroines: who yours are, and why

Humanity: what you think is important about being human, what you think is our function

Love: what you think about its nature and importance, along with all its related words—compassion, forgiveness, grace

Moral issues: which ones you believe are the most important for us to pay attention to, wrestle with, help solve

Paradox: what your attitude is toward its presence in life

Purpose: why we are here, what life is all about

Reality: what you think is its nature, and components

Self: deciding whether physical self is the limit of your being, deciding what trust-in-self means

Spirituality: what its place is in human life, how we should treat it

Stewardship: what we should do with God's gifts to us

Supreme Being: your concept of, and what you think holds the universe together

Truth: what you think about it, which truths are most important

Uniqueness: what you think makes each of us unique

Values: what you think about humanity, what you think about the world, prioritized as to what matters most (to you)

When you are done writing, put a summary paragraph on Petal #4, your Goal, Purpose, or Mission in Life, on pages 116–17.

Now, on to another side of Who You Are.

I Am a Person Who . . .
ALREADY HAS (AND LOVES) THESE PARTICULAR KNOWLEDGES (OR INTERESTS)

Knowledges

Fifth Petal

My Favorite Knowledges, Interests, Subjects

Goal in Filling Out This Petal: To summarize all that you have stored in your brain. *Required:* From your past, subjects you already know a lot about, and enjoy talking about. *Optional:* For your future, what you would like to learn.

What You Are Looking For: Some guidance as to what field you would most enjoy working in.

Form of the Entries on Your Petal: Basically, they will all turn out to be nouns, but see below.

Example of a Good Petal: Graphic design, data analysis, mathematics, how to repair a car, video games, cooking, music, principles of mechanical engineering, how to run an organization, Chinese language, etc.

Example of a Bad Petal: Prompt, thorough, analyzing, persistent, communicating.

> **Why Bad:** Knowledges are always nouns. The words in the bad example above are not. In case you're curious, they are, in order, a trait (adjective), a trait (adjective), a transferable skill (verb), a trait (adjective), and a transferable skill (verb). All in all, that is one mixed bag! All are important, but you want only knowledges on this particular petal.

As mentioned in Petal #3, there are three things traditionally called skills: knowledges, as here; functions, *also known as transferable skills;* and traits or self-management skills. And as we saw there, a general rule throughout this inventory is that *knowledges are nouns; transferable skills are verbs;* and *traits are adjectives or adverbs.* If it helps knowing that, great; if not, *forget it!* Our overarching principle throughout this book is that if a generalization, or metaphor, or example, helps you, use it. But if it just confuses you, then ignore it!!!

On this Petal #5, you will eventually write your final results—your Favorite Knowledges/Fields of Interest, prioritized in the order of importance to you—on pages 116–17.

Petal Five, Worksheet #1

Q&A: TEN SHORTCUTS FOR IDENTIFYING YOUR FAVORITE KNOWLEDGES, SUBJECTS, FIELDS, OR INTERESTS (WHATEVER YOU WISH TO CALL THEM)

On a blank sheet of paper jot down your answers to any or all of these ten shortcuts:

1. What are your favorite hobbies or fields where you like to spend a lot of your time? (Computers? Gardening? Spanish? Law? Physics? Department stores? Hospitals? etc., etc.) Start a list.

2. What do you love to talk about? Ask yourself: If you were stuck on a desert island with a person who only had the capacity to speak on a few subjects, what would you pray those subjects were?

   If you were at a get-together, talking with someone who was covering two of your favorite subjects at once, which way would you hope the conversation would go? Toward which subject?

   If you could talk about something with some world expert, all day long, day after day, what would that subject or field of interest be? Add any ideas that these questions spark in you to your list.

3. What magazine articles or blogs do you love to read? I mean, what subjects? You get really interested when you see a blog that deals with . . . what subject? Add any ideas to your list.

4. What newspaper articles do you love to read or podcasts do you listen to? You get really interested when you see a newspaper special report that deals with . . . what subject? Add any ideas to your list.

5. If you're browsing in a bookstore, what sections of the bookstore do you tend to gravitate toward? What subjects there do you find really fascinating? Add any ideas to your list.

6. What sites on the Internet do you tend to gravitate toward? What subjects do these sites deal with? Do any of these really fascinate you? Add any ideas to your list.

7. What television shows do you tend to watch? What do you enjoy about them? Add any ideas to your list.

8. When you look at a catalog of courses that you could take in your town or city (or on the Internet), which subjects really interest you? Add any ideas to your list.

9. If you could write a book, and it wasn't about your own life or somebody else's, what would be the subject of the book? Add it to your list.

10. There are moments, in most of our lives, when we are so engrossed in a task, that we lose all track of time. (Someone has to remind us that it's time for supper, or whatever.) If this ever happens to you, what task, what subject, so absorbs your attention that you lose all track of time? Add it to your list.[5]

5. I am indebted, again, to Daniel Porot of Geneva, Switzerland, for many of these suggestions.

Petal Five, Worksheet #2

CHART OF ALL THE THINGS YOU'VE LEARNED: THE FISHERMAN'S NET

You may want to copy the following chart onto a larger piece of paper, leaving much more space beneath the title for each of the four parts, before you start filling it in.

CHART: THE FISHERMAN'S NET

Notes About the Knowledges, Subjects, or Interests I've Picked Up Thus Far in My Life
1. What I Know from My Previous Jobs
2. What I Know About or Picked Up, Outside of Work
3. What Fields, Careers, or Industries Sound Interesting to Me
4. Any Other Hunches, Bright Ideas, Great Ideas, etc. That Occur to Me

This chart is like a commercial fisherman's net, where you want to cast it into the sea in order to capture the largest haul of fish possible, and only later do you pick out the best from your haul. But we start *big*.

How to fill out this chart? Well, that's your choice. You may want to fill this out at one sitting; or you may prefer to keep it in your pocket and jot down anything that occurs to you over a period of two or three weeks: every bright idea, every hunch, every remembered dream, every intuition that pops up. *This is an important petal—very important— as it may help you unearth a field or fields where you would really like to work. So it's worth spending some time on.*

Now here are some hints to help you fill in the first three parts of the chart.

PART 1. WHAT YOU KNOW FROM YOUR PREVIOUS JOBS

If you've been out there in the world of work for some time, you've probably learned a lot of things that you now just take for granted. *"Of course I know that!"* But such knowledges may be important, in and of themselves, or they may point you to something important, down the line. So don't be afraid to really get detailed.

Examples: It can be things such as *bookkeeping, handling applications, credit collection of overdue accounts, hiring, international business, management, marketing, sales, merchandising, packaging, policy development, problem solving, troubleshooting, public speaking, recruiting, conference planning, systems analysis, the culture of other countries, other languages, government contract procedures,* and so on.

Think of each job you've ever held, and then for each job jot down any system or procedure that you learned there. For example: *"Worked in a warehouse; learned how to use a forklift and crane, inventory control, logistics automation software, warehouse management systems, teamwork principles, and how to supervise employees."*

Or, *"Worked at a fast food place; learned how to prepare and serve food, how to wait on customers, how to make change, how to deal with complaints, how to train new employees, etc."*

PART 2. WHAT YOU KNOW, OUTSIDE OF WORK

Jot down any bodies of knowledge that you picked up on your own just because the subject fascinated you, such as *antiques, gardening, cooking, budgeting, decorating, photography, crafts, spirituality, sports, camping, travel, repairing things, flea markets, scrapbooking, sewing, art appreciation at museums, how to run or work in a volunteer organization,* and so on.

a. Also think of anything you learned in high school (or college) that you prize knowing today. *Keyboarding? Chinese? Accounting? Geography?* Is this knowledge important to you? Figure that out later; for now, your goal is to just cast as wide a net as possible.

b. Think of anything you learned at training seminars, workshops, conferences, and so on, possibly in connection with a job you had at the time. Or something you decided to attend on your own. Jot it all down. Is this knowledge important to you? Figure that out later; for now, your goal is to just cast as wide a net as possible.

c. Think of anything you studied at home, via online courses, mobile apps, CDs (likely played in your car while commuting), PBS television programs, etc. Is this knowledge important to you? Figure that out later; for now, your goal is to just cast as wide a net as possible. Jot it all down.

d. Think of anything you learned out there in the world, such as *how to assemble a flash mob, how to organize a protest, how to fundraise for a particular cause, how to run a marathon, how to repair a toilet,* etc. Is this knowledge important to you? Figure that out later; for now, your goal is to just cast as wide a net as possible. Jot it all down, in the second section of the chart.

PART 3. WHAT FIELDS, CAREERS, OR INDUSTRIES SOUND INTERESTING TO YOU

Broadly speaking, the workplace consists of the following six branches: *agriculture, manufacturing, information, technology, finance,* and *services.* Any ideas about which of these six is most attractive to you, right off the bat? If so, jot your answer down, in the third section of the chart.

In order to drill further into these six, your best bet is the government's O*NET OnLine (www.onetonline.org).

O*NET OnLine has various lists of career clusters or industries or job families. Below is a mashup of these. Please read over the following list, and copy down any of these that you want to explore (*multiple choices preferred here, in order to have alternatives and therefore hope*) in the third section of the chart.

- ❏ Accommodation and Food Services
- ❏ Administrative and Support Services
- ❏ Agriculture, Food, and Natural Resources
- ❏ Architecture, Engineering, and Construction
- ❏ Arts, Audio/Video Technology, and Communications
- ❏ Business, Operations, Management, and Administration
- ❏ Community and Social Services
- ❏ Computer and Mathematical
- ❏ Design, Entertainment, Sports, and Media
- ❏ Distribution and Logistics
- ❏ Education, Training, and Library
- ❏ Entertainment and Recreation
- ❏ Farming, Forestry, Fishing, and Hunting
- ❏ Finance and Insurance
- ❏ Food Preparation and Serving
- ❏ Government and Public Administration
- ❏ Green Industries or Jobs
- ❏ Health Care, Health Science, and Social Assistance
- ❏ Hospitality and Tourism
- ❏ Human Services
- ❏ Information and Information Technology

- ❑ Law, Public Safety, Corrections, and Security
- ❑ Life, Physical, and Social Sciences
- ❑ Management of Companies and Enterprises
- ❑ Manufacturing
- ❑ Marketing, Sales, and Service
- ❑ Military Related
- ❑ Mining, Quarrying, and Oil and Gas Extraction
- ❑ Personal Care and Service
- ❑ Production
- ❑ Professional, Scientific, and Technical Services
- ❑ Protective Services
- ❑ Real Estate, Rental, and Leasing
- ❑ Religion, Faith, and Related
- ❑ Retail Trade, Sales, and Related
- ❑ Science, Technology, Engineering, and Mathematics
- ❑ Self-Employment
- ❑ Transportation, Warehousing, and Material Moving
- ❑ Utilities

With the O*NET OnLine, once you have chosen anything on the list above, the site has drop-down menus, which allow you to go deeper into each *career cluster, industry,* or *job family* that you have checked off. It drills down to career pathways, and then drills down further to individual occupations, and then drills down still further to tasks, tools, technologies, knowledges, skills, abilities, work activities, education, interests, work styles, work values, related occupations, and salary.

Remember: Jobs, industries, and careers are *mortal*; they are born, they grow, they mature, they flourish, then decline and ultimately die. Sometimes it takes centuries, sometimes merely decades, sometimes even sooner than that. But, eventually, most jobs, industries, and careers *are* mortal. It doesn't matter if they were killed off by China or Mexico, or other supposed villains. They would have died anyway. Eventually.

We are mortal. So are jobs. Understand that truth and you will avoid a life of bitterness and blame. In today's world, you must *always* have a plan B up your sleeves.

Petal Five, Worksheet #3

PRIORITIZING YOUR KNOWLEDGES: FAVORITE SUBJECTS MATRIX

Okay, now you've completed Worksheet #2. You've cast as wide a commercial fisherman's net—so to speak—as possible, using Worksheet #1 and Worksheet #2 for this Petal. What now?

Well, it's time to pick the best of your haul, as we indicated earlier. Time to look it all over, and decide which knowledges, subjects, or interests are your favorites. Time for prioritizing. But we're going to use a different kind of prioritizing aid here: not our familiar Grid, but four boxes/compartments/"bins" along the axes of "Expertise" and "Enthusiasm." In other words, a matrix (above).

You should copy this matrix onto a much larger piece of paper, before you begin.

Then copy everything—*everything*—you have written down on Worksheet #1 (Ten Shortcuts) and Worksheet #2 (the Chart) and decide which of the four bins it belongs in, as you weigh your expertise (or lack of it) and your enthusiasm (or lack of it) with that particular subject or knowledge.

(You don't have to copy anything into bin #4, if you don't want to. Except if you want bin #4 to stand there, filled with subjects and knowledges that you don't care about—as a cautionary tale. I'll state the obvious: any knowledge that you have neither any expertise in nor any enthusiasm for, is a knowledge you will want to avoid at all costs in a future job, if it's up to you. And it is.)

Once you have finished copying every knowledge from Worksheets #1 and #2 into one of these bins, go back and study only what you put into bin #1: *High Expertise, High Enthusiasm.* Copy what you consider to be your top four or five favorites from that bin—*use a Prioritizing Grid if you need to*—and maybe, just maybe, one item from bin #2, and put them on Petal #5, found on pages 116–17.

Bueno! Your Favorite Subjects, Knowledges, Fields, Interests—whatever you want to call them—is done. Now you're ready to move on, to consider the sixth side of Who You Are.

I Am a Person Who . . .
PREFERS A CERTAIN LEVEL
OF RESPONSIBILITY AND SALARY

Salary

Sixth Petal

My Preferred Level
of Responsibility and Salary

Goal in Filling Out This Petal: To gain a realistic picture of how much money you will need to earn, or want to earn, at whatever job you find.

What You Are Looking For: A range, because most employers are thinking in terms of a range, too. When you negotiate salary, as you will almost certainly have to, if the employer is of any significant size, you want the bottom of your range to be near the top of theirs.

Form of the Entries on Your Petal: Total dollars needed, weekly, monthly, or annually. Stated in thousands (symbol: K).

Example of a Good Petal: $75K to $85K

Example of a Bad Petal: $500K

> **Why Bad:** Well, it's not a range, which it needs to be; and it's too high unless you have a reason why such a high income is expected, and—more important—justified.

A CRASH COURSE ABOUT MONEY

Money is important. Or else we're reduced to bartering for our food, clothing, and shelter. So, when we're out of work, unless we have huge amounts of money in our savings account or investments, we are inevitably thinking "What am I going to do, so that I have enough money to put food on the table, clothes on my back, and a roof over our heads for myself—and for my family or partner (*if I have one*)?"

Happiness is important, too. So, we may find ourselves thinking "How much do I really need to be earning, for me to be truly happy with my life?"

Are these two worries—money and happiness—related? Can money buy happiness?

Partly, it turns out. Partly. A study, published in 2010, of the responses of 450,000 people in the US to a daily survey, found that the less money they made, the more unhappy they tended to be, day after day.[6] No surprise there. And, obviously, the more money they made, measured in terms of percentage improvement, the happier they tended to be, *as measured by the frequency and intensity of moments of smiling, laughter, affection, and joy all day long, vs. moments of sadness, worry, and stress.*

So, money does buy happiness. *But only up to a point.* That point was found to be around $75,000 annual income (*at the end of 2017, median household income was $61,372[7]*). If people made more money than $75,000, it of course further improved their *satisfaction* with how their life was going, but it did not increase their happiness. Above $75,000, they started to report reduced ability to spend time with people they liked, to enjoy leisure, and to savor small pleasures. Happiness depends on things like that, and on other factors too: good health; a loving relationship; loving friends; and a feeling of competence, gaining mastery, respect, praise, or even love because we are really good at what we do.

---

6. Daniel Kahneman and Angus Deaton, *Proceedings of the National Academy of Sciences*, Early Edition, September 6, 2010.
7. Lorie Konish, "US Median Household Income Climbs to New High of $61,372," CNBC Personal Finance, September 14, 2018, www.cnbc.com/2018/09/12/median-household-income-climbs-to-new-high-of-61372.html.

So, this petal cannot be filled out all by itself. It is inextricably tied to the other petals—most particularly, to what you love to do, and where you love to do it.

Still, salary is something you must think out ahead of time, when you're contemplating your ideal job or career. Level goes hand in hand with salary, of course. So here are a couple of questions you should be asking yourself:

1. At what level would you like to work, in your ideal job?

Level is a matter of how much responsibility you want, in an organization:

- ❏ Boss or CEO (this may mean you'll have to form your own business)
- ❏ Manager or someone under the boss who carries out orders
- ❏ The head of a team
- ❏ A member of a team of equals
- ❏ One who works in tandem with one other partner
- ❏ One who works alone, as an employee, a consultant to an organization, or a one-person business

Think carefully about your answer, talk it over with your friends or family, then enter a two- or three-word summary of your answer (for now) on Petal #6, the Preferred Salary and Level of Responsibility, of your Flower Diagram, pages 116–17.

2. What salary would you like to be aiming for?

Here you have to think in terms of a range, not a single figure. One way to do this is to think of your minimum or maximum desired.

Minimum is what you would need to make, if you were just barely "getting by." And incidentally, you do need to know this *before* you go in for a job-interview with anyone (*or before you form your own business, and need to know how much profit you must make, just to survive*). You can't survive on a negative income stream.

Maximum could be any astronomical figure you can think of, but it is more useful here to put down the salary you realistically think you could make, with your present competency and experience, were you working for a real, *but generous*, boss. (If this maximum figure is still depressingly low, then put down the salary you would like to be making five years from now.)

Petal Six, Worksheet #1

A BUDGET: KEEPING TRACK OF HOW MUCH YOU DO SPEND AND HOW MUCH YOU'D LIKE TO SPEND

Many job-hunters and career-changers want to begin by making up a budget of what they think they will need. On the next page you will find a simple guide to the categories you will need to think about. Figure out what you think you will need *monthly*, in each category. And if you see any categories missing, do not hesitate to add them.

Many do not want to start with a budget of how they *should* spend their money. They want to start by first keeping track of how, in actual fact, they *do* spend their money. You can just jot down notes at the end of each day. Lots of apps make this task much easier. For example, there is Spending Tracker, Pocket Expense, Goodbudget, and for all those who want to sync with their bank accounts, Mint.com.

The good news: All are simple, and all are free.

Once you figure out what you *do* spend, you'll be much better able to lay out a realistic budget of what you *want* to spend.

In any event, by hook or by crook, once you have your monthly budget, it's time to do some math. Fill out your monthly expenses chart on the next two pages.

Multiply the total amount you need each month by 12, to get the yearly figure.

Divide the yearly figure by 2,000, and you will be reasonably near the *minimum* hourly wage that you need. Thus, if you need $3,333 per month, multiplied by 12 that's $40,000 a year, and then divided by 2,000, that's $20 an hour.

You will also want to put down the *maximum* salary you would like to make (dream, dream, dream). Once you are done, enter both salary figures—minimum and maximum—and any notes you want to add such as to justify the maximum (*you may also want to add any "nonmonetary" rewards you seek from the Optional Exercise on page 104*) and add all of this onto Petal #6, the Preferred Salary and Level of Responsibility petal, found on pages 116–17.

MONTHLY EXPENSES

Housing

Rent or mortgage payments . . . . $_____

Electricity/gas. . . . . $_____

Water . . . . $_____

Phone/Internet. . . . . $_____

Garbage removal . . . . $_____

Cleaning, maintenance, repairs[8] . . . . $_____

Food

What you spend at the supermarket
and/or farmers' market, etc. . . . . $_____

Eating out . . . . $_____

Clothing

Purchase of new or used clothing. . . . . $_____

Cleaning, dry cleaning, laundry . . . . $_____

Automobile/transportation

Car payments . . . . $_____

Gas (*who knows?*[9]). . . . . $_____

Repairs. . . . . $_____

Public transportation (*bus, train, plane*) . . . . $_____

Insurance

Car . . . . $_____

Medical or health care. . . . . $_____

House and personal possessions. . . . . $_____

Life . . . . $_____

Medical expenses

Doctors' visits. . . . . $_____

Prescriptions. . . . . $_____

Fitness costs . . . . $_____

---

8. If you have extra household expenses, such as a security system, be sure to include the quarterly (or whatever) expenses here, divided by three.
9. Your checkbook stubs and/or online banking records will tell you a lot of this stuff. But you may be vague about your cash or credit card expenditures. For example, you may not know how much you spend at the supermarket, or how much you spend on gas, etc. But there is a simple way to find out. Keep notes on your smartphone or iPad for two weeks (there are apps for that, such as DailyCost—$0.99). Jot down everything you pay cash (or use credit cards) for—on the spot, right after you pay it. At the end of those two weeks, you'll be able to take that record and make a realistic guess of what should be put down in these categories that now puzzle you. (Multiply the two-week figure by two, and you'll have the monthly figure.)

Support for other family members

    Child-care costs (*if you have children*)............$_____

    Child support (*if you're paying that*).............$_____

    Support for your parents (*if you're helping out*).....$_____

Charity giving/tithe (*to help others*) ....$_____

School/learning

    Children's costs (*if you have children in school*) .....$_____

    Your learning costs (*adult education,*

    job-hunting classes, etc.).......................$_____

Pet care (*if you have pets*) ....$_____

Bills and debts (*usual monthly payments*)

    Credit cards................................$_____

    Local stores.................................$_____

    Other obligations you pay off monthly...........$_____

Taxes

    Federal[10] (*next April's due, divided by*

    twelve months) ....$_____

    State (*likewise*) ....$_____

    Local/property (*next amount due, divided by*

    twelve months) ....$_____

    Tax help (*if you ever use an accountant, or*

    pay a friend to help you with taxes, etc.) ....$_____

Savings ....$_____

Retirement (*Keogh, IRA, SEP, etc.*)..................$_____

Amusement/discretionary spending

    Movies, Netflix, etc...........................$_____

    Other kinds of entertainment ....$_____

    Reading, newspapers, magazines, books.........$_____

    Gifts (*birthdays, holidays, etc.*)..................$_____

    Vacations...................................$_____

Total Amount You Need Each Month.............$_____

---

10. Incidentally, for US citizens, looking ahead to next April 15, be sure to check with your local
IRS office or a reputable accountant to find out if you can deduct the expenses of your job-hunt
on your federal (and state) income tax returns. At this writing, some job-hunters can, if—big
IF—this is not your first job that you're looking for, if you haven't been unemployed too long, and
if you aren't making a career-change. Do go find out what the latest "ifs" are. If the IRS says
you are eligible, keep careful receipts of everything related to your job-hunt, as you go along:
telephone calls, stationery, printing, postage, travel, etc.

Petal Six, Worksheet #2

AN OPTIONAL EXERCISE:
OTHER REWARDS BESIDES MONEY

If you do check off things on this list, arrange your answers in order of importance to you, and then add them to the petal.

Now, on to the seventh side of Who You Are.

Optional Exercise:
Nonmonetary Rewards

You may wish to put down other rewards, besides money, that you would hope for from your next job or career. These might be:

❏ Adventure

❏ Challenge

❏ Respect

❏ Influence

❏ Popularity

❏ Fame

❏ Power

❏ Intellectual stimulation from the other workers there

❏ A chance to be creative

❏ A chance to help others

❏ A chance to exercise leadership

❏ A chance to make decisions

❏ A chance to use your expertise

❏ A chance to bring others closer to God

❏ Other:

I Am a Person Who . . .
PREFERS CERTAIN PLACES TO LIVE

Geography

Seventh Petal

My Preferred Place(s) to Live

Goal in Filling Out This Petal: To define in what part of the country or the world you would most like to work and live, and be happiest, *if you ever have a choice.* Also to resolve a conflict (should it arise) between you and your partner as to where you want to live after you retire or make your next career move.

What You Are Looking For: Having a clearer picture about what you hope for in life, now or later. Now, if you're able to move and want to make a wise decision as to *where.* Later, if you're currently tied down to a particular place because "I need to be near my kids or my ailing parents," or whatever, in which case this becomes a planning for the future—retirement, or earlier. It's important to think about the future *now*, because an opportunity may come along when you least expect it, and you might pass right by it, unless you've given it some thought, and instantly recognize it.

Form of the Entries on Your Petal: You can stay general (*city, suburbs, rural, up in the mountains, on the coast,* or *overseas*) or you can get very specific if you're really ready to move, naming names and places—as this exercise will teach you to do.

Example of a Good Petal: First preference—Austin, Texas; second preference—Honolulu; third preference—New York City.

Example of a Bad Petal: The West; a suburb; snow.

> **Why Bad:** Too broad. Doesn't really offer any help in making a decision. And it isn't prioritized, as a good petal must be.

Petal Seven, Worksheet #1

A CHART: WHAT I LIKED OR DISLIKED
ABOUT PLACES I HAVE LIVED

Copy the chart found on pages 108–9, onto a larger (11" x 17") piece of
paper or cardboard. And if you are doing this exercise with a partner,
make a copy for them too, so that each of you is working on a clean
copy of your own, and can follow these instructions independently.

Now, as to how you fill out this chart:

Column 1. In *Column 1*, you should list all the places where you
have ever lived.

Column 2. In *Column 2*, you should list all the factors you disliked
(and still do) about each place. The negative factors do not have
to be put exactly opposite the place in *Column 1*. The names in
Column 1 exist simply as pegs on which to hang your memory.

If the same factors keep repeating, just put a check mark after
the first listing of that factor, every time it repeats.

Keep going until you have listed all the factors you disliked
or hated about each and every place you named in *Column 1*. Now,
in effect, throw away *Column 1*; discard it from your thoughts. The
negative factors were what you were after. *Column 1* has served
its purpose.

(*As you go, if you recall some things you liked about any place, list
those factors at the bottom of the next column, Column 3.*)

Column 3. Look at *Column 2*, your list of negative factors, and
in *Column 3* try to list each one's opposite (or near opposite).
For example, "the sun never shone there" would, in *Column 3*, be
turned into "mostly sunny, all year-round." It will not always
be *the exact opposite*. For example, the negative factor "rains all
the time" does not necessarily translate into the positive "sunny
all the time." It might be something like "sunny at least 200 days
a year." It's your call. Keep going, until every negative factor in
Column 2 is turned into its opposite, a positive factor, in *Column 3*.

Don't forget to note any positive factors you listed at the bottom of *Column 3*, when you were working on *Column 2*.

Column 4. In *Column 4*, now, list the positive factors in *Column 3*, in the order of most important (to you), down to least important (to you). For example, if you were looking at and trying to name a new town, city, or place where you could be happy and flourish, what is the first thing you would look for? Would it be good weather? Or lack of crime? Or good schools? Or access to cultural opportunities, such as music, art, museums, or whatever? Or would it be inexpensive housing? etc., etc. Rank all the factors in *Column 4*. Use the ten-item Prioritizing Grid on page 111 if you need to.

Show and tell. Once done, list on a blank sheet of paper those top ten factors, in order of importance to you, and show it to everyone you meet for the next ten days, with the ultimate question: "Can you think of any place that has all ten of these factors, or at least the top five?" Jot down any and all of their suggestions on the back of the sheet. When the ten days are up, look at the back of that sheet and circle the three places that seem the most interesting to you. If there is only a partial overlap between your dream factors and the places your friends and acquaintances can come up with, *make sure the overlap is in the factors that count the most*. Google can help, too. Try searching "cities with lowest crime rates" or "best places for sunshine in US" and see what shows up.

Column 5. Now you have some names that you will want to find out more about, so that you can eventually figure out which would be your absolute favorite place to live, and your second, and your third, as backups. Enter those three places in *Column 5*, then copy them plus your top five geographical factors onto Petal #7, Preferred Place(s) to Live, on the Flower Diagram on pages 116–17.

Column 6. If you are doing this with a partner, skip *Column 5*. Instead, when you have finished your *Column 4*, look at your partner's *Column 4*, and copy it into *Column 6*. The numbering of *your* list in *Column 4* was 1, 2, 3, 4, etc. So, you need a different numbering system for your partner's list, as you copy it into *Column 6*; let us say a, b, c, d, etc.

My Geographical Preferences
DECISION MAKING FOR JUST YOU

Column 1	Column 2	Column 3	Column 4
Names of Places I Have Lived	From the Past: Negatives	Translating the Negatives into Positives	Ranking of My Positives
	Factors I Disliked and Still Dislike About Any Place		1.
			2.
			3.
			4.
			5.
			6.
			7.
			8.
		Factors I Liked and Still Like About Any Place	9.
			10.

Column 5		Column 6	Column 7	Column 8
Places That Fit These Criteria		Ranking of His/Her Preferences	Combining Our Two Lists (Columns 4 & 6)	Places That Fit These Criteria

Our Geographical Preferences

DECISION MAKING FOR YOU AND A PARTNER

Column 5	Column 6	Column 7	Column 8
Places That Fit These Criteria	Ranking of His/Her Preferences	Combining Our Two Lists (Columns 4 & 6)	Places That Fit These Criteria
	a.	a.	
		1.	
	b.	b.	
		2.	
	c.	c.	
		3.	
	d.	d.	
		4.	
	e.	e.	
		5.	
	f.	f.	
		6.	
	g.	g.	
		7.	
	h.	h.	
		8.	
	i.	i.	
		9.	
	j.	j.	
		10.	

Column 7. Now, in *Column 7*, both of you can combine your *Column 4* with *Column 6*, on your respective worksheets. Combine the two lists in this manner: first your partner's top favorite geographical factor ("a"), then *your* top favorite geographical factor ("1"), then your partner's second most important favorite geographical factor ("b"), then yours ("2"), etc., until you have twenty favorite geographical factors (*yours and your partner's*) listed, in order, in *Column 7*. Both of you are now working on the same list.

Show and tell (for two people). For now, don't work on all twenty; narrow it down to the top ten in column 7, and list these on a blank sheet of paper. Then both of you should show that list to everyone you meet, for the next ten days, with the same question "Can you think of any place that has these ten factors, or at least the top five?" Jot down their suggestions on the back of the sheet. When the ten days are up, you and your partner should look at the back of your sheets and agree on which three places look the most interesting to the two of you. If there is only a partial overlap between your dream factors and the places your friends and acquaintances suggested, make sure the overlap is in the factors that matter the most to the two of you, i.e., those at the top of your list in *Column 7*.

Column 8. Now you have the names of places that you will want to find out more about, until you are sure which is the absolute favorite place to live for both of you, plus your second, and your third, as backups. Enter in *Column 8*.

Finally, both of you should put the names of those top three places, plus your top five geographical factors, onto Petal #7, the Preferred Place(s) to Live petal, on both of your Flower Diagrams, pages 116–17.

Conclusion for Petal 7

Does all this seem like just too much work? Well, there are two shortcuts you *may* want to try. The first is a website called Teleport (teleport.org). Try it! See if it helps you at all. One reader said, about a similar site, "I found it useful. It showed me towns I'd never thought about."

PRIORITIZING GRID FOR 10 ITEMS OR FEWER

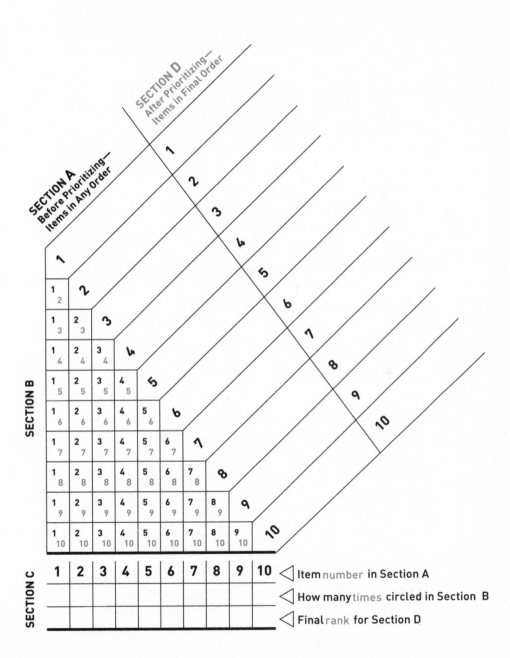

Other alternative: Have everyone in the house throw darts at a map (of the US or wherever) that you've pinned to a dartboard. One family did this, after they couldn't agree on anything. See what place the most darts came near. (For them it came out "Denver"! So, Denver it was!)

I Am a Person Who . . .
HAS COMPLETED MY FLOWER

Readers have asked to see an example of "That One Piece of Paper" all filled out. Rich W. Feller—a student of mine back in 1982, now a world-famous professor and past president of the National Career Development Association—filled out his flower as you see on the facing page. He said "That One Piece of Paper" has been his lifelong companion ever since, and his guiding star. (The petals then were slightly different.)

Rich Feller first put his personal "picture" together over thirty years ago. Here are his comments about its usefulness since, and how "That One Piece of Paper" helped him, how he's used it, and how it's changed.

WHAT THE PARACHUTE FLOWER HAS MEANT TO ME

More than anything I've gained from an academic life, my Flower has given me hope, direction, and a lens to satisfaction. Using it to assess my life direction during crisis, career moves, and stretch assignments, it helps me define and hold to personal commitments. In many ways it's my "guiding light." Data within my Flower became and remain the core of any success and satisfaction I have achieved.

After I first filled out my own Flower Diagram in a two-week workshop with Dick Bolles back in 1982, I decided to teach the Flower to others. My academic position has allowed me to do this, abundantly. Having now taught the

(continued)

Example
(Rich Feller's Flower)

Favorite Values

1. Improve the human condition 2. Promote interdependence and futuristic principles 3. Maximize productive use of human/material resources 4. Teach people to be self-directed/self-responsible 5. Free people from self-defeating controls (thoughts, rules, barriers) 6. Promote capitalistic principles 7. Reduce exploitation 8. Promote political participation 9. Acknowledge those who give to the community 10. Give away ideas

Favorite People-Environment

1. Strong social, perceptual skills 2. Emotionally and physically healthy 3. Enthusiastically include others 4. Heterogeneous in interests and skills 5. Social changers, innovators 6. Politically, economically astute 7. Confident enough to confront/cry and be foolish 8. Sensitive to nontraditional issues 9. I and R (see page 46) 10. Nonmaterialistic

Favorite Interests

1. Large conference planning 2. Regional geography and culture 3. Traveling on $20/day 4. Career planning seminars 5. Counseling techniques/theories 6. American policies 7. Fundamentals of sports 8. Fighting sexism 9. NASCAR auto racing 10. Interior design

Favorite Skills

1. Observational/learning skills • continually expose self to new experiences • perceptive in identifying and assessing potential of others 2. Leadership skills • continually search for more responsibility • see a problem/act to solve it 3. Instructing/interpreting/guiding • committed to learning as a lifelong process • create atmosphere of acceptance 4. Serving/helping/human relations skills • shape atmosphere of particular place • relate well in dealing with public 5. Detail/follow-through skills • handle great variety of tasks • resource broker 6. Influencing/persuading skills • recruiting talent/leadership • inspiring trust 7. Performing skills • getting up in front of a group (if I'm in control) • addressing small and large groups 8. Intuitional/innovative skills • continually develop/generate new ideas 9. Develop/plan/organize/execute • designing projects • utilizing skills of others 10. Language/read/write • communicate effectively • can think quickly on my feet

Favorite Working Conditions

1. Receive clinical supervision 2. Mentor relationship 3. Excellent secretary 4. Part of larger, highly respected organization with clear direction 5. Near gourmet and health food specialty shops 6. Heterogeneous colleagues (race, sex, age) 7. Flexible dress code 8. Merit system 9. Can bike/bus/walk to work 10. Private office with window

Geography

1. Close to major city 2. Mild winters/low humidity 3. Change in seasons 4. Clean and green 5. 100,000 people 6. Nice shopping malls 7. Wide range of athletic options 8. Diverse economic base 9. Ample local culture 10. Sense of community (pride)

Salary and Level of Responsibility

1. Can determine 9/12 month contract 2. Can determine own projects 3. Considerable clout in organization's direction without administrative responsibilities 4. Able to select colleagues 5. 3 to 5 assistants 6. $35K to $50K 7. Serve on various important boards 8. Can defer clerical and budget decisions and tasks 9. Speak before large groups 10. Can run for elected office

Flower to thousands of counselors and career development and human resource specialists, I continually use it with clients, and in my own transitional retirement planning.

I'm overwhelmed with how little has changed within my Flower, over the years. My Flower is the best of what I am. Its petals are my compass, and using my "favorite skills" is the mirror to a joyful day. I trust the wisdom within "That One Piece of Paper." It has guided my work and my life, ever since 1982, and it has helped my wife and me define our hopes for our son.

The process of filling out and acting on "That One Piece of Paper" taught me a lot. Specifically, it taught me **the importance of the following ten things, often running contrary to what my studies and doctoral work had taught me previously.**

I learned from my Flower the importance of:

1. Chasing after passions, honoring strengths, and respecting skill identification

2. Challenging societal definitions of balance and success

3. Committing to something bigger than oneself

4. Living authentically and with joy

5. Being good at what matters to oneself and its relationship to opportunity

6. Finding pleasure in all that one does

7. Staying focused on well-being and life satisfaction

8. Personal clarity and responsibility for designing "possible selves"

9. Letting the world know, humbly but clearly, what we want

10. "Coaching" people amid a world of abundance where individuals yearn for meaning and purpose more than they hunger for possessions, abject compliance with society's expectations, or simply fitting in

This technologically enhanced, global workplace we now face in the twenty-first century certainly challenges all we thought we knew about our life roles. Maintaining clarity, learning agility, and identifying development plans have become elevated to new and critical importance, if we are to maintain choice. As a result I've added the following four emphases to "Rich's Flower"—Have, do, learn, and give. That is to say, I try to keep a running list (constantly updated) of ten things that I want to:

1. Have

2. Do

3. Learn

4. Give

Through the practice of answering the four questions listed above, I can measure change in my growth and development.

I feel so fortunate to have the opportunity to share with others how much I gained from the wisdom and hope embedded within "Rich's Flower."

I humbly offer my resume, home location and design, and family commitments on my website at *www.mychhs .colostate.edu/Rich.Feller*. I'd be honored to share my journey, and encourage others to nurture and shine light on their garden as well. I believe you'll find about 90 percent of the Flower's items influence our daily experience.

Rich Feller
Professor of Counseling and Career Development
University Distinguished Teaching Scholar
Colorado State University
Fort Collins, CO

Okay, like Rich, you've now got your completed Flower. Nice diagram. What do you do with it?

Well, that's the subject of our next chapter.

The Flower

"That One Piece of Paper"

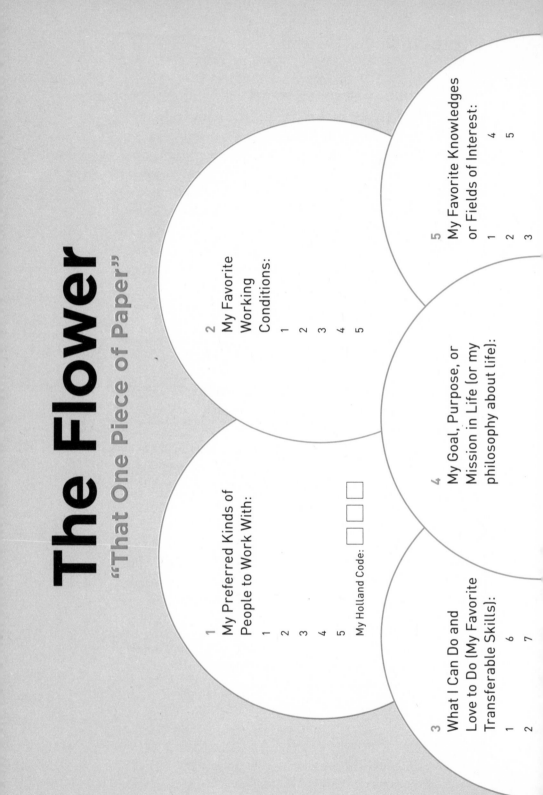

2 My Favorite Working Conditions:

1
2
3
4
5

5 My Favorite Knowledges or Fields of Interest:

1   4
2   5
3

1 My Preferred Kinds of People to Work With:

1
2
3
4
5

My Holland Code: ☐ ☐ ☐

4 My Goal, Purpose, or Mission in Life (or my philosophy about life):

3 What I Can Do and Love to Do (My Favorite Transferable Skills):

1   6
2   7

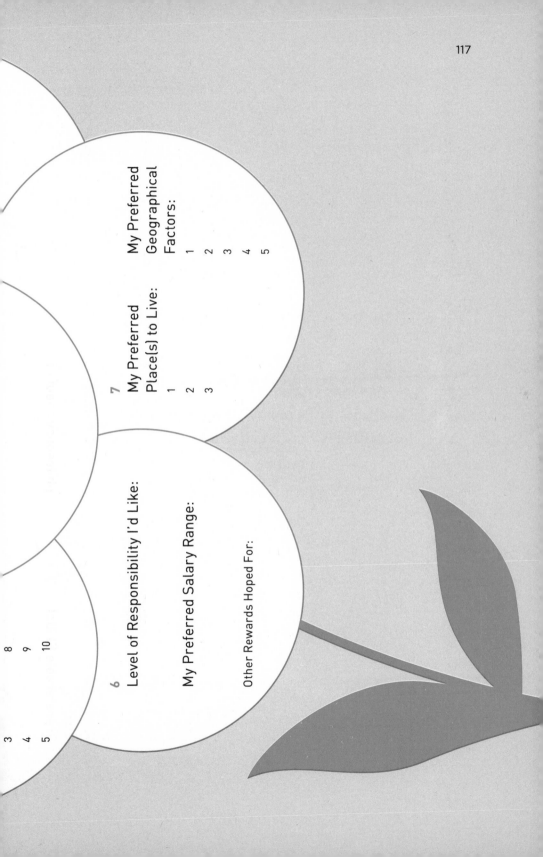

My Preferred Geographical Factors:
1
2
3
4
5

My Preferred Place(s) to Live:
1
2
3

6

Level of Responsibility I'd Like:

My Preferred Salary Range:

Other Rewards Hoped For:

7

3
4
5

8
9
10

This is the real secret of life—to be completely engaged with what you are doing in the here and now. And instead of calling it work, realize it is play.
         —Alan Watts

CHAPTER 6

You Get to Choose Where You Work

Some of you will look at your completed Flower Exercise and have an instant flash of recognition. *Wow, I see what I want to do with my life! I'm excited.* Others of you will need a more carefully reasoned series of steps to find that out.

Here are five steps that job-hunters or career-changers have found tremendously helpful to take—*and in this order*:

#1. Find Out What Careers or Work Your Flower Points To.
#2. Try On Jobs Before You Decide Which Ones to Pursue.
#3. Find Out What Kinds of Organizations Have Such Jobs.
#4. Find Names of Particular Places That Interest You.
#5. Learn as Much as You Can About a Place Before Formally Approaching Them.

First, You Need to Find Out What Careers or Work Your Flower Points To

1. Look at your completed Flower Diagram, and from the fifth petal of the Flower choose the top *three* of your favorite Knowledges (or fields of interest, favorite fields, or fields of fascination—whatever you want to call them). All nouns. On one piece of blank paper, say, 8½" x 11", or on your mobile device, copy these in the top half of that page, in their order of importance to you (most important at the top). Beneath them all, midway down the page, draw a line, straight across.

2. Then, look at the Skills petal on your completed Flower Diagram and choose your top *five* favorite Transferable Skills. All verbs. Copy them down, in order, below the line.

3. Now, take this page and show it to at least five friends, family members, or professionals whom you know. Ask them what jobs or work this page suggests to them. Tell them you just want them to take some wild guesses, combining as many of the eight factors on that page, as possible. *Plan B:* If they absolutely draw a blank, tell them that interests or special knowledges (in the top half of the page) usually point toward a career field, while transferable skills (in the bottom half) usually point toward a job-title or job-level, in that field. So, ask them, in the case of your favorite special knowledges, "What career fields do these suggest to you?" And in the case of your transferable skills, "What job-title or jobs do these skills suggest to you?" If possible, you or they must combine two or three of your knowledges (fields) into one specialty: that's what can make you unique, with very little competition from others.

Here is how to go about doing that: Let us say your three favorite knowledges are gardening and carpentry and a limited knowledge of psychiatry. What you want to do is use all three expertises, not just one of them—if you possibly can. So, put those three favorite knowledges on a series of overlapping circles, as seen above. Now, to figure out how to combine these three, imagine that each circle is a person; that is, in this case, Psychiatrist, Carpenter, and Gardener. You ask yourself which person took the longest to get trained in their specialty. The answer, here, is the psychiatrist. The reason you ask yourself this question, is that the person with the longest training is most likely to have the broadest overview of things. So, you go to see a psychiatrist, either at a private clinic or at a university or hospital. You ask for fifteen minutes of his or her time, and pay them if necessary. Then you ask the psychiatrist if he or she knows how to combine psychiatry with *one*—just one, initially—of your other two favorite knowledges. Let's say you choose gardening here. "Doctor, do you know anyone who combines a knowledge of psychiatry with a knowledge of gardening or plants?" Since I'm talking about a true story here, I can tell you what the psychiatrist said: "Yes, in working with catatonic patients, we often give them a plant to take care of, so they know there is something that is depending on them for its future, and its survival." "And how would I also employ a knowledge of carpentry?" "Well, in building the planters, that's a start, isn't it?" This is the way you learn how to combine your three favorite knowledges, all at once, no matter what those three may be.

4. Jot down *everything* these people suggest to you, on your computer, iPad, smartphone, or small pad of paper. Whether you like their suggestions, or not. This is just brainstorming, for the moment.

5. After you have done this for a week or so, with everyone you meet, sit down and look at all these notes. Anything helpful or valuable here? If you see some useful suggestions, circle them and determine to explore them. If nothing looks interesting, go talk to five more of your friends, acquaintances, or people you know in the business world or nonprofit sector. Repeat, as necessary.

6. As you ponder any suggestions that look worth exploring, consider the fact we saw in chapter 5, that all jobs can be described as working primarily with *people* **or** working primarily with *information/ data* **or** working primarily with *things*. Most jobs involve all three, but which is your *primary* preference? It is often your *favorite* skill that will give you the clue. If it *doesn't*, then go back and look at the *whole* Transferable Skills petal, on your Flower Diagram. What do you think? Are your favorite skills weighted more toward working with *people,* or toward working with *information/ data,* or toward working with *things*?

7. Just remember what you are trying to do here: find some names for your Flower. Typically, if you show it to enough family, friends, or colleagues, you will end up with about forty suggestions.

Don't ever think to yourself "Well, I see what it is that I would die to be able to do, but I know there is no job in the world like that." Dear friend, you don't know any such thing. Now I grant you that after you have completed it, you may not be able to find all that you want—down to the last detail. But you'd be surprised at how much of your dream you may be able to find. Sometimes it will be found in stages. One retired man I know, who had been a senior executive with a publishing company, found himself bored to death in retirement, after he turned sixty-five. He decided he didn't care what field he worked in, at that point, so he contacted his favorite business acquaintance, who told him apologetically, "Times are tough. We just don't have anything open that matches or requires your abilities; right now all we need is someone in our mail room." The sixty-five-year-old executive said, "I'll take that job!" He did, and over the ensuing years steadily advanced once again, to just the job he wanted: as a senior executive in that organization, where he utilized all his prized skills, for a number of years. Finally, he retired for the second time, at the age of eighty-five.

Always keep in mind your dream. Get as close to it as you can. Then be patient. You never know what doors will open up.

Second, You Need to Try On Jobs Before You Decide Which Ones to Pursue

You know when you go shopping at a clothing store, you try on different outfits that you see in their window or on their racks. Why do you try them on? Well, the clothes that look *terrific* in the window don't always look so hot when you see them on *you*. They don't hang quite right, etc.

It's the same with careers. Ones that *sound* terrific in your imagination don't always look so great when you actually see them up close and personal.

What you want of course is a career that looks terrific—in the window, *and* on you. So you need to go talk to people who are already doing the kind of job or career that you're thinking about. The website LinkedIn should be invaluable to you, in locating the names of such people.

Once you find them, if they live nearby ask for nineteen minutes of their time face-to-face—Starbucks?—and keep to your word, unless during the chat they *insist* they want to go on talking. *Some* workers—not all—are desperate to find someone who will actually listen to them; you may come as an answer to their prayers.

Here are some questions that will help when you're talking *with workers who are actually doing the career or job you think you might like to do*:

- "How did you get into this work?"
- "What do you like the most about it?"
- "What do you like the least about it?"
- And, "Where else could I find people who do this kind of work?" (*You should always ask them for more than one name here, so that if you run into a dead end at any point, you can easily go visit the other name[s] they suggested.*)

If at any point in these informational interviews with workers, it becomes more and more clear to you that this career, occupation, or job you are exploring definitely doesn't fit you, then the last question (above) gets turned into a different kind of inquiry:

- "Do you have any ideas as to who else I could talk to—*about my skills and special knowledges or interests*—who might know what other careers use the same skills and knowledge?" If they come up with names, go visit the people they suggest. If they can't think of anyone, ask them, "If you don't know of anyone, who do you think might know?"

Sooner or later, as you do this informational interviewing with workers, you'll find a career that fits you just fine. It uses your favorite skills. It employs your favorite special knowledges or fields of interest. Okay, then you must ask how much training etc. it takes, to get into that field or career. You ask the same people you have been talking to previously.

More times than not, you will hear *bad news*. They will tell you something like "In order to be hired for this job, you have to have a master's degree and ten years' experience at it."

Is that so? Keep in mind that no matter how many people tell you that such-and-such are the rules about getting into a particular occupation, and there are no exceptions—believe me there *are* exceptions to almost *every* rule, except for those few professions that have rigid entrance examinations as, say, medicine or law. Otherwise, *somebody* has figured out a way around the rules. You want to find out who these people are, and go talk to them, to find out *how they did it*.

So, in your informational interviewing, you press deeper; you search for *exceptions:*

- "Yes, but do you know of anyone in this field who got into it without that master's degree, and ten years' experience?"
- "And where might I find him or her?"
- "And if you don't know of any such person, who do you think might know?"

But in the end, maybe—just maybe—you can't find any exceptions. It's not that they aren't out there; it's just that you don't know how to find them. So, what do you do when everyone tells you that such-and-such a career takes *years* to prepare for, and you can't find *anyone* who took a shortcut? What then?

Good news. Every professional specialty has one or more *shadow* professions, which require much less training. For example, instead of becoming a doctor, you can go into paramedical work; instead of becoming a lawyer, you can go into paralegal work; instead of becoming a licensed career counselor, you can become a career coach. There is always a way to get *close*, at least, to what you dream of. Think about your career ideas more broadly. You can Google "careers related to _____" and discover ideas you never considered. For example, let's go back to the psychiatrist career mentioned on page 120. If you discover through your research you can't or don't want to go to medical school, a Google search of careers related to psychiatry lists options such as mental health counselor, hospital social worker, and marriage counselor, all of which require less education and training. There is a field called horticultural therapy, which would closely relate to the individual's interests in the example.

Third, You Need to Find Out What Kinds of Organizations Have Such Jobs

Before you think of individual places where you might like to work, it is helpful to stop and think of all the *kinds* of places where one might get hired, so you can be sure you're casting the widest net possible.

Let's take an example. Suppose in your new career you want to be a teacher. You must then ask yourself *"What kinds of places hire teachers?"* You might answer, *"Just schools"*—and finding that schools in your geographical area have no openings, you might say, *"Well, there are no jobs for people in this career."*

But wait a minute! There are countless other *kinds* of organizations and agencies out there, besides schools, that employ *teachers*. For example, corporate training and educational departments, workshop sponsors, foundations, private research firms, educational consultants, teachers' associations, professional and trade societies, military bases, state and local councils on higher education, fire and police training academies, and so on and so forth.

"Kinds of places" also means places with different *hiring options*, besides full-time, such as:

- places that would employ you part-time (maybe you'll end up deciding, or having, to hold down two or even three part-time jobs, which together add up to one full-time job);
- places that take temporary workers, on assignment for one project at a time;
- places that take consultants, one project at a time;
- places that operate primarily with volunteers etc.;
- places that are nonprofit;
- places that are for-profit;
- and, don't forget, places that you yourself could start up, should you decide to be your own boss (more in chapter 12).

During this interviewing for information, you should not only talk to people who can give you a broad overview of the career that you are considering, you should also talk with actual workers, who can tell you in more detail what the tasks are in the kinds of organizations that interest you.

Fourth, You Need to Find Names of Particular Places That Interest You

As you interview workers about their jobs or careers, somebody will probably innocently mention, somewhere along the way, actual names of organizations that have such kinds of workers—plus what's good or bad about the place. This is important information for you. Jot it all down. Keep notes religiously!

But you will want to supplement what they have told you, by seeking out other people to whom you can simply say "I'm interested in this kind of organization, because I want to do this kind of work; do you know of particular places like that, that I might investigate? And if so, where they are located?" Use face-to-face interviews, use LinkedIn, use search engines, to try to find the answer(s) to that question. Incidentally, you must not care, at this point, if they have *known* vacancies or not. The only question that should concern you for the moment is whether or not the place looks interesting, or even intriguing to you. (*The only caveat is that you will probably want to investigate smaller places— one hundred or fewer employees—rather than larger; and newer places, rather than older.*) But for a successful job-hunt you should choose places based on *your interest in them,* and not wait for them to open up a vacancy. Vacancies can suddenly open up in a moment, and without warning.

What will you end up with, when this step is done? Well, you'll likely have either *too few names* or *too many* to go investigate. There are ways of dealing with either of these eventualities.

TOO MANY NAMES

You will want to cut the territory down, to a manageable number of *targets*.

Let's take an example. Suppose you discover that the career that interests you the most is *financial services*. You want to be a financial adviser. Well, that's a beginning. You've cut the 23 million US job markets down to:

I want to work in a place that hires financial advisers.

But the territory is still too large. There are thousands of places in the country that use financial advisers. You can't go visit them all. So, you've got to cut down the territory further. Suppose that on your Preferred Place to Live petal you said that you really want to live and work in the San Jose area of California. That's helpful; that cuts down the territory further. Now your goal is:

I want to work in a place that hires financial advisers, within the San Jose area.

But, the territory is still too large. There could be 100, 200, 300 organizations that fit that description. So you look at your Flower Diagram for further help, and you notice that under *working conditions* you said you wanted to work for an organization with fifty or fewer employees. Good, now your goal is:

I want to work in a place that hires financial advisers, within the San Jose area, that has fifty or fewer employees.

This territory may still be too large. So you look again at your Flower Diagram for further guidance, and you see that you said you wanted to work for an organization that works with people who are close to retiring. So now your statement of what you're looking for becomes:

I want to work in a place that hires financial advisers, within the San Jose area, has fifty or fewer employees, and helps people with their pending retirement.

Using your Flower Diagram, you can thus keep cutting down the territory, until the *"targets"* of your job-hunt are no more than ten places. That's a manageable number of places for you to *start with*. You can always expand the list later, if none of these ten turns out to be promising or interesting.

TOO FEW NAMES

In this case, you want to expand the territory. Your salvation here is probably not going to be informational interviewing face-to-face, but digital directories. Indeed.com can give you a general idea of the openings and opportunities in your area. Also, see if the local chamber of commerce publishes a business directory; often it will list not only small companies but also local divisions of larger companies, with names of department heads; sometimes they will even include the North American Industry Classification System (NAICS) codes, which is useful if you want to search by the code of your chosen field. Third, see if your town or city publishes a business newsletter, directory, or even a Book of Lists on its own. It will, of course, cost you, but it may be worth it. Some metropolitan areas (San Francisco comes to mind) have particularly helpful ones. Forty of them are listed at www.bizjournals .com. Your local public library can be a terrific source of free assistance. Ask a librarian to help you find print and online resources, including databases such as Reference USA or the Small Business Resource Center.

If you are diligent here, you won't lack for names, believe me— unless it's a very small town you live in, in which case you'll just have to cast your net a little wider, to include other towns, villages, or cities that are within commuting distance from you.

Fifth, You Need to Learn as Much as You Can About a Place Before Formally Approaching Them

At some point you will be happy. You've found a career that you would die to do. You've interviewed people *actually doing that work*, and you like it even more. You've found names of places that hire people in that career.

Okay, now what? Do you rush right over there? No, you research those places first. This is an absolute *must*. Remember, companies and organizations love to be loved. You demonstrate you love them when you have taken the trouble to find out all about them, before you walk in. That's called *research*.

What is it you should research about places before you approach them for a hiring-interview? Well, first of all, you want to know something about the organization from the inside: what kind of work they do there. Their style of working. Their *corporate culture*. And what kinds of goals they are trying to achieve, what obstacles or challenges they are running into, and how your skills and knowledges can help them. In the interview you must be prepared to demonstrate that you have something they need. That begins with finding out *what* they need.

Second, you want to find out if you would enjoy working there. You want to take the measure of those organizations. Everybody takes the measure of a workplace, but most job-hunters or career-changers only do it *after* they are hired there. In the US, for example, a survey of the federal/state employment service once found that 57 percent of those who found a job through that service were not working at that job just thirty days later, and this was *because* they used the first ten or twenty days *on the job* to find out they didn't really like it there at all.

You, by doing this research ahead of time, are choosing a better path by far. Yes, even in tough times, you do want to be picky. Otherwise, you'll take the job in desperation, thinking, "Oh, I could put up with anything," and then finding out after you take the job that you were kidding yourself. So you have to quit, and start your job-hunt all over again. By doing this research now, you are saving yourself a lot of grief. So, you need to know, ahead of time, if this place just doesn't fit. Now, how do you find that out? There are several ways, some face-to-face, some not:

- **Friends and Neighbors.** Ask *everyone* you know, if they know anyone who works at the places that interest you. And, if they do, ask them if they could arrange for you and that person to get together, for lunch, coffee, or tea. At that time, tell them why the place interests you, and indicate you'd like to know more about it. (*It helps a lot if your mutual friend is sitting there with the two of you, so the purpose of this little chat won't be misconstrued.*) This is the vastly preferred way to find out about a place. However, obviously you need a couple of additional alternatives up your sleeve, in case you run into a dead end here.

- **People at the Organizations in Question, or Similar.** LinkedIn has an extensive menu where you can find a company's name. They will tell you who works there, or used to work there. An email will sometimes produce an interesting contact; but in this increasingly busy busy life, even the best-hearted people may sometimes say they just cannot give you any time, due to over-load. If so, respect that.

  You can go in person to organizations and ask questions about the place. This is not recommended with large organizations that have security guards and so on. But with small organizations (in this case, fifty employees or fewer) you sometimes can find out a great deal by just showing up. Here, however, I must caution you about several *dangers.*

  First, make sure you're not asking them questions that are in print somewhere, which you could easily have read for yourself instead of bothering *them*. This irritates people.

  Second, make sure that you approach the gateway people—front desk, receptionists, customer service, etc.—*before* you ever approach people higher up in that organization.

  Third, make sure that you approach subordinates rather than the top person in the place, if the subordinates would know the answer to your questions. Bothering the boss there with some simple questions that someone else could have answered is com-mitting job-hunting suicide.

  Fourth, make sure you're not using this approach simply as a sneaky way to get in to see the boss, and make a pitch for them to hire you. You said this was just information gathering. Don't lie. Don't ever lie. They will remember you, but not in the way you want to be remembered.

- **What's on the Internet.** Many job-hunters or career-changers think that every organization, company, or nonprofit has its own website, these days. Not true. Sometimes they do, some-times they don't. It often has to do with the size of the place, its access to a good web designer, its desperation for custom-ers, etc. Easy way to find out: Type the name of the place into your favorite search engine and see what that turns up. Try more than one search engine. Sometimes one knows things the others don't. There are, in fact, sites particularly devoted to getting feedback on organizations from actual employees who are working there or recently used to. The most famous of these is Glassdoor (www.glassdoor.com/Reviews/index.htm). Approximately half of all job-seekers consult Glassdoor.[1] It has employee reviews from almost 800,000 companies or organiza-tions worldwide. It will even tell you which companies are (supposedly) the best to work for, etc. Similar review sites are Take This Job or Shove It (http://takethisjoborshoveit.com) and Career Bliss (www.careerbliss.com/reviews).

- **What's in Print.** Not books; their time lag is too great. But often the organization has timely stuff—in print, or on its website—about its business, purpose, etc. Also, the CEO or head of the organization may have given talks, and the front desk there may have copies of those talks. In addition, there may be bro-chures, annual reports, etc. that the organization has put out about itself. How can you get copies? The person who answers the phone there, if you call, will know the answer, or at least know who to refer you to. Also, if it's a decent-size organiza-tion, public libraries in that town or city may have files on that organization—newspaper clippings, articles, etc. You never know; and it never hurts to ask your friendly neighborhood research librarian.

---

1. Erin Osterhaus, "Half of All Job Seekers Consult Glassdoor Reviews," *ERE*, January 23, 2014, www.eremedia.com/ere/half-of-all-job-seekers-consult-glassdoor-reviews.

- **Temporary Agencies.** Many job-hunters and career-changers have found that a useful way to explore organizations is to go and work at a temporary agency. To find these, put into Google the name of your town or city and (on the same search line) the words "Temp Agencies" or "Employment Agencies." Employers turn to such agencies in order to find (a) job-hunters who can work part-time for a limited number of days; and (b) job-hunters who can work full-time for a limited number of days. The advantage to you of temporary work is that if there is an agency that loans out people with your particular skills and expertise, you get a chance to be sent to a number of different employers over a period of several weeks, and see each one from the inside. Maybe the temp agency won't send you to exactly the place you hoped for, but sometimes you can develop contacts in the place you love, even while you're temporarily working somewhere else—if both organizations are in the same field. At the very least you'll pick up experience that you can later cite on your resume.

- **Volunteering.** If you're okay financially for a while, but can't find work, you volunteer to work for nothing, short term, at a place that has a "cause" or mission that interests you. You can find a directory of places that are known to do this, in what are called "internships" (www.internships.com) or "volunteer opportunities" (listed at www.volunteeringinamerica.gov—see their data infographic about volunteering leading to employment—and www.volunteermatch.org). Also, you can put into your search engine the name of the city or town where you live, together with the phrase "volunteer opportunities," and see what that turns up. Or you can just walk into an organization or company of your choice, and ask if they would let you volunteer your time there.

  Your goal is, first of all, to find out more about the place.

  Second, if you've been out of work a lengthy period of time, your goal is to feel useful. You're making your life count for something.

Third, your distant hope is that maybe somewhere down the line they'll actually want to hire you to stay on, for pay. The odds of that happening in these hard times are pretty remote, so don't count on it and don't push it; but *sometimes* they may ask you to stay. For pay. The success rate of this as a method for finding jobs isn't terrific. But it does happen.

You Must Send Thank-You Notes, *Please, Please, Pleeze*

After anyone has done you a favor, anytime during your job-hunt, you must be sure to send them a thank-you note by the very next day, at the latest. I cover this more in chapter 8. It's just as important here. Such a note should be sent by you to anyone who helps you, or who talks with you. That means friends, people at the organization in question, temporary agency people, receptionists, librarians, workers, or whomever.

Ask them, at the time you are face-to-face with them, for their business card (if they have one), or ask them to write out their name and work address, on a piece of paper, for you. You don't want to misspell their name. It is difficult to figure out how to spell people's names simply from the sound of it. What sounds like "Laura" may actually be "Lara." What sounds like "Smith" may actually be "Smythe," and so on. Get that name and address, but get it right, please.

And let me reiterate: thank-you notes must be prompt. Email the thank-you note that same night, or the very next day at the latest. Follow it with a lovely copy, handwritten or printed, nicely formatted, and sent through the mail. Most employers these days prefer a printed letter to a handwritten one, but if your handwriting is beautiful, then go for it.

Don't ramble on and on. Your mailed thank-you note can be just two or three sentences. Something like *"I wanted to thank you for talking with me yesterday. It was very helpful to me. I much appreciated your taking the time out of your busy schedule to do this. Best wishes to you."* Of course, if there's any additional thought you want to add, then add it. And when you're done, remember to sign it.

What If I Get Offered a Job Along the Way, While I'm Just Gathering Information?

Not likely. Nonetheless, an occasional employer *may* stray across your path during all this Informational Interviewing. And that employer *may* be so impressed with you, that they want to hire you, on the spot. So, it's *possible* that you'd get offered a job while you're still doing your information gathering. Not very *likely,* but *possible.* And if that happens, what should you say?

Well, if you're desperate, you will probably have to say *yes.* I remember one wintertime when I was in my thirties, with a family of five, when I had just gone through the knee of my last pair of pants, we were burning pieces of old furniture in our fireplace to stay warm, the legs on our bed had just broken, and we were eating spaghetti until it was coming out our ears. In such a situation, you can't afford to be picky. You've got to put food on the table, and stave off the debt collectors. Now.

But if you're not *desperate,* if you have time to be more careful, then you respond to the job offer in a way that will buy you some time. You tell them what you're doing: that the average job-hunter tries to screen a job *after* they take it. But you are examining careers, fields, industries, jobs, and particular organizations *before* you decide where you would do your best and most effective work. And you're sure this employer would do the same, if they were in your shoes. (If they're not impressed with your thoroughness and professionalism, at this point, then I assure you this is not a place where you want to work.)

Add that your informational interviewing isn't finished yet, so it would be premature for you to accept their job offer, until you're *sure* that this is the place where you could be most effective, and do your best work.

Then, you add: "Of course, I'm excited that you would want me to be working here. And when I've finished my personal survey, I'll be glad to get back to you about this, as my preliminary impression is that this is the kind of place I'd like to work in, and the kind of people I'd like to work for, and the kind of people I'd like to work with."

In other words, *if you're not desperate yet,* you don't walk immediately through any opened doors, but neither should you allow them to shut.

As I said, this scenario is highly unlikely. You're networking with *workers.* But it's nice to be prepared ahead of time, in your mind, just in case it does ever happen.

A Final Word on Contacts

A word about contacts in general: Research has revealed that the more of a social life you have, the more people you know, the more time you spend with people outside of work, the more likely you are to find a job. Some surveys estimate that as many as 85 percent of positions are found through networking.[2] And the more people you know who are in other fields than your own, the more likely you are to be able to effectively change careers. Often, in fact, your contacts will turn up job opportunities for you even before you go out formally searching. Problem: One in four workers don't network at all. And 41 percent would like to network more but don't feel they have time. Those statistics are for the UK,[3] but similar findings are found around the world.

Another discovery from research is that the farther afield these contacts are from your usual social circles, the more likely they are to help your job-hunt. If you ask yourself how much time you spend with your contacts, your contacts will divide into those with whom you have "strong ties" and those with whom you have "weak ties," the latter being defined as people you see only occasionally or rarely—maybe only once a year, or even less. These "weak ties" will strengthen your job-search immeasurably.

The findings from the research have been summarized by Mark Granovetter, professor at Stanford, as "the strength of weak ties." As he writes in his classic *Getting a Job: A Study of Contacts and Careers*, "There is . . . a structural tendency for those to whom one is only *weakly* tied, to have better access to job information one does not already have. Acquaintances, as compared to close friends, are more prone to move in different circles than one's self. Those to whom one is closest are likely to have the greater overlap with those one already knows, so that the information to which they are privy is likely to be much the same as that which one already has."[4]

Now, once you've found a place that interests you and you want to get an interview there, there is a particular kind of contact that will

2. Gina Belli, "How Many Jobs Are Found Through Networking, Really" Payscale.com, April 6, 2017, www.payscale.com/career-news/2017/04/many-jobs-found-networking.
3. Julia Hobsbawm, "Fully Connected," *EY*, http://ukcareers.ey.com/beingconnected.
4. Mark Granovetter, *Getting a Job: A Study of Contacts and Careers*, Second Edition (Chicago: University of Chicago Press, 1995), pp. 52–53.

save your neck. I call such a contact a "Bridge-Person." What I mean by that title, is that they know you; and they know them (your target), and thus bridge the gap between you and a job there.

You can't identify a bridge-person until you have a target company or organization in mind. But when that time comes, here's how you go about identifying *bridge-people*:

1. LinkedIn is your best friend here. Each employer you want to pursue should have a Company Profile page. (Unless the company is just *too small*.) Identify what place you want to approach, and look up its Company Profile page; go there.

2. Start with the company. LinkedIn will tell you the people in your network who work for the company you are targeting. Then sort that list. You can sort it by *employees* there, who share:

   a. A LinkedIn group with You

   b. A former employer with You

   c. A school with You

   d. An industry with You

   e. A language with You

   f. A specific location with You

3. Then go to your school. On that same Company Profile page, look for your school—if you ever attended vo-tech school, community college, college, university, or grad school, ask LinkedIn to tell you who among your fellow alumni work for the company or organization you are targeting.

4. Then go to the company activity. On that same Company Profile page, ask LinkedIn to tell you new hires (who), departures (who), job-title changes, job-postings, number of employees who use LinkedIn, where current employees work, where current employees worked before they worked for *this* company, where former employees went after they worked for this company, etc. Insightful statistics!

5. As for connecting with the bridge-people whose names you discover, currently LinkedIn requires you to have one of their *paid* memberships, rather than the *free* one, to send a note to someone

who's not a direct connection. But if they're still working at the company, you can phone the company and ask for them. Or you can search for their contact information through a larger search engine (Google their name!).

6. If you come up blank, both on LinkedIn and all the other places you search for names, such as family, friends, Facebook, etc. (no bridge-person can be found who knows *you* and also knows *them*), you can advertise on LinkedIn, for such connections. They have "ads by LinkedIn Members" available to you, for modest cost (so far!). You can also browse LinkedIn groups, and join those (ten at the most) that seem most likely to be seen by the kinds of companies you are trying to reach. However, don't just join them! Post intelligent questions, respond to intelligent "post-ers" that you think make sense. In other words, attain as high visibility there as you can; maybe *employers* will then come after *you*.

Once you get an introduction to a place, follow the instructions about interviews in chapter 8 of this book. And, good luck!

He or she who gets hired is not necessarily
The one who can do that job best;
But, the one who knows the most
About how to get hired.

—*Richard Lathrop*

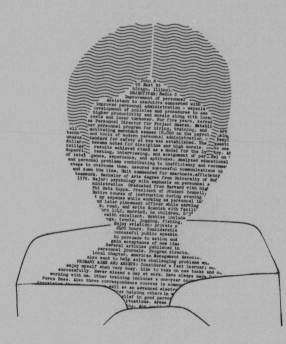

CHAPTER 7

Google Is Your New (but Not Only) Resume

I know what you're thinking. *I'm out of work, I've got to go job-huntin'. So the first thing I have to do is put together my resume.*

Yeah, that used to be true.

In "the old days."

Before the Internet came on the scene.

Back then, the only way an interviewer could learn much about you was from a piece of paper that you yourself wrote—with maybe a little help from your friends—called your resume, or CV (an academic term meaning "curriculum vitae").

On that paper was a summary of where you had been and all you had done in the past. From that piece of paper, the employer was supposed to *guess* what kind of person you are in the present and what kind of employee you'd be in the future.

The good thing about this—from your point of view—was that you had absolute control over what went on that piece of paper.

You could omit anything you didn't want the employer to see, anything that was embarrassing, or anything from your past that you have long since regretted.

Short of their hiring a private detective, or talking to your previous employers, a prospective employer couldn't find out much else about you.

That was nice. But those days are gone forever.

Today, there's a new resume in town, and it's called Google.

All any prospective employer has to do now is *Google* your name—yes, *Google* has become both noun and verb—and there's your new resume, using the word *resume* loosely.

If you've been anywhere near the Internet—and as of 2018, more than 89 percent of adults in the US have—and if you've posted anything on Facebook, Twitter, LinkedIn, Instagram, Pinterest, or YouTube, or if you have your own website or webcasts or photo album or blog, or if you've been on anyone else's Facebook page, every aspect of you may be revealed (depending on your privacy settings). *Bye, bye, control.*

Depending on which study you read, the numbers vary; but it's safe to say that virtually all recruiters will look at your social media, and more than 57 percent of employers have rejected some applicants on the basis of what they found. Things that can get you rejected: bad grammar or gross misspelling on your Facebook or LinkedIn profile; anything indicating you lied on your resume; any bad-mouthing of previous employers; any signs of racism, prejudice, or screwy opinions about stuff; anything indicating alcohol or drug abuse; and any—to put it delicately—*inappropriate content*, etc.

What is sometimes forgotten is that this works both ways. Sometimes—44 percent of the time, as it turns out—an employer will offer someone a job because they liked what Google turned up about them. Things such as the creativity or professionalism you demonstrate online; your expressing yourself extremely well online; their overall impression of your personality online; the wide range of interests you exhibit online; and evidence online that you get along well and communicate well with other people. And according to a survey conducted by the Harris Poll for CareerBuilder in 2018, about 47 percent of employers indicate that if they can't find a social media presence for someone, they won't bring them in for an interview. So if you're thinking the easiest way to avoid problems is not to use social media, think again.[1]

Is there anything you can do about this new Google resume of yours? Well, yes, actually, there are four things you can do.

You can edit, fill in, expand, and add. Let's see what each of these involves.

1. Cision PR Newsire, "More Than Half of Employers Have Found Content on Social Media That Caused Them NOT to Hire a Candidate, According to Recent CareerBuilder Survey," August 9, 2018, www.prnewswire.com/news-releases/more-than-half-of-employers-have-found-content-on-social-media-that-caused-them-not-to-hire-a-candidate-according-to-recent-careerbuilder-survey-300694437.html.

1. Edit

First of all, think of how you would like to come across, when you are being considered for a job. Make a list of adjectives you'd like the employer to think of, when they consider hiring you. For example, how about: professional? experienced? inventive? hard working? disciplined? honest? trustworthy? kind? What else? Make a list.

Then Google yourself and read over everything the search engine pulls up about you. Go over any pages you have put up on social sites, like Facebook, LinkedIn, Twitter, Instagram, Pinterest, or YouTube, and remove anything you posted there, or allowed others to post, that contradicts the impression you would like to make, anything that might cause a would-be employer to think, *"Uh, let's not call them in, after all."* You have the list, on the facing page, of what to look for.

If you don't know how to remove an item from a particular site, type or speak the following into a search engine such as Google: "How to remove an item from *[Facebook]*" or whatever.

The site itself may not tell you, but using your favorite search engine, you should have no trouble finding somebody's detailed, step-by-step instructions for scrubbing any site.

I guarantee you're hardly the first one with this need, so someone clever has already figured out how to do it, and posted the answer. But you want current instructions, so look at the date on the list of items the search engine pops up. Pick the most recent, and do what they say.

If you want to be thorough, you should do this editing on any and all sites that you find you're on.

Now to the second of the four things you can do about your new Google resume (so to speak).

2. Fill In

On any site, but on LinkedIn and Twitter in particular, if they allow you to fill out a profile, fill it out completely: cross every *t*, dot every *i*, and have someone check your spelling. Leave no part of the profile blank unless you have a very good reason.

Most important, be sure to keep each profile up-to-date. Really up-to-date. Week by week, or at the least, month by month. There is nothing that makes you look less professional than having an obviously outdated profile.

LinkedIn

Last thought in this section: I mentioned LinkedIn; be sure to get on it, if you're not already (www.linkedin.com/reg/join). It's the site of first resort when some employer is curious about you. It allows corporate and agency headhunters to avoid advertising an open position, but nonetheless to go searching on LinkedIn for what employers call "passive job-seekers." (You ain't lookin' for them, but they are lookin' for you.) Of course you have no control over whether they find you, except for being sure you have a completely filled-out profile. They search by keywords.

Any job-hunter working online these days will want to pay large attention to LinkedIn. Here are some of the reasons why:

Background: This is "the Swiss army knife" of job-sites; it is a multi-tool. It is used (at this writing) by at least 500 million people worldwide, 133 million of them in the US. Employers from around the world who are searching for prospective employees are among them.

General Description: LinkedIn gives you a "profile" page on which you can write anything about yourself and your history that you want to, using the standardized format or template that LinkedIn provides.

Usefulness to Job-Hunters: If you have contacted a particular employer, most of them now search to see what there is about you on LinkedIn (and on the Internet in general, anywhere and everywhere) before inviting you in, or deciding to hire you.

Ways to Make It More Effective:[2] Remember, this is a *professional* site. If you are looking for work, don't post anything here that isn't related to your professional goal. (Needless to say, leave out parties, dating, summer vacations, etc.) Make your profile page really

---

2. I am indebted here to Patrick Schwerdtfeger, Susan Joyce, Alison Doyle, Jason Alba, Dan DeMaioNewton, and other colleagues for their ideas.

stand out from others' profile pages, when employers go browsing. Fortunately, LinkedIn provides a variety of helpful training on its site as well as videos on YouTube (www.youtube.com/user /Linkedin). Here are some hints:

1. Sign in with an email account you use regularly.

2. Once you create an account, immediately go to "Settings and Privacy" and turn off "sharing profile edits." (If you don't every time you make even a minor change, your network will be notified.) You can choose to share a major update (like new employment status) later.

3. A PHOTO is mandatory. Every survey has revealed that not having your photo posted there is a turnoff for most employers. The likelihood that your LinkedIn profile will get viewed increases eleven times if you include a photo. Make it a shot just of your head and shoulders; in fact, fill the frame with just your head and shoulders. Make it sharply focused and well lit, even if taken with an iPhone. Dress up for this one. And smile.

4. In the section called HEADLINE, if you aren't searching for a career-change, and you like what you've been doing, but the title they gave you doesn't contain the words that a hiring manager would normally use to search for someone who does what you do, put in a slash mark, then add the title they would use. Alternatively, if you are looking for a change, after you list your current job-title in this title section, enter a slash and then add the industry you want to find a job in (so that an employer's search engine will pick you up). Pack this section with keywords related to the position you're seeking.

5. In describing your PAST JOBS OR EXPERIENCE, don't just make a list of tasks or achievements. LinkedIn gives you enough space to tell a story, so tell a story. Summarize some major achievement of yours, in that job, and then tell a story of how you did it, and what the measurable results were (time or money saved, or the profit created, etc.). List your skills: you increase the likelihood that your LinkedIn profile will be looked at by thirteen times, if you do.

6. In the SUMMARY be sure to state whatever you think gives you a competitive advantage in your field—i.e., what makes you a better hire than nineteen other people who might compete for the kind of job you want. This is a place to highlight what makes you the best (*or, for the modest, what makes you a better*) choice for that kind of job.

7. Under SPECIALTIES list every keyword you can think of that would lead a search engine to find you for the job you *want*. If you don't know what keywords to list, find someone on LinkedIn who already has a job like the one you want, and see what keywords *they* listed. Copy the ones that seem relevant in your case.

8. LIST any hobbies, interests, education, training, community service, associations you belong to, etc.

9. ADD LINKS TO ANY WEBSITE you feel would help you stand out: *your blog*? (if you have one, and posts there are *solely* devoted to your area of expertise); *your Twitter account*? (if you have one, and if you've only been posting tweets that manifest your expertise in your field); *your Facebook page*? (doubtful, unless it looks very focused and professional—if it's sloppy, real personal, and all over the map in its content, it is unlikely to help you get hired, and may in fact hinder you). Consider filming a video of you discussing some area of your expertise (with numbers if possible), post it on YouTube, and link to it on your profile page here. If you don't know how to shoot and upload the video, there are loads of free instructions (even on YouTube) telling you step-by-step how to do this.

10. JOIN one or more LinkedIn group, related to your expertise. Post sparingly but regularly, when they are discussing something you are an expert on. You want to get a name and reputation in your field. "Groups" are in the bar across the top of your home page. Once you've filled out your profile completely, click on "Groups" and then on the subheading "Groups You May Like." It will make suggestions, based on your profile, with information about each group, as to whether it is *Very Active, Active,* or very neglected. Join ones, related to your expertise, which are at least *Active*. Be aware, if you join a group and then don't ever contribute, LinkedIn has

a cute little habit of summarily removing you from that group without any advance warning. Just a nice brief note after the fact, saying "We removed you" due to your inactivity there. (And you thought they weren't paying attention! Oh yes, they do. They are. They will.)

11. You can use LinkedIn to DESCRIBE a project you're proud of, post a photo, or report on a recent professional event. As every job contributes to "the bottom line," mention any way you did that in past jobs: say how you controlled costs or generated revenue. To post this also on Twitter, always begin not with Twitter but with LinkedIn. Write your update here, check the box with the Twitter icon, and then click "Share."

Now to the third thing you can do about your new Google resume.

3. Expand

Expand your presence on the Internet. How to do this? Several ways:

Forums. Professional sites such as LinkedIn have forums, or groups, organized by subject matter. Other social networking sites, like Facebook, have pages devoted to particular subjects. Look through the directory of those groups or forums, choose one or two that are related to your industry or interests, and after signing up, speak up regularly whenever you have something to say that will quietly demonstrate you are an expert in your chosen subject area. Otherwise, keep quiet. Don't speak up about just anything. You want to be seen as a specialist—knowledgeable and focused. You want to get noticed by employers when they're searching for expert talent in your field or specialty.

Blogs. Start a blog, if you don't already have one. It doesn't matter what your expertise is; if it's related to the job you are looking for, do a blog, and update it regularly. And if you don't know how to blog, there are helpful sites such as Blogger.com that give you detailed instructions. Incidentally, there are reportedly up to 300 million blogs on the Internet. Figure out how to make yours stand out.

If you already have a blog, but it roams all over the country-side in terms of subject matter, then start a new blog that is more narrowly preoccupied with your particular area of expertise. Post helpful articles there, focused on action steps, not just thoughts. Let's say you are an expert plumber; you can post entries on your blog that deal with such problems as "how to fix a leaky toilet," etc. Generally speaking, employers are looking for blogs that deal with concrete action, rather than lofty philosophical thought. Unless, of course, they represent a think tank.

Twitter. Some experts claim that blogs are so *yesterday.* Communication, they say, is moving toward brief, and briefer. Texting has become hugely, hugely, popular. So has Twitter: 24 percent of US adults use Twitter and that number jumps to 40 percent in those aged eighteen to twenty-nine. Twitter's advantage is that it has hashtags, and Google is indexing all those tags and "tweets." Savvy employers know how to do Twitter searches on Google (or on Twitter itself, for that matter). All you have to figure out is which hashtags employers are likely to look for, when they want to find someone with your expertise and experience.

Videos. Presentation is moving strongly these days toward the visual. People like to *see* you, not just *read* you. Expensive equipment not required. Smartphones can produce surprisingly good video.

As for where to post your video, once you've shot and edited it, the champion of course is YouTube—1.5 billion monthly users, 5 billion views per day. But there are other choices: see PCGDigitalMarketing's list, found at http://tinyurl.com/8owtlbo.

Now to the fourth and final thing you can do about your new Google resume.

4. Add

It will take any employer or HR department some time to sift through all the stuff about you that may appear when they do a Google search. You would help them by summarizing and organizing the pertinent information about yourself. You do this by—*surprise!*—composing an old-type resume. And you can post it on the Internet (where Google will find it), as well as taking or sending it to an interested employer.

You wanna do this? Of course you do. Here's an outline you may find useful for gathering that information about yourself.

Since a resume is about your past, this gives you a framework for recalling that past.

A Starter Kit for Writing Your Resume

Think of your working and personal skills that you believe you possess innately, or have picked up along the way. Which ones are you proud of? What things have you done in your life or work experience that no one else has done, in quite the same way? Take some blank sheets of paper and fill in any answers that occur to you.

It is important to be quantitative when you do this (e.g., mention dates, percentages, dollars, money or time saved, brand names, etc.).[3]

Volunteer, Community, and Unpaid Work

1. Have you completed any voluntary or unpaid work for any organization or company? (e.g., church, synagogue, mosque, school, community service, or special needs organization)

Educational

2. Did you work while you were studying? If so, did you receive any promotions or achievements in that role?
3. Did you gain any scholarships?
4. Were you involved in any committees etc.?
5. Did you win any awards for study?
6. Did you have any high (e.g., A or A+) grades? If so, what were the subjects—and grades?

---

3. This is adapted, with the written permission of my friend Tom O'Neil, from an original document of his, which was and is copyright protected under the New Zealand Copyright Act (1994) © cv.co.nz 2001. You may contact Tom at www.cv.co.nz.

Sales or Account Management

Have you ever been in sales? If so, what were some of your achievements? For example:

7. Have you ever consistently exceeded your set budget in that role? If so, by what percent or dollar value?

8. Have you exceeded your set budget in a particular month(s)/quarter(s) in a role? If so, by what percent or dollar value?

9. What level were you, compared to other sales professionals in your company? (e.g., "Number three out of twenty on the sales team.")

10. Have you ever increased market share for your company? If so, by what percent or dollar value?

11. Have you ever brought in any major clients to your company?

12. What major clients are/were you responsible for managing and selling to?

13. Did you ever manage to generate repeat business or increase current business? If so, by what percent or dollar value?

14. Have you won any internal or external sales awards?

15. Did you develop any new successful promotional or marketing ideas that increased sales?

Administration, Customer Service, and Accounts

Have you ever been in customer service or helped run a business unit? If so:

16. Did you assist in reducing customer complaints etc.?

17. Did you set up or improve any systems and/or processes?

18. Was there a quantifiable difference in the company or business unit when you first joined the business or project and when you completed the project or left the business?

19. Did you take any old administration or paperwork-based systems and convert them into an IT-based system?

Responsibility

20. Have you ever been responsible for the purchase of any goods or services in some job? (e.g., air travel or PC acquisition)

21. Have you ever had any budget responsibility? If so, to what level? (e.g., "Responsible for division budget of $200,000 per annum.")

22. Have you ever been responsible for any staff oversight? If so, in what capacity and/or how many staff members were you responsible for?

23. Were you responsible for any official or unofficial training? If so, what type, for whom, and how many people have you trained? (e.g., "Responsible for training twelve new staff in customer service as well as in using the in-house computer system.")

24. Were you responsible for any official or unofficial coaching or mentoring of other staff?

Events or Conference Planning or Logistical Management

25. Have you organized any events or conferences? If so, how large were they (both people attending and total budget if possible) and where and when was the event(s) held?

26. Have you been involved in any major relocation projects?

27. Have you had responsibility with regard to any major suppliers? If so, who?

Computers

28. What systems, software, and hardware experience do you have? Desktop, notebook, mobile, smartphones? Mac OS, Android, or Windows? And how deep is your expertise with any of these?

29. What software have you utilized? Or what software have you developed? Mobile apps? Systems software?

30. Have you developed any websites? If so, what were they, and did they positively affect any business you were doing? Are you on LinkedIn, Plaxo, Twitter, Facebook, YouTube, etc., and if so, how deep an expertise do you have with any of these sites?

31. Were you involved in any special projects that were outside of your job description?

Mechanical

32. Other than computers, have you had experience on any kinds of machines or equipment? Please list them together with the number of years.

33. If you ever worked on transportation devices, what were the airplane, farm equipment, truck, car, machine, or bike brands that you serviced, maintained, or repaired?

Building, Construction, Electrical, and Plumbing

34. If you ever worked in such fields, were there any major projects you worked on? How much did the project(s) cost? (e.g., "Reception refurbishment—ABC Bank [Auckland Central Head Office] $1.2 m.")

General

35. How long have you spent within any industry? (e.g., "Twelve years' experience within the fashion industry.")

36. Were you promoted in any of your roles? If so, in what years and to which roles?

37. Was extra authority awarded to you after a period of time within a role? (e.g., "Commenced as receptionist; then, after three months, awarded by being given further clerical responsibilities including data entry and accounts payable.") It is not necessary that these responsibilities awarded to you should have changed your job-title and/or salary.

38. Have you been asked to take part in, or lead, any trainee management courses or management development programs?

39. Were you asked to get involved in any special projects outside your job description? Or, did you ever volunteer for such? What was the result?

Positive Feedback

40. Have you ever received any written or verbal client, customer, or managerial commendations or letters of praise?

41. Can you think of any occasions where you gave excellent customer service? If so, how did you know the customer was satisfied? (Also: What was the outcome? How did it benefit the company?)

42. Did you receive any awards within your company or industry? (e.g., "Acknowledged for support or service of clients or staff.")

Memberships

43. Have you been a representative on any committees (e.g., health and safety committee)? Any special responsibilities there?

44. Do you belong or have you belonged to any professional clubs such as Toastmasters, Lions, or Rotary?

Published or Presented Work

45. Have you had any articles, papers, or features published in any magazines, journals, or books? If so, what publications and when? Have you written any books?

46. Have you presented any topics at any conferences or completed any public speaking? If so, what subjects have you talked about and how large was the audience? List in detail.

Looking Ahead

47. What value do you think you would add to a potential employer's business? How would you be "a resource" or even "a resource-broker" for them, rather than just "a job-beggar"? What kind of problems are you good at solving?

48. How do you think you would stand out compared to other applicants who have about the same qualifications as you have?

That should give you a good start. Modify the list any way you want to—add items and questions to it, change the wording, whatever.

If you need additional guidance, search Google for the topic "keywords on an electronic resume" or "examples of resumes." Or "how to write a resume," or "tips on writing a resume." This will turn up thousands of sample resumes and templates, many of which are free. Entire books are devoted to resume-writing.[4]

As for what is the proper form for a resume, there are no rules (well, except correct spelling and grammar). The only question is, Is there a particular place or kind of place where you'd like to work, and if so, will the person there who has the power to hire you for the kind of job you want, be persuaded by your resume to invite you in? If the answer is, Yes, then it matters not what form your resume takes.

To illustrate my point, I used to have a hobby of collecting "winning" resumes—that is, resumes that had actually gotten someone an interview and, ultimately, a job. Being playful by nature, I would show these without comment, to employer friends of mine, over lunch. Many of them didn't like these winning resumes at all. "That resume will never get anyone a job," they would say. Then I would reply, "Sorry, you're wrong. It already has. I think what you mean is that it wouldn't get them a job with *you*." Keep in mind that the more conservative the field (e.g., finance) the more traditional your resume should be. A creative field will allow more creativity in your resume. See the chart on page 156 for guidance.

---

4. Oh, and speaking of books, a supplement to this chapter is found in my little *What Color Is Your Parachute? Guide to Rethinking Resumes* (Ten Speed Press, 2014).

Key Tips for Resume Design

1. You can look up resume formats on a variety of Internet sites. Even most word-processing programs have sample templates that you can adjust to fit your needs.

2. Double-check spelling and grammar. Employers often eliminate resumes containing errors.

3. Be prepared to alter your resume for every position you're applying to. Adjust your descriptions of your experience and education to best fit the skills needed for the position.

4. Use your resume to tell your story. Describe all education and experience in ways that are relevant to the position you're seeking.

5. Sell your strengths. Don't make the employer dig for information.

6. Use keywords related to your field.

7. Avoid describing yourself in positive terms that can't be supported ("hardworking," "energetic," etc.). Focus on facts and what you did.

8. Include numbers and statistics when relevant. If you raised funds, indicate the amount; if you increased customer satisfaction, by how much?

9. Include Contact Information:
   Name.
   City, State (if relevant; no need for street address).
   Phone number.
   Email.
   LinkedIn address.

10. Include Education and Training:
    If it's recent and most relevant to your work, place before experience section. If older or less relevant, place after experience section.

11. Include GPA if 3.0 or above.

12. Include honors, awards, and scholarships.

13. Include Experience.

14. Use action verbs and bullet points to highlight key information.

15. You can list your experience from most recent to most distant (reverse chronological) or by type (functional or combination). For instance, if you want a banking career and have worked in several banks, but most recently held a position in a retail store, you could create an experience section called "Banking Experience" and then list just your banking jobs under that heading. The retail experience could go under "Other Experience," "Related Experience," or another category.

16. Optional sections include a summary of your experiences at the top of the resume (generally not needed), a job objective (also not needed when there's a cover letter or when your objective is clear), and a section for hobbies or interests. Hobbies or interests, if included, should always be at the end of the resume and limited to a few interesting and relevant selections.

17. Do not include photos, birthdate, marital status, information about children, etc.

The brutal truth is, no matter how skillfully you write and post your resume, some employers will like it, some won't. Trouble is, if you're interested in some employer, you don't know which category they fit into. That's why many job-hunters, if they use resumes, pray as they post their resume: *Please, dear God, let them be employers who like resumes in general, and may the form of my resume appeal to those employers I care about, in particular.*

Post your resume right on the actual website of companies that interest you, if they have a site, and if their site permits that. You can also post your resume on any of the major job-posting sites, like Monster or CareerBuilder. *I recommend you pay particular attention to small employers (first try those with twenty-five or fewer employees, then fifty or fewer, and then one hundred or fewer). Also you're likely to have better luck with newer organizations (seven years old or younger).*

If you post your resume on the sites of particular employers, large or small, don't count on any acknowledgment or reply. Just post the thing, cross your fingers, and pray it arrives at the right time, at the right place, into the hands of the right person: *the one who actually has the power to hire you.* Sad truth: Many employers don't even look at the resumes posted on their site.

Wild Life, by John Kovalic, ©1989 Shetland Productions. Reprinted with permission.

Alternatives to the Classic Resume

A cover letter was, for decades, something you sent along with your resume. Now, many employers prefer a cover letter *instead* of your resume. That brief cover letter can summarize all that a longer resume might have covered. I get this kind of report all the time, from successful job-hunters: *"Cover letter. Make it personal and specific to THAT job. I was directly told in two interviews that my unique cover letter got me in the door. I researched the companies. . . ."*

If you don't know what a cover letter is, or how to write it, the Internet can rescue you handily. Check out Novoresume's guide at https://novoresume.com/career-blog/how-to-write-a-cover-letter-guide. You can also consult the cover letter chapter in my little book, *What Color Is Your Parachute? Guide to Rethinking Resumes* (Ten Speed Press, 2014).

Another alternative to a classic resume is a Job or Career Portfolio. A portfolio may be electronic (posted on the Internet) or on paper/in a notebook/in a large display case (as with artists), demonstrating your accomplishments, experience, training, commendations, or awards from the past. Artists have a portfolio, with samples of their work. You probably knew that. But portfolios are equally apt in other fields.

Instead of "portfolio" we might just call them "Evidence of What I Can Do and Have Done," or "Proof of Performance." For guidance on how to prepare a job portfolio, and what to include, simply type "job or career portfolio" into Google; you'll get a wealth of tips and information, such as www.livecareer.com/career/advice/jobs/job-search-portfolio.

Types of Resumes Chart

	Reverse	Functional
Basic Structure	Divide resume by education, experience, and other sections. Place entries in reverse chronological order, beginning with most recent.	Divide resume by skills or competencies. Use education and experiences to illustrate and support these competencies. Doesn't always include dates of experience or education.
Purpose/Value	Most traditional and common. Works for most stages of life. Easiest to construct. Works best when you have a consistent employment record that fits the field you're seeking.	By focusing on experiences and skills, and not dates, this resume can help when you want to highlight skills rather than how you attained them, when you're switching to a completely new career field, when there are gaps in employment, or when you're returning to the workplace after significant time away.
Downsides to This Approach	If your most recent education or experiences don't fit position you're seeking, this will not show you at your best.	Because it's generally used by people with gaps in experience, employers may be concerned that you're hiding something. (If you have gaps, be prepared to explain them in your cover letter or interview.)
How to Choose Which to Use	Use when you have a list of experiences that directly relate to the position you seek.	Use, with caution, when you want the employer to focus on your skills and competencies rather than dates, or how you acquired the experience.

Combination	Creative
Divide experience into categories based on work area ("marketing") or theme/skill ("leadership") most relevant to employer. Within each category use reverse chronological order.	Varies according to the position sought and skills needed. Can involve unique colors, fonts, structure, or illustrations.
Generally, most powerful format for most positions. Works best when you want to highlight related education and experience that may not be your most recent experience, or when you want to combine experiences from different areas.	Directly demonstrates creative skills and ability to use Photoshop, Illustrator, or other creative computer software.
Harder to write initially. Requires you to consider the subcategories you will create that an employer would want to see.	Creativity is subjective. What is creative to one employer may be seen as odd or inappropriate to another. Harder to gauge audience reaction since resume may be viewed by non-creative types.
Use when you can divide your education or experience into categories that relate to your desired field.	Use, with caution, when a creative approach would fit directly with the position you seek. You might still want to create a more traditional resume to accompany your creative effort.

Some Friendly Reminders About Your "Pre-Google Resume"

1. If you're blanketing the Internet with that resume, be cautious about including any stuff on the resume that would help someone find out where you live or work. Sad to say, there are some sick people out there. Sick in the head, that is. If I were you, I'd be sure to leave out my address and home phone number. Just an email address should more than suffice.

2. If you are targeting particular employers, rather than or in addition to broad job-sites, keep in mind that a resume is best not sent solely by email, particularly if it's an attachment, and not embedded in the body of the email. Many employers, leery of viruses, will not even open email attachments (and that includes your resume). Send it by email if you must, but always send a nicer version of it by the postal service, or UPS, or FedEx, etc.

3. If you're going to snail-mail a resume to a target employer, pay attention to the paper you write or print it on. Picture this scenario: an employer is going through a whole stack of resumes, and on average he or she is giving each resume about eight seconds of their time (true: we checked!). Then that resume goes into either a pile we might call "Forgeddit," or a pile we might call "Bears further investigation." And what determines which pile it goes into? *Surprise! It's the feel of the paper.* Yes, that employer's first contact with your resume is with their fingers, assuming this is in a stack of printed resumes (not digital ones). By the pleasure or displeasure of their fingers, as they first pick up your resume, they are prejudiced for or against you before they even start reading. Usually, they are blissfully unaware of this. Anyway, this is why you want the paper to feel good. That usually means using paper weighing at least 28 pounds (a paper's weight is on the outside of every package). And you want it to be easy to read—so be sure it's nicely laid out or formatted, using a decent-size font, size 12 or even 14.

4. A resume should have a purpose, at least in *your* mind. It might be that you're posting it online, just to collect and organize all pertinent information about yourself in one place, so that when an employer Googles you they find *this*, nice and concise, in contrast to all the other stuff about you that Google will find, scattered all over the Internet.

5. Your sole purpose, for your resume, if you're targeting individual employers, is to get yourself invited in for an interview. Period. This truth, unfortunately, is not widely known. Most job-hunters (and more than a few resume writers) assume a resume's purpose is to "sell you," or secure you a job. It does happen. But primarily the purpose of a resume is just to get invited in for an interview, where it will then be time for you to sell yourself. In person. Face to face. Not on paper. So, once written, go back and read over every single sentence in your resume and evaluate it by this one standard: "Will this item help to get me invited in? Or will this item seem too puzzling, or off-putting, or a red flag?" If you doubt a particular sentence will help get you invited in for an interview, then omit that sentence. If it's important to you, give yourself a note to be sure to cover it *in the interview*. And if there is something you feel you will ultimately need to explain, or expand upon, save that explanation also for the interview. Your resume is, above all, no place for "true confessions." (*"I kind of botched up, at the end, in that job; that's why they let me go, as I'm sure they'll tell you when you check my references."*) If you want the interviewer to know that, in the interest of full disclosure, don't put it in your resume. Save true confessions for the end of the interview, and only if you're confident at that point that they really want you, and you really want them.

6. The same advice applies to discussing any nonvisible or non-obvious disability or issue you may have. Generally speaking—there are exceptions—don't mention it as early as the resume. And even when you're in the interview, don't discuss right off the bat what you *can't* do. Focus all their attention, initially, on what you can do—that you can perform all the tasks required in this job. Save what you can't do for the moment when they say they really want you.

7. If you're coming out of some subculture that has its own language (*e.g., the military, the clergy*) get some help in translating your experience into the language of employers. For example, "preached" should be replaced by "taught." "Commanded" should be replaced by "supervised," etc.

8. "Keywords" are important if you're posting your resume without specific employers in mind. A good article about keywords—what they are, and how to insert them into your resume—can be found in Squawkfox's article, "8 Keywords That Set Your Resume on Fire," at www.squawkfox.com/8-keywords-that-set-your-resume-on-fire.

9. Finally, don't include references on your resume. Some career counselors and resume writers will disagree with me on this, but I think references are better offered after prospective employers have had a chance to see and talk with you. And please, please, please, *never list somebody as a reference, at any time in your job-hunt, without first getting their written permission to do so*. Be aware that your references, if they are checked out, will often be checked out over the phone, rather than in writing. But in case you may need something in writing, if your references permit you to use their name, ask them to give the letter of recommendation to *you*. You want to screen your references, believe me you do! *Don't assume they'll give you a raving recommendation*. Some of your preferred reference writers may turn out to be people who are by nature brutally honest. If they've never actually seen you at work, for example, they may say so, and decline to say whether you'd be an asset or not. That kind of "recommendation" is honest, but it won't do you any good. You want to find this out before any prospective employer sees it. Then you can decide whether you want to use it or deep-six it, before you go into the interview.

10. Hard fact to learn, but you must learn it: Some employers *hate* resumes. Why should that be any surprise? Currently, according to experts, 82 percent of all resumes have to be checked out, concerning the facts stated or the experience claimed. Lies are spreading like a plague, on resumes. Another hard fact: Some employers *love* resumes. Unfortunately, it's not for the reasons

you think. They love them because they offer an easy way to cut down the time they have to spend interviewing candidates for a vacancy. Don't forget this: for an employer, hiring is essentially *an elimination game*. Particularly where a lot of people are applying, they're reading over your resume looking for one thing: a reason—any reason—to eliminate you, so they can cut that stack of resumes down to a manageable number for face-to-face interviewing (say, three to eight). Surveys show it only takes a skilled human resources person about eight seconds to scan a resume (thirty seconds, if they're really dawdling), so getting rid of fifty job-hunters—I mean getting rid of fifty resumes—takes only half an hour or less. Whereas, interviewing those fifty job-hunters in person would have required a minimum of twenty-five hours. Great time savings—for them! No wonder employers invented resumes!

Where You Post Your Resume Makes a Difference

Let's say that again: *where* you post your resume makes all the difference in the world. Research has discovered that the number of face-to-face interviews that employers need to conduct before they find someone they want to hire, stays pretty constant—around 5.4—once they've sifted through all the resumes or applications. So, to conserve their energy, they instinctively ask themselves, "Where would I have to sift through the least number of resumes, before I decide who to do those 5.4 interviews with?" Fortunately, we know the answer. Somebody did a study.[5]

If employers post their vacancy on a job-board such as Monster.com, Indeed.com, or CareerBuilder.com, they typically have to look through **219** resumes from job-hunters who respond, before they find someone to interview and hire.

---

5. From an analysis, released in April 2011, by Jobs2web Inc., of 1,300,000 job applications and 26,000 hires in 2010.

If employers consider resumes from job-hunters who come through social media sites, such as LinkedIn or Facebook, they typically have to look through **116** resumes, before they find someone to interview and hire.

If employers post their vacancy on their own website, they typically have to look through **33** resumes from job-hunters who respond, before they find someone to interview and hire.

And if the job-hunter takes the initiative to find a very specific job, rather than waiting to find a vacancy, and does this, say, by typing the name of that kind of job into a search engine, then sending resumes to any companies whose name turns up, employers only have to look through **32** applications, before they find someone to interview and hire.

And if the job-hunter takes even more initiative, chooses a company where they'd like to work, and gets a referral (i.e., gets some employee within that company to recommend them), employers have to look through only **10** such candidates, before they find someone to interview and hire.

Summary

Okay, one more time: *Do you need a resume?*

Well, no you don't, and yes you do.

You already have a kind of resume without lifting a finger, if you've been posting anything on the Internet. Google is your new resume. What an employer finds out about you simply by *Googling* your name, helps determine whether you get hired or not.

You've got to clean up what they'll find, *before* they find it. Edit, fill in, expand, and add to it, before they see it.

But that, alone, is not enough. You need to summarize and organize the information about yourself in one place, online or off. And that means, you need to write the traditional resume.[6]

Once written, you can go two ways with it. The first way is just to post it everywhere on the Internet, which is akin to nailing it to a tree in the town square, where everyone can see it. You just post it *as is*.

---

6. For additional reading and guidance: *What Color Is Your Parachute? Guide to Rethinking Resumes*, a little over $10 online or at bookstores.

The second way is to send it to particular employers whom you have targeted, hoping that resume will get you an interview. Here you will need to *edit it*, before sending it to any employer. You will need to weigh every sentence in it by one criterion and one only: Will this help get me invited in, for an interview *at this place*? If the answer is *No*, you must edit or remove that sentence.

Because, these are the most fundamental truths about approaching individual employers:

The primary purpose of a resume is *to get yourself invited in for an interview.*

The primary purpose of that interview is *to get yourself invited back* for a second interview.

The primary purpose of the second and subsequent interviews there is *to help them decide that they like you and want you*, once you've decided that you like them and could do some of your best work there.

THE TEN GREATEST MISTAKES
MADE IN JOB-INTERVIEWS

Whereby Your Chances of Finding a Job Are Greatly Decreased

I. Going after large organizations only (such as the Fortune 500).

II. Hunting all by yourself for places to visit.

III. Doing no homework on an organization before going there.

IV. Allowing the Human Resources department to interview you (their primary function is to look for reasons to screen you OUT).

V. Setting no time limit when you first begin the interview, and then overstaying your welcome.

VI. Letting your resume be the only agenda discussed during the job-interview.

VII. Talking primarily about yourself throughout the interview, and what benefit the job will be for you.

VIII. Failing to give examples of the skills you claim you have.

IX. Basically approaching the employer as if you were a job-beggar, hoping they will offer you any kind of a job, however humble.

X. Not sending a thank-you note right after the interview.

CHAPTER 8

Sixteen Tips About Interviewing for a Job

Now, hunting for one of those ten million vacancies that are out there each month, will inevitably involve interviewing, sooner or later. And the word *interview* strikes terror into the hearts of many—if not most—job-hunters. Well, it needn't. Interviews aren't just "for a job." There are many types of interviews, so this topic shouldn't be intimidating. I can think of three kinds of interviews right off the bat that arise during a job-hunt. They are distinguished from each other by *what you are looking for*, and more important, *who you are talking to*.

a. **Interviews for fun or practice.** Here you are talking with people who are passionate about something that you are, too—be it Hawaii, scrapbooks, travel, physical fitness, running, or whatever. *Oh, you would just call these "conversations"? Okay, then: conversations.*

b. **Interviews for information.** This is where you are talking with employees who did or do the job you are exploring; or maybe you're talking with information specialists, or with experts in the industry that interests you. *Oh, you would just call these "conversations"? Okay, then: conversations.*

c. **Interviews for a job.** Where you are talking with employers, and most particularly with the person who actually has the power to hire you for the job you want, rather than an HR interviewer whose first job is to screen out as many candidates as possible. You want information. *Oh, you wouldn't call these "conversations"? Well, I would.*

This chapter is about this third kind of interview or conversation: the one for a job.[1] Keep in mind that the interview *may* not be face-to-face, 75 percent of companies now report that they sometimes do video interviews. Many via Skype. If you're not familiar with Skype, it's never too late to start. Load it onto your computer, test it by calling a friend. See how you come across; get honest feedback, not just backstroking.

Also keep in mind that "interview" is usually plural. You are very likely to have a whole series of interviews at one particular place, before they decide to hire you (and you decide you really want to work there)—unless it's a small "mom and pop" kind of enterprise.

In any event, there are sixteen tips about the hiring conversation(s), at one particular place, that you would do well to keep in mind:

Conversation Tip #1

There is no such thing as "employers." I'm referring to the way job-hunters use that word to reach conclusions after just two interviews at two different places. You conclude *"Employers just won't hire me or someone with my background or someone with my disability,"* or nonsense like that. My friend, you're reaching way beyond the facts.

Fact: You interviewed with two employers (or six, or twelve) and they wouldn't hire you. Those two. Those six. Or those twelve. They hardly speak for all 28.8 million active businesses that are out there.

Fact: "Employers" are individuals, as different from one another as night and day. "Employers" span a wide range of attitudes, wildly different ideas about how to hire, a wide range of ways to conduct hiring-interviews, and as many different viewpoints as you can possibly think of. You cannot possibly predict the attitude of one employer from the attitude of another. All generalizations about "employers" (*including those in this book*) are just mental *conveniences*.

Fact: There are millions of separate, distinct, unrelated employers out there with very different requirements for hiring. Unless you look dirty, wild, and disreputable, and smell really bad, if you know what

---

1. The other two are discussed on pages 224–30.

your *talent* is, I guarantee some employer is looking for *you*. You have to keep going. Some employers out there *do* want you, no matter what the others think. Your job is to find *them*.

Fact: There is a big difference between large employers (those with hundreds or thousands of employees) and small employers (alternately defined as those with twenty-five or fewer employees, or as those with fifty or fewer employees, or—the most common definition—as those with one hundred or fewer employees). The chief difference is that large employers are harder to reach, especially if the-person-who-has-the-power-to-hire-you-for-the-job-you-want is in some deep inner chamber of that company, and the company's phone has a voice menu with eighteen impenetrable layers. Don't think your interviewing experience with small employers will necessarily be at all like that.

Fact: There is a big difference between new companies or enterprises, and those that have been around for some time, so far as hiring is concerned. A recent study by the Bureau of Labor Statistics found that newer companies with fewer than one hundred employees, which were less than five years old, created a net gain of 2.8 million jobs in 2017, while *older* similar firms had a net loss of 1.4 million jobs.[2] So when hiring is tight, you will want to concentrate on small firms, and *newer* small firms at that. Don't think your interviewing experience with new companies will necessarily be at all like the rejection you had with old ones.

Moral: Don't get discouraged by your interview turn-downs. Job expert Tom Jackson[3] brilliantly described the outcomes of job-interviews at a whole bunch of places as follows:

NO NO NO NO NO NO NO NO NO NO NO NO NO NO
NO NO NO NO NO NO NO NO NO NO NO YES YES

As Tom points out, every "NO" you get out of the way, gets you one step closer to YES. (Or, preferably, two YESes.)

---

2. Bureau of Labor Statistics, US Department of Labor, Table 1-A-E, "Annual Gross Job Gains and Gross Job Losses by Age and Average Size of Establishment," December 2017.
3. Author of *The Perfect Resume: Today's Ultimate Job Search Tool*, 2004.

Conversation Tip #2

An interview (or series of interviews there) should be prepared for, before you ever go in. Naturally, you want to go into the interview(s) with this employer curious to know more about *you*, but the employer is first of all curious about what you know about *them*. Do a lot of research on them before you go in. Why? Because organizations love to be loved. If you've gone to the trouble of finding out as much as you can about them, before you interview with them, they will be flattered and impressed, believe me.

So don't skip this step. It may make the difference between your being hired, or not being hired. Find out everything you can about them. Google them. Go to their website if they have one, and read all their press releases, plus everything there that is hidden under the heading "About Us." If this organization is local, and your town has a public library, ask your local librarian for help in finding any news clippings or other information about the place. And, finally, ask all your friends if they know anyone who ever worked there, or works there still, so you can take that person to lunch or tea or Starbucks and find out any inside stories, before you approach the place. (And, of course, maybe after you hear these stories you'll decide not to explore them any further. Better to know that now, than later.)

Conversation Tip #3

Honor agreements. If it was you who asked for the interview, not them, remove their dread of this visit by specifying how much time you are asking of them. You are the one in control of how long the interview lasts. Specify some oddball period, like nineteen minutes (*twenty* sounds vague, *nineteen* sounds precise—like you are really serious).

If they grant you the interview, keep to this time limit as though your life depended on it. It builds trust. You mean what you say. You do what you say you're gonna do. If you have a cell phone with a timer that allows you to select "Vibrate" without any sound, set its timer before you go in to your appointment, to *seventeen* minutes (that leaves you two minutes to wrap up). But don't activate the timer yet. Wait for the time you actually are about to enter their office for the interview, then activate it by tapping it on or go. Keep the phone in a pocket or purse, where you can feel it. At the seventeen-minute vibration warning, tap it off, and prepare to end the interview by saying, *"I said I would only take nineteen minutes of your time, and I like to honor my agreements."* This will usually make a huge impression on an employer!

Don't obsess about time during the interview; just stay quietly aware of it, in the background of your mind, as you focus sharply on what the employer is saying.

And at the end, don't stay one minute longer than the nineteen minutes, unless the employer begs you to—and I mean, begs, Begs, BEGS. A courteous interviewer will say, *"Oh, do you have to?"* But don't mistake that for anything other than what it is: *courtesy.* Just graciously go.

Of course, if it was they who invited you in for the interview, then it is up to them as to how long the interview lasts.

Conversation Tip #4

An interview for a job is a lot like dating. I remind you of what I said in chapter 2: the other human activity that job-hunting most resembles is *dating*, not *marketing* a used car. This conversation is two people attempting to decide if you both want to "try going steady." (Or maybe it's you plus six or nine others, depending on how many from the employer's team are sitting in on the interview.) It's got to be a *two-way* decision. What the employer decides is critical, of course; but so is what you decide.

This interview is a data-collecting process for the employer. Whether one person or a team is interviewing you, they are using the interview to find out, "Do we like you? Do we want you to work here? Do you have the skills, knowledge, or experience that we really need? Do you have the work ethic that we are looking for? And, how will you fit in with our other employees?"

All well and good. But, this interview is part of *your* data-collecting process, too—the one you have been engaged in, or should have been engaged in, throughout your whole job-hunt. You are sitting there, now, with the employer or their team, and the question you are trying to find an answer to is, *"Do I like you all? Do I want to work here, or not?"*

You don't begin an interview—as some so-called experts would have it—by "marketing yourself." Not now. Not in the beginning. Not until you have gathered all the information you need to know about the place, and are weighing the question "Do I want to work here?" and have concluded "Yes," or "I think so," do you then turn your energy toward *marketing* yourself.

Let me emphasize this: your side of the conversation (or conversations) has two steps to it. First, gentle questioning about the place, then quiet, self-confident marketing of yourself, if—but only if—you've decided this is the place for you. Because there are two steps, you'll save yourself a lot of grief if you realize the first interview, there, has only one main purpose: to be invited back for a second interview.

Conversation Tip #5

Questions to expect from them, then questions you can ask. The principal question, the first question, the most important question they are likely to ask you is *"Tell me about yourself."* How you answer that question will determine your fate during the rest of the interview. So, here are some key points to keep in mind about your answer to *Tell me about yourself*:

a. With this question they are giving you a kind of test. They want to see how you respond to an open-ended, unstructured situation, the kind of unanticipated challenge that life (and a job) are continually presenting to each of us.

b. Employers feel you have flunked the test if you respond with a question instead of any answer. Every job-hunter's favorite response—*Well, what do you want to know about me?*—is every employer's *least* favorite. They interpret this to mean you have no idea what to answer, and are stalling for time.

c. What employers are looking for here, is an answer to a somewhat different question than the one they posed. That unspoken real question the employer has is, *What experience, skills, or knowledges do you have that are relevant to the job I am trying to fill?*

That's what you should try to answer here. Not your personal history, where you grew up, your tastes, or hobbies. Employers want your work history, and more particularly your work history as it relates to this job that you are discussing with them.

d. Incidentally, it will help if you ask yourself, before going to the interview(s), "What are *the three most important* competencies, for this job?" If you haven't a clue, then that's what you want to ask *them*, early on in the interview(s). Then, of course, during the interview(s) you will want to emphasize and demonstrate that you *have* those three—for the job that you are applying for.

e. But here we're pondering your answer to "tell me about yourself." Employers expect you to have this answer at your fingertips, well-summarized, well-rehearsed. (This is the famous "elevator speech" job coaches are always recommending to job-hunters. In the length of time it takes to ride an elevator up a tall building, you should be able to give your entire answer *to this question*, rehearsed and rehearsed beforehand, until you could say it in your sleep.)

Okay, what other questions may you expect the employer to ask you, during your interview there? Books on *interviewing*, of which there are many, often publish long lists of questions employers may ask you, along with some timeworn, semiclever answers. Their lists include such questions as:

- Tell me about yourself. (As we have seen.)
- What do you know about this company, business, or organization?
- Why are you applying for this job?
- How would you describe yourself?
- What are your major strengths?
- What is your greatest weakness?
- What type of work do you like to do best?
- What are your interests outside of work?
- What accomplishment thus far in your life, gave you the greatest satisfaction?

- Why did you leave your last place of work?
  Or, *Why were you fired* (if you were)?

- Where do you see yourself five years from now?

- What are your goals in life?

- How much did you make at your last job?

And their lists go on. But really there are only *five basic questions* that you need pay attention to. The people-who-have-the-power-to-hire-you are most curious about your answers to these five, which they may ask directly or try to find out without *even mentioning the questions per se*:

1. "Why are you here?" This means, *"Why are you knocking on my door, rather than someone else's door?"*

2. "What can you do for us?" This means, *"If we were to hire you, will you help me with the challenges I face? What are your skills, and how much do you know about the subject or field that our organization is in?"*

3. "What kind of person are you?" This means, *"Will you fit in? Do you have the kind of personality that makes it easy for people to work with you, and do you share the values that we have at this place?"*

4. "What exactly distinguishes you from nineteen or nine hundred other people who are applying for this job?" This means, *"Do you have better work habits than the others, do you show up earlier, stay later, work more thoroughly, work faster, maintain higher standards, go the extra mile, or . . . what?"*

5. "Can I afford you?" This means, *"If we decide we want you here, how much will it take to get you, and are we willing and able to pay that amount—governed, as we are, by our budget, and by our inability to pay you as much as the person who would be next above you, on our organizational chart?"*

These are the principal questions that employers want to know the answers to. *This is the case, as I said, even if the interview begins and ends with these five questions never once being mentioned explicitly by the employer.* Nonetheless, these questions are still *floating* beneath the surface of the conversation, beneath all the things being discussed. So, anything you can do, during the interview(s) there, to help the employer with these five curiosities, will make you stand out, in the employer's mind.

Of course, it's not just the employer who has questions. This is a two-way conversation, remember? You have questions too. And—no surprise!—they are the same questions as the employer's (in only slightly different form). Here is what you are probably quietly thinking about during your half of the conversation:

1. **"What does this job involve?"** You want to understand exactly what tasks will be asked of you, so that you can determine if these are the kinds of tasks you would really like to do, and can do.

2. **"What are the skills a top employee in this job would have to have?"** You want to find out if your skills match those that the employer thinks a top employee in this job has to have, in order to do this job well.

3. **"Are these the kinds of people I would like to work with, or not?"** Do not ignore your intuition if it tells you that you would not be comfortable working with these people! You want to know if they have the kind of personalities that would enable you to accomplish your best work. If these people aren't it, keep looking!

4. **"If we like each other, and we both want to work together, can I persuade them there is something unique about me, that makes me different from nineteen or nine hundred other people who are applying for this job?"** You need to think out, way ahead of time, what does make you different from other people who can do the same job. For example, if you are good at analyzing problems, how do you do that? (1) Painstakingly? (2) Intuitively, in a flash? (3) By consulting with greater authorities in the field? You see the point. You are trying to put your finger on the "style" or "manner" in which you do your work, that is distinctive and hopefully appealing, to this employer, so that they choose you over other people they are interviewing. (These are called your "self-management skills," as we saw in chapter 5.)

5. **"Can I persuade them to hire me at the salary I need or want?"** This requires some knowledge on your part of how to conduct salary negotiation. (Key things to know: It should always take place at the end of the interviews there, and whoever mentions a salary figure first generally loses in the negotiation.) That's covered in the next chapter.

You will probably want to ask questions one and two out loud. You should *observe* quietly the answer to question three. You will be prepared to make the case for questions four and five, when the *appropriate* time in the interview arises.

Further questions you may want to ask:

- What significant changes has this company gone through in the past five years?
- What values are sacred to this company?
- What characterizes the most successful employees this company has?
- What future changes do you see in the work here?
- Who do you see as your allies, colleagues, or competitors in this business?

How do you first raise these questions of yours, if you initiated the interview? Well, you might begin by reporting just exactly how you've been conducting your job-hunt, and what impressed you so much about *this* organization during your research, that you decided to come in and talk to them about a job. From there, and thereafter, you can fix your attention on the five questions that are inevitably on the employer's mind.

Incidentally, these five questions pop up (yet again), if you're there to talk *not* about a job that already exists, but rather, a job that you hope they will *create* for you. In that case, these five questions change form only slightly. They get changed into five *statements* that you make to the person-who-has-the-power-to-*create*-this-job.

1. You tell them what you like about this organization.
2. You tell them what sorts of needs you find intriguing in this field, in general, and in this organization, in particular (by the way, unless you first hear the word coming out of their mouth, don't use the word *"problems,"* as most employers prefer synonyms that sound gentler to their ears, such as *"challenges"* or *"needs"*).
3. You tell them what skills seem to you to be necessary in order to meet such needs, and you give them brief stories from your past experience that demonstrate you have those very skills.

Employers, in these days of "behavioral interviews," are not impressed with vague statements like "I'm good at. . . ." They want concrete examples, from your past experience, that prove you have the transferable skills, special knowledges skills, or self-management skills, i.e., traits, that you are claiming to have.

4. You tell them what is unique about the way *you* perform those skills. Every prospective employer wants to know *what makes you different* from nineteen or nine hundred other people who can do the same kind of work as you. You *have* to know what that is. And then not merely talk about it, but actually demonstrate it by the way you conduct your side of the hiring-interview.

5. And you tell them how the hiring of you will not cost them, in the long run. You need to be prepared to demonstrate that you will, in the long run, bring in more money than the salary they pay you. Emphasize this!

Conversation Tip #6

During the interview(s), determine to observe "the 50-50 rule." Studies have revealed that, in general, the people who get hired are those who mix speaking and listening fifty-fifty in the interview(s). That is, half the time they let the employer do the talking, half the time in the interview(s) they do the talking. People who didn't follow that mix were the ones who didn't get hired, according to the study.[4] My hunch as to the reason why this is so, is that if you talk too much about yourself, you come across as one who would ignore the needs of the organization; if you talk too little, you come across as trying to hide something about your background.

---

4. This one was done by a researcher at Massachusetts Institute of Technology, whose name has now been lost in the mists of time.

Conversation Tip #7

In answering the employer's questions, observe "the twenty-second to two-minute rule." Studies have revealed that when it is your turn to speak or answer a question, you should plan not to speak any longer than two minutes at a time, if you want to make the best impression.[5] In fact, a good answer to an employer's question sometimes only takes twenty seconds to give. (But not less than that, else you will be assumed to be "a grunter," lacking any communication skills.)

Conversation Tip #8

The employer is primarily concerned about risk. As I mentioned earlier, employers *hate* risks. One risk stands above all the others: that they may hire you, but you won't work out. In which case, you are going to cost the employer a lot of money. Put the term "cost of a bad hire" into your favorite Internet search engine (Google?), and see what it turns up. As you can see, hiring the wrong person can cost the employer one to five times the *bad hire's* annual salary, or more.

So, during the interview, you may think you are sitting there, scared to death, while the employer (individual or team) is sitting there, blasé and confident. But in actual fact you and they may both be quite anxious.

The employer's anxieties include any or all of the following:

a. That if hired, you won't be able to do the job; that you lack the necessary skills or experience, and the hiring-interview didn't uncover this.

b. That if hired, you won't put in a full working day, more often than not.

c. That if hired, you'll take frequent sick days, on one pretext or another.

---

5. This one was conducted by my friend and colleague, Daniel Porot, of Geneva, Switzerland.

d. That if hired, you'll only stay around for a few weeks or at most a few months, until you find a better job.

e. That if hired, it may take you too long to master the job, and thus it will be too long before you turn a profit for that organization.

f. That you won't get along with the other workers there, or that you will develop a personality conflict with the boss.

g. That you will only do the minimum that you can get away with, rather than the maximum that the boss was hoping for. Since every boss these days is trying to keep their workforce as small as possible, they are hoping for the maximum productivity from each new hire.

h. That you will always have to be told what to do next, rather than displaying initiative.

i. That you will turn out to have a disastrous character flaw not evident in the interview, and ultimately reveal yourself to be either dishonest, or irresponsible, a spreader of dissension at work, lazy, an embezzler, a gossip, a sexual harasser, a drunk, a drug user or substance abuser, a liar, incompetent, or to put it bluntly, an employer's worst nightmare.

j. (*If this is a large organization, and your would-be boss is not the top person there*) That you will bring discredit upon them, and upon their department/section/division, etc., for ever hiring you in the first place—making them lose face, possibly also costing them a raise or a promotion, from the boss upstairs.

In the end, what employers want to hire are people who can bring in more money than they are paid. Every organization has two main preoccupations for its day-by-day work: challenges they are facing, and what solutions to those challenges their employees and management are coming up with. Therefore, the main thing the employer is trying to figure out during the hiring-interview with you is, Will you be part of the solution there, or just another part of the challenge.

In trying to allay their worries here, you should figure out prior to the interview how a *bad* employee would "screw up," in the position you are discussing with the employer, individual or team—such things as *come in late, take too much time off, follow his or her own agenda instead of the employer's, etc.* By your actions and words before, during, and after the interview, plan to show the employer how much you are the very opposite: you show up on time or ahead of time, during the interview you are preoccupied with the employer's agenda, not your own, and your sole goal "is to increase the organization's effectiveness, service, and bottom line."

Conversation Tip #9

It's the small things that are the killers, in a job interview. Okay, you're in the interview. You're ready with your carefully rehearsed summary of your experience, skills, and knowledges. *But the employer isn't listening.* Because, sitting across from you, they are noticing things about you that will kill the interview. And the job offer.

I think of this as losing to mosquitoes when you were prepared to fight dragons. And losing in the first two minutes (*ouch*).

So what's going on? Simply this.

The best interviewers operate intuitively on the principle that microcosm reveals macrocosm. They believe that what you do in some small "universe" reveals how you would and will act in a larger "universe."

They watch you carefully, during the small universe of the interview, because they assume that each of your behaviors there reveals how you would act in a larger "universe"—like: *the job!*

They scrutinize your past, as in your resume, for the same reason: *microcosm* (your behavior in the past) *reveals macrocosm* (your likely behavior in the future).

So let us look at what mosquitoes (as it were) can fly in, during the first thirty seconds to two minutes of your interview so that the person-who-has-the-power-to-hire-you starts muttering to themselves, "I sure hope we have some other candidates besides this one."

1. Your appearance and personal habits. Survey after survey has revealed that you are much more likely to get the job if:

- you have obviously freshly bathed and groomed; and
- you have on freshly laundered clothes, pants, or pantsuits with a sharp crease, and shoes, not flip-flops, freshly polished; and
- you have freshly brushed and flossed your teeth, so that you do not have bad breath, do not dispense the odor of garlic, onion, stale tobacco, or strong drink or mouthwash (a dead give-away) into the enclosed office air; and equally
- you are not wafting tons of aftershave cologne or overwhelming perfume fifteen feet ahead of you, when you enter the room. Employers have become super-sensitive these days to the fact that many employees (and employers!) are allergic to certain scents.
- you do not have a whole lot of tattoos clearly visible in the interview. Now, to be sure, not all tattoos are offensive. Tattoos are everywhere these days—on movie stars, singers, dancers, athletes, and everyday people. Some body art is tiny and discrete. In which case this doesn't apply to you. But if you have tattoos that are gang-related, or otherwise off-putting, and you're afraid a particular employer that you want very much to work for is going to think badly of you upon seeing them, weigh carefully if you value the tattoo more than a job (there). At the very least, cover your tattoos with a long-sleeved shirt, blouse, or jacket.

2. Nervous mannerisms. It is a turnoff for many employers if:

- you continually avoid eye contact with the employer (in fact, this is a big, big no-no), or
- you give a limp handshake, or
- you slouch in your chair, endlessly fidget with your hands, crack your knuckles, or constantly play with your hair during the interview. Note, many of these mannerisms are unconscious and increase under stress. One of the best ways to learn if you're doing them is to record a mock interview on your phone or computer. Play it back, but turn off the sound, and watch.

3. Lack of self-confidence. It is a turnoff for many employers if:

- you are speaking so softly you cannot be heard, or so loudly you can be heard two rooms away, or

- you are giving answers in an extremely hesitant fashion, or

- you are giving only one-word answers (*no, yes, maybe, not yet, I think so*) to all the employer's questions, or

- you are constantly interrupting the employer, or

- you are downplaying your achievements or abilities, or are continuously being self-critical in comments you make about yourself during the interview.

4. The consideration you show to other people. It is a turnoff for many employers if:

- you show a lack of courtesy to the receptionist, assistant, and (if at lunch) to the server, or

- you display extreme criticalness toward your previous employers and places of work, or

- you drink strong stuff during the interview process. Ordering a drink if the employer takes you to lunch has become a complete no-no, as it raises the question in the employer's mind, *"Do they normally stop with one, or do they normally keep on going?"* Don't . . . do . . . it! . . . *even if they do*; or

- you forget to thank the interviewer as you're leaving, or forget to send a thank-you note afterward, that same day. Says one human resources expert, *"A prompt, brief... letter thanking me for my time along with a (brief!) synopsis of his/her unique qualities communicates to me that this person is an assertive, motivated, customer-service-oriented salesperson who utilizes technology and knows the rules of the 'game.' These are qualities I am looking for. . . . At the moment I receive approximately one such letter . . . for every fifteen candidates interviewed."*

5. Your values. It is a complete turnoff for many employers, if they see in you:

- any sign of arrogance or excessive aggressiveness; any sign of tardiness or failure to keep appointments and commitments on time, including these interviews; or

- any sign of laziness or lack of motivation; or

- any sign of constant complaining or blaming things on others; or

- any signs of dishonesty or lying—especially on your resume or during the interviews; or

- any signs of irresponsibility or tendency to goof off; or

- any sign of not following instructions or obeying rules; or

- any sign of a lack of enthusiasm for this organization and what it is trying to do; or

- any sign of instability, inappropriate response, and the like; or

- the other ways in which you evidence your values, such as: what things impress you or don't impress you in their office; or what you are willing to sacrifice in order to get this job and what you are not willing to sacrifice in order to get this job; or your enthusiasm for work; or the carefulness with which you did or didn't research this company before you came in; and blah, blah, blah.

- Incidentally, many an employer will watch to see if you smoke, either in the office or at lunch. In a race between two equally qualified people, the nonsmoker will win out over the smoker 94 percent of the time, according to a study done by a professor of business at Seattle University. Sorry to report this, but take it seriously!

So, there you have it, these are the *metaphorical* mosquitoes that can kill you, when you're on the watch for dragons, during the hiring-interviews.

One favor I ask of you: do not write me, telling me how picayune or asinine some of this is. I know that. I'm not reporting the world *as it should be,* and certainly not *as I would like it to be.* I'm only reporting what study after study has revealed about the world *as it is.* And how it affects your chances of getting hired.

But here's the good news, when all is said and done: you can kill all these mosquitoes. Yes, you control and can change every one of these factors. Go back and read the list and see!

Conversation Tip #10

Be aware of the skills most employers are looking for, these days, regardless of the position you are seeking.
They are looking for employees:

- who are punctual, arriving at work on time or better yet, early; who stay until quitting time, or even leave late;
- who are dependable;
- who have a good attitude;
- who have drive, energy, and enthusiasm;
- who want more than a paycheck;
- who are self-disciplined, well-organized, highly motivated, and good at managing their time;
- who can handle people well;
- who can use language effectively;
- who can work on a computer;
- who are committed to teamwork;
- who are flexible, and can respond to novel situations, or adapt when circumstances at work change;
- who are trainable, and love to learn;
- who are project-oriented, and goal-oriented;
- who have creativity and are good at problem solving;
- who have integrity;
- who are loyal to the organization; and
- who are able to identify opportunities, markets, and coming trends.

So, plan on claiming all of these that you **legitimately** can, and prior to the interview, sit down, make a list, and jot down some experience you have had, for each, that proves you have that skill.

Conversation Tip #11

Try to think of some way to bring evidence of your skills to the hiring-interview. For example, if you are an artist, a craftsperson, or anyone who produces a product, try to bring a sample of what you have made or produced—in scrapbook or portfolio form, on a flash-drive, on YouTube, in photos, or if you are a programmer, examples of your code. And so on. Just keep relevance in mind. Only bring evidence of skills needed in this new position.

Conversation Tip #12

Do not bad-mouth your previous employer(s) during the interview, even if they were terrible people. Employers sometimes feel as though they are a fraternity or sorority. During the interview you want to come across as one who displays courtesy toward *all* members of that fraternity or sorority. Bad-mouthing a previous employer only makes this employer who is interviewing you worry about what you would say about *them*, after they hire you.

(I learned this in my own experience. I once spoke graciously about a previous employer during a job-interview. Unbeknownst to me, the interviewer already knew that my previous employer had badly mistreated me. He therefore thought very highly of me because I didn't bad-mouth the guy. In fact, he never forgot this incident; talked about it for years afterward.)

Plan on saying something nice about any previous employer, or if you are pretty sure that the fact you and they didn't get along will surely come out, then try to nullify this ahead of time, by saying something simple like, "I usually get along with everybody; but for some reason, my past employer and I just didn't get along. Don't know why. It's never happened to me before. Hope it never happens again."

Conversation Tip #13

Throughout the interview, keep in mind: employers don't really care about your past; they only ask about it in order to try to predict your future (behavior) with them, if they decide to hire you. They have fears, of course; don't we all?

Legally, US employers may only ask you questions that are related to the requirements and expectations of the job. They cannot ask about such things as your creed, religion, race, age, sexual orientation, or marital status. But, any other questions about your past are *fair game*. And they *will* ask them, if they know what they're doing.

Therefore, during the hiring-interview, before you answer any question the employer asks you about your past, you should pause to think, "What fear about the *future* caused them to ask this question about my past?" and then address *that fear*, subtly or directly.

Here are some *examples*:

Employer's Question	The Fear Behind the Question	The Point You Try to Get Across	Phrases You Might Use to Get This Across
"Tell me about yourself."	The employer is afraid he/she isn't going to conduct a very good inter-view, by failing to ask the right questions. Or is afraid there is something wrong with you, and is hoping you will blurt it out.	You are a good employee, as you have proved in the past at your other jobs. (Give the briefest history of who you are, where born and raised, interests, hobbies, and kind of work you have enjoyed the most to date.) Keep it to two minutes, max.	In describing your work history, use any honest phrases you can about your work history that are self-complimentary: "Hard worker." "Came in early, left late." "Always did more than was expected of me." Etc. Back up your state-ments with examples.

Employer's Question	The Fear Behind the Question	The Point You Try to Get Across	Phrases You Might Use to Get This Across
"What kind of work are you looking for?"	The employer is afraid that you are looking for a different job than that which the employer is trying to fill. E.g., he/she wants an assistant, but you want to be an office supervisor.	You are looking for precisely the kind of work the employer is offering (but don't say that, if it isn't true). Repeat back to the employer, in your own words, what he/she has said about the job, and emphasize the skills you have to do that.	If the employer hasn't described the job at all, say, "I'd be happy to answer that, but first I need to understand exactly what kind of work this job involves." Then answer, as at left.
"Have you ever done this kind of work before?"	The employer is afraid you don't possess the necessary skills and experience to do this job.	You have skills that are transferable, from whatever you used to do; and you did it well.	"I pick up stuff very quickly." "I have quickly mastered any job I have ever done." Share how your past relates with examples.
"Why did you leave your last job?"—or "How did you get along with your former boss and coworkers?"	The employer is afraid you don't get along well with people, especially bosses, and is just waiting for you to "bad-mouth" your previous boss or coworkers, as proof of that.	Say whatever positive things you possibly can about your former boss and co-workers (without telling lies). Emphasize you usually get along very well with people—and then let your gracious attitude toward your previous boss(es) and co-workers prove it, right before this employer's very eyes (and ears).	If you left voluntarily: "My boss and I both felt I would be happier and more effective in a job where [here describe your strong points, such as] I would have more room to use my initiative and creativity." If you were fired: "Usually, I get along well with everyone, but in this particular case the boss and I just didn't get along with each other. Difficult to say why." You don't need to say anything more than that. If you were laid off and your job wasn't filled after you left: "My job was terminated."
"How is your health?"—or "How much were you absent from work during your last job?"	The employer is afraid you will be absent from work a lot, if they hire you. Unfortunately for them, and fortunately for you, this is a question they cannot legally ask you.	Just because the question is illegal, doesn't mean you can't address their hidden fear. Even if they never mention it, you can try to disarm that fear.	You can find a way to say, "My productivity always exceeded other workers in my previous jobs." Share a story or example to back this up.

Employer's Question	The Fear Behind the Question	The Point You Try to Get Across	Phrases You Might Use to Get This Across
"Can you explain why you've been out of work so long?"—or "Can you tell me why there are these gaps in your work history?" (Usually said after studying your resume.)	The employer is afraid that you are the kind of person who quits a job the minute you don't like something about it; in other words, that you have no "stick-to-it-iveness."	You love to work, and you regard times when things aren't going well as challenges, which you enjoy learning how to conquer.	"During the gaps in my work record, I was studying/doing volunteer work/raising my children/doing some hard thinking about my mission in life/ finding redirection." (Choose one.)
"Wouldn't this job represent a step down for you?"—or "I think this job would be way beneath your talents and experience."—or "Don't you think you would be underemployed if you took this job?"	The employer is afraid you could command a bigger salary somewhere else, and will therefore leave him/her as soon as something better turns up.	You will stick with this job as long as you and the employer agree this is where you should be.	"I like the duties of this position and I have the skills to do it well." "We have mutual fears; every employer is afraid a good employee will leave too soon, and every employee is afraid the employer might fire him/her, for no good reason." "I like to work, and I give my best to every job I've ever had."
And, last, "Tell me, what is your greatest weakness?"	The employer is afraid you have some character flaw, and hopes you will now rashly blurt it out, or confess it.	You have limitations just like anyone else, but you work constantly to improve yourself and be a more and more effective worker.	Mention a weakness and then stress its positive aspect, e.g., "I don't like to be oversupervised, because I have a great deal of initiative, and I like to anticipate problems before they even arise."

Conversation Tip #14

As the interview proceeds, you want to quietly notice the time frame of the questions the employer is asking, because it's a way of measuring how the interview is going. If it's going favorably for you, the time frame of the employer's questions will often move—*however slowly*—through the following stages.

1. Distant past: *e.g., "Where did you attend high school?"*
2. Immediate past: *e.g., "Tell me about your most recent job."*
3. Present: *e.g., "What kind of a job are you looking for?"*
4. Immediate future: *e.g., "Would you be able to come back for another interview next week?"*
5. Distant future: *e.g., "Where would you like to be five years from now?"*

Well, you get the point. The more the time frame of the interviewer's questions moves from the past to the future, the more favorably you may assume the interview is going for you. On the other hand, if the interviewer's questions stay firmly in the past, the outlook is not so good. *Ah well, ya can't win them all!*

When the time frame of the interviewer's questions moves firmly into the future, *then* is the time for you to get more specific about the job in question. Experts say it is essential for you to ask, at that point, these kinds of questions, *if* you don't already know the answers:

- What is the job, specifically, that I am being considered for?
- If I were hired, what duties would I be performing?
- What would you be hiring me to accomplish?
- What responsibilities would I have?
- Would I be working with a team, or group?
- To whom would I report? (*Remember, the communication skills and personal warmth of an employee's supervisor are often crucial in determining the employee's tenure and performance. In fact, recent research shows that the quality of the supervisor may be more important than the experience and individual attributes of the workers themselves.*)

- Whose responsibility is it to see that I get the training I need here, to get up to speed?
- How would I be evaluated, how often, and by whom?
- What were the strengths and weaknesses of previous people in this position?
- May I meet the persons I would be working with and for (if it isn't you)?
- (Optional) If you don't mind my asking, I'm curious as to why *you* yourself decided to work at this organization?
- (Optional) What do you wish you had known about this company before you started here?

Conversation Tip #15

Before you leave the (final) interview there, assuming you have decided that you like them and maybe they like you, you have a decision to make. The last questions you ask in the process are going to be the most memorable, so tread carefully. In some situations a direct approach is appropriate, so you could ask:

"Can you offer me this job?" If after hearing all about this job at this place, you decide you'd really like to have it, you can ask for it. The worst thing the employer can say is "No," or "We need some time to think about all the interviews we're conducting." Be prepared for the employer to say no.

You could also ask, "What is the next step in the hiring process?" or "When may I expect to hear from you?" If the employer says, "We need some time to think about this," or "We will be calling you for another interview," you could then ask:

"Might I ask what would be the latest I can expect to hear from you?" The employer will probably give you their best guess, but just know that hiring is often a process with several layers of approval, and it can take longer than anyone, including your interviewer, thinks. A delay is not a denial.

You can then ask, "May I contact you after that date, if for any reason you haven't gotten back to me by that time?" Some employers resent this question. You'll know that is the case if they snap at you. But most employers appreciate your offering them what is in essence a safety net. They know they can get busy, become overwhelmed with other things, forget their promise to you. It's reassuring, in such a case, for you to offer to rescue them. Just keep in mind it can be frustrating to have several candidates constantly "checking in," so use this action judiciously, if at all. You can always call the human resources office and ask if the position has been filled.

If ultimately the employer says "No," you can ask, "Can you think of anyone else who might be interested in my skills and experience?" This question is invoked only if they replied "No" to your first question.

Jot down any answers they give you, then stand up, thank them sincerely for their time, give a firm handshake, and leave.

In the following days, rigorously keep to all that you said, and don't contact them except with that mandatory thank-you note, until after the latest deadline you two agreed upon. If you do have to contact them after that date, and if they tell you things are still up in the air, you could ask these questions again, but tread lightly.

Conversation Tip #16

Every expert on interviewing will tell you two things:

1. Thank-you notes must be sent after every interview, by every job-hunter; and

2. Most job-hunters ignore this advice.

Indeed, it is safe to say that it is the most overlooked step in the entire job-hunting process.

If you want to stand out from the others applying for the same job, send thank-you notes—to everyone you met there that day. Ask if they have a business card, and if not, ask them to write out their name and address. Do this with the administrative assistants (who often hold the keys to the kingdom) as well as with your interviewer.

If you need any additional encouragement to send thank-you letters (besides the fact that it may get you the job), here are six more reasons for sending a thank-you note, especially to the one who interviewed you:

First, you were presenting yourself as one who has good skills with people. Your actions with respect to the job-interview must back this claim up. Sending a thank-you note does that. The employer can see you are good with people; you remembered to thank them.

Second, it helps the employer recall who you are. Very helpful if they've seen a dozen people that day.

Third, if a committee will be involved in the hiring process, but only one member was at the first interview, the man or woman who first interviewed you has something to show the others on the committee.

Fourth, if the interview went rather well, and the employer seemed to show an interest in further talks, the thank-you note can reiterate your interest in further talks.

Fifth, the thank-you note gives you an opportunity to correct any wrong impression you left behind. You can add anything you forgot to tell them that you want them to know. And from among all the things you two discussed, you can underline the two or three points that you most want to stand out in their minds.

Last, if the interview did not go well, or you lost all interest in working there, and this thank-you note is sort of "good-bye, and thanks," keep in mind that they may hear of openings elsewhere that would be of interest to you. In the thank-you note, you can mention this, and ask them to please let you know if they hear of anything anywhere. If this was a kind man or woman who interviewed you, they may send you additional leads.

Conclusion

There is no magic in job-hunting. No techniques work all the time. I hear regularly from job-hunters who report that they paid attention to all the tips I have mentioned in this chapter and the book, and are quite skilled at securing interviews—but they never get hired. And they want to know what they're doing wrong.

Sometimes it is because there are levels of screening, some within your sight, some beyond your sight. And everything may appear to be going well, on the levels you can see; but not necessarily on the levels you can't see.

Still puzzled about why you're not getting hired? Sometimes, unfortunately, the answer is "You're not doing anything wrong." I don't know how often this happens, but I know it does happen: namely, some employers play despicable tricks on job-hunters, whereby they invite you in for an interview despite the fact that they have already hired some-one for the position in question, and they know from the beginning that they have absolutely no intention of hiring you—not in a million years!

You are cheered, of course, by the ease with which you get these interviews. But unbeknown to you, the manager who is interviewing you (we'll say it's a he) has a personal friend he already agreed to give the job to. Only one small problem remains: the state or the federal government gives funds to this organization, and has mandated that this position be opened to all. So this manager must pretend to inter-view ten candidates, including his favorite, as though the job opening were still available. But, he intended, from the beginning, to reject the other nine and give the job to his favorite. You were selected for the honor of being among those nine rejectees.

You will, of course, be baffled as to why you got turned down. Trouble is, you will never know.

On the other hand, maybe no games are being played. You are getting rejected, at place after place, because there is something really wrong with the way you are coming across, during these hiring-interviews.

Employers will rarely ever tell you this. You will never hear them say something like, "You came across as just too cocky and arrogant during the interview." You will almost always be left in the dark as to what it is you're doing wrong.

If you feel daring, there is a strategy you can try. If you've been interviewed by a whole bunch of employers, whoever was the friend-liest of them all may want to help you. I said *may*.

You can always try phoning, reminding them of who you are, and then asking the following question—deliberately kept generalized, vague, unrelated to just that place, and above all, future-directed.

Something like: *"I'd appreciate some advice. I've been on several interviews at several different places now. From what you've seen, is there something about me in an interview that you think might be causing me not to get hired at those places? If so, I'd really appreciate your giving me some pointers so I can do better in my future hiring-interviews."*

Most of the time they'll duck. Their legal adviser, if they have one, will certainly advise against it. First of all, they're afraid of lawsuits. Second, they don't know how you will use what they might have to say. (Said an old military veteran to me one day, *"I used to think it was my duty to tell everyone the truth. Now I only give it to those who can use it."*)

But occasionally you will run into a compassionate and kind employer who is willing to risk giving you the truth, because they think you will use it wisely. If so, thank them from the bottom of your heart, no matter how painful their feedback is. Such advice, seriously heeded, can bring about just the changes in your interviewing strategy that you most need, in order to win during interviews in the future.

In the absence of any such help from employers who interviewed you, you might want to get a good business friend of yours to role-play a mock hiring-interview with you, in case they immediately see something glaringly wrong with how you're "coming across."

When all else fails, I would recommend you go to a career coach who charges by the hour, and put yourself in their tender, knowledgeable hands. Role-play an interview with them, and take their advice seriously (you've just paid for it, after all).

In interviewing, as elsewhere in your job-hunt, the secret is to find out anything that is within your control, even if it's only 2 percent; and change it!

And if you do get the job, make one resolution to yourself right there, on the spot: plan to keep track of your accomplishments at this new job, on a weekly basis—jotting them down, every weekend, in your own private log. Career experts recommend you do this without fail. You can then summarize these accomplishments annually on a one-page sheet, for your boss's eyes, when the question of a raise or promotion comes up.[6]

---

6. For additional reading and guidance: *What Color Is Your Parachute? Guide to Rethinking Interviews*, a little over $10 online or at bookstores.

THE TEN COMMANDMENTS FOR JOB-INTERVIEWS

Whereby Your Chances of Finding a Job Are Vastly Increased

I. Go after new, small organizations with fewer than fifty employees, at first, since they create nearly two-thirds of all new jobs. Only if you turn up nothing should you broaden the search to slightly larger organizations, those with fifty employees; then if that doesn't prove to be a successful strategy, organizations with one hundred employees.

II. Hunt for places to interview using the aid of, say, eighty friends and acquaintances—because a job-hunt requires eighty pairs of eyes and ears. But first do homework on yourself so you can tell them exactly what you are looking for. (This is discussed further in chapter 5.)

III. As for who to interview, once you've identified a place that interests you, you really need to find out who has the power to hire you there, for the position you want, and use "bridge-people" (those who know you and also know them) to get an introduction to that person. Employ LinkedIn.com and similar, to find these people. (See chapter 6.)

IV. Do thorough homework on an organization before going there, using Informational Interviews (see chapter 6) plus the Internet to find out as much about them as you possibly can. If you have a public library in town, ask there too.

V. Then prepare for the interview with your own agenda, your own questions and curiosities about whether or not this job fits you. This will always impress employers.

VI. If you initiated the appointment, ask for just nineteen minutes of their time; and keep to your word strictly. Set a timer.

VII. When answering a question of theirs, talk only between twenty seconds and two minutes, at any one time. Try to be succinct. Don't keep rattling on, out of nervousness.

VIII. Basically approach them not as a "job-beggar" but humbly as a resource person, able to produce better work for that organization than any of the people who worked in that position previously.

IX. At the end of the interviewing process, find out the timeline for the process and stay in touch about your continued interest. Salary negotiation should only happen when they have definitely said they want you; prior to that, it's pointless.

X. Always write a thank-you note the same evening as the interview, and mail it at the latest by early next morning. This in addition to emailing it. The tendency these days is for job-hunters to only email a thank-you note. You will stand out from the others if you do both.

Pick up a camera. Shoot something. No matter how small, no matter how cheesy, no matter whether your friends and your sister star in it. Put your name on it as director. Now you're a director. Everything after that you're just negotiating your budget and your fee.

—*James Cameron*

CHAPTER 9

The Six Secrets of Salary Negotiation

Salary.

It must be discussed, before you finally agree to take the job. Once they've offered it to you.

I hope you know that. I remember talking to a breathless high school graduate, who was elated at having just landed her first job. "How much are they going to pay you?" I asked. She looked startled. "I don't know," she said, "I never asked. I just assume they will pay me a fair wage." Boy! Did she get a rude awakening when she received her first paycheck. It was so miserably low, she couldn't believe her eyes. And thus did she learn, painfully, what you must learn too: Before accepting a job offer, *always* ask about salary.

Indeed, ask and then negotiate.

It's the "negotiate" that throws fear into our hearts. So many of us feel ill prepared to do that.

Well, set your mind at ease; it's not all that difficult.

While whole books can be—and have been—written on this subject, there are basically just six secrets to keep in mind.

The First Secret of
Salary Negotiation

Before You Go to the Interview, Do Some
Careful Research on Typical Salaries for Your
Field and in That Organization

Salary negotiation is required any time the employer does not openly state the salary and indicate that it's not negotiable.

Okay, so here is the $64,000 question: How do you tell whether the figure the employer first offers you is only their starting bid, or is their final offer? The answer is, by doing some research on the field and that organization, before you ever go in for an interview.

Oh, come on! I can hear you say. *Isn't this more trouble than it's worth?* No, it's not. If you want to win the salary negotiation. There is a financial penalty exacted from those who are too lazy, or in too much of a hurry, to go gather this information. In plain language: If you don't do this research, it'll cost ya!

Let's say it takes you from one to three days to run down this sort of information on the three or four organizations that interest you the most. And let us say that because you've done this research, when you finally come to the end of the final interview for a job there, you are able to ask for and obtain a salary that is—oh, let's say—$15,000 a year *higher* than you would otherwise have gotten. (That's not unrealistic.)

In the next three years, then, you will be earning $45,000 extra because of your salary research. Not bad pay, for just one to three days' work! And it can be even more.

It doesn't always happen; but I know many job-hunters and career-changers to whom it has. It's certainly worth a shot.

Okay, then, how do you do this research? Well, there are two ways to go: online, and off. Let's look at each, in turn.

Salary Research Online

If you want to research salaries for particular geographical regions, positions, occupations, or industries, or even (sometimes) organizations, here are some free sites that may give you just what you're looking for:

- www.glassdoor.com: This site allows you to search job-titles, and their corresponding average salaries, in your area. It also features employee reviews from more than 600,000 companies.

- www.payscale.com: By answering a few questions about your field of interest, experience, and preferred geographic location, you will get an expected salary range. (Note: You don't have to answer every question—only those with a red asterisk. But answering more will give you a more accurate result.)

- www.salary.com: The most visited of all the salary-specific job-sites, with a wide variety of information about salaries.

- www.indeed.com: While not specifically a salary site, Indeed posts salaries for specific openings when available and also sorts job-listings by salary range. Enter a job-title and geographic location to see what is available and the approximate pay range.

- www.bls.gov/ooh: The Bureau of Labor Statistics' survey of salaries in individual occupations, from the *Occupational Outlook Handbook* 2018–2019. It lists jobs that are highest paying, and/or jobs that are the fastest growing, and/or jobs that have the highest number of openings.

- www.MyPlan.com: This site has several lists of the highest-paying jobs in America, including a list for those without a college degree (under Careers, click on Top Ten Lists).

- www.salaryexpert.com: When you need a salary expert, it makes sense to go to "the Salary Expert." Lots of stuff on the subject of salaries here, including a free "Salary Report" for hundreds of job-titles, varying by area, skill level, and experience. It also has some salary calculators.

If you "strike out" on all the above sites, then you're going to have to get a little more clever, and work a little harder, and pound the pavement, as I shall describe next.

Salary Research off the Internet

Okay, so how do you do salary research offline? Well, there's a simple rule: *generally speaking, abandon books, and go talk to people.*

Use books and libraries only as a second, or last, resort because print publication time frames will render the information out-of-date. You can get much more complete and up-to-date information from people who are doing the kind of job you're interested in, maybe at another company or organization than the one(s) you're interested in.

If you don't know where to find them, talk to people at a nearby university or college who train such people, whatever their department may be. Teachers and professors will usually know what their graduates are making, and some university career centers will post salary data for their alumni. Also you can go visit actual workplaces.

Let's look at some concrete examples.

First Example: A fast food place. You may not need to do any salary research. They pay what they pay. You can walk in, ask for a job application, and interview with the hiring manager. He or she will usually tell you the pay, outright. It's usually set in concrete. But at least it's easy to discover what the pay is. (*Incidentally, filling out an application, or even having an interview there, doesn't mean you have to take that job—but you probably already know that. Just say,* "I need to go home and think about this." *You can decline any offer from any place. That's what makes this approach harmless.*)

Second Example: A construction company. This is typical of a place where you can't discover what the pay is, right off the bat. If you're actually going to try to get work at that construction company but you want to research salaries before you go for an interview, the best way to do this research is to go visit a different construction company in the same town or geographical area—one that isn't of much interest to you—and ask what *people* make *there.* Or, if you don't know who to talk to there, fill out one of their applications, and talk to the hiring person about what kinds of jobs they have (or might have in the future)—at which time prospective wages is a legitimate subject of inquiry. Then, having done this research on a place you don't care about, go back to the place that really interests you, and apply. You still don't know exactly what they pay, but you do know what their competitor pays—which will usually be close to what you're trying to find out.

There's a lot you can find out by talking to people. But another way to do salary research—if you're out of work and have time on your hands—is to find a Temporary Work Agency that places different kinds of workers, and let yourself be farmed out to various organizations: the more, the merrier. It's relatively easy to do salary research when you're inside a place. (Study what that place pays the agency, not what the agency pays you after they've taken their "cut.") If you're working temporarily at a place where the other workers really like you, you'll be able to ask questions about a lot of things there, including salary. Keep in mind, it's best not to ask someone their specific salary but rather "What's the general range of pay for this type of position?" Some companies have policies against discussing salaries.

The Second Secret of Salary Negotiation

Never Discuss Salary Until the End of the Whole Interviewing Process at That Organization, When (and If) They Have Definitely Said They Want You

"The end of the interviewing process" is difficult to define. It's the point at which the employer says, or thinks, "We've got to get this person!" That may be at the end of the first (and therefore the last) interview; or it may be at the end of a whole series of interviews, often with different people within the same company or organization, or with a whole bunch of them all at once.

But assuming things are going favorably for you, whether after the first, or second, or third, or fourth interview, *if you like them* and they increasingly like you, a job offer will be made. Then, and only then, is it time to deal with the question that is inevitably on any employer's mind: *How much is this person going to cost me?* And the question that is on your mind: *How much does this job pay?* This is the time to complete any research on salaries for this field or job-title.

If the employer raises the salary question earlier, say, near the beginning of the interview, asking (innocently), *"What kind of salary are you looking for?"* you should have three responses ready—at your fingertips.

Response #1: If the employer seems like a kind man or woman, your best and most tactful reply might be, *"Until you've decided you definitely want me, and I've decided I definitely could help you with your tasks or projects here, I feel any discussion of salary is premature."*

That will work, in most cases. There are instances, however, where that doesn't work. Then you need:

Response #2: You may be face-to-face with an employer who demands within the first two minutes of the interview to know what salary you are looking for. So, here, you may need a backup response, such as, *"I'll gladly answer that, but could you first help me understand what this job involves?"*

That is a good response, in most cases. But what if it doesn't work? Then you'll need to fall back on:

Response #3: The employer with rising voice says, *"Come, come, don't play games with me. I want to know what salary you're looking for."* Okay, that's that. You have to come clean. But you don't have to mention a single figure; instead you can answer in terms of *a range.* For example, *"I'm looking for a salary in the range of $35,000 to $45,000 a year."*

If that still doesn't satisfy them, then clearly you are being interviewed by an employer who has no range in mind. Their beginning figure is their ending figure. No negotiation is possible.[1] This happens, when it does, because many employers are making salary their major if not sole criterion for deciding who to hire, and who not to hire. It's an old game: among two equally qualified candidates, the one who is willing to work for the least pay, wins. And *that* is *that!*

---

1. One job-hunter said his interviews *always* began with the salary question, and no matter what he answered, that ended the interview. Turned out, this job-hunter was doing all the interviewing over the phone. That was the problem. Once he went face-to-face, salary was no longer the first thing discussed in the interview.

If you run into this situation, you may decide this isn't the kind of place you want to work at, for if they're inflexible in this, what else will they be inflexible about, once you take the job? You've been warned. Microcosm equals macrocosm.

On the other hand, if you're flat broke and you need this job—any job—desperately, you will have no choice but to give in. Ask what salary they have in mind, and make your decision. (Of course you can always try postponing your decision a day or so, by saying, "I need a little time to think about this.")

However, all the foregoing is merely the worst-case scenario. Usually, things won't go this badly, where you feel so powerless.

In most interviews these days, the employer, alone or in a group, *will* be willing to save salary negotiation until they've finally decided they want you (and you've decided you want them). And at that point, the salary will be negotiable. I'll explain *why* in the next Secret.

For now, let me hammer home this second Secret: it is in your best interest to *not* discuss salary until all of the following conditions have been fulfilled:

- Not until they've gotten to know you, at your best, so they can see how you stand out above the other applicants, and therefore how you're worth more than they would pay *them*.
- Not until you've gotten to know them, as completely as you can, so you can tell if this really is a place where you want to work.
- Not until you've found out exactly what the job entails.
- Not until they've had a chance to find out how well you match their job requirements.
- Not until you're in the final interview at that place, for that job.
- Not until you've decided, "I *really* would like to work here."
- Not until they've conveyed to you their feelings, such as, "Well that's good, because we want you."
- Or, better yet: Not until they've conveyed the feeling, "We've *got* to have you."

If you'd prefer this in the form of a diagram, see the next page.

WHEN TO NEGOTIATE SALARY

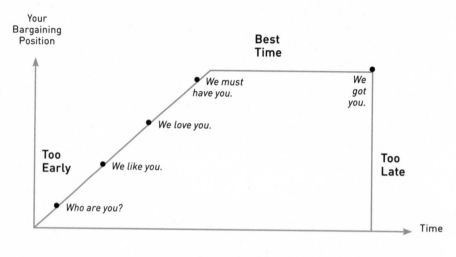

It all boils down to this: if you really shine during the hiring-interview, they may—at the end—offer you a higher salary than they originally had in mind when the interview started. And this is particularly the case when the interview has gone so well that they're now *determined* to obtain you.

The Third Secret of Salary Negotiation

The Purpose of Salary Negotiation Is to Uncover the Most That an Employer Is Willing to Pay to Get You

Negotiation. There's the word that strikes terror into the hearts of most job-hunters or career-changers. Why do we have to negotiate?

Simple. It would never be necessary if every employer in every hiring-interview were to mention, right from the start, the top figure they are willing to pay for that position. A few employers do. And that's the end of any salary negotiation. But most employers don't.

They know, from the beginning of the interview, the top figure they're willing to pay for this position under discussion. But. But. They're hoping they'll be able to get you for less. So they *start* the bidding (*for that is what it is*) lower than they're ultimately willing to go.

And this creates a range.

A range between the lowest they're hoping to pay vs. the highest they can afford to pay. And that range is what the negotiation is all about.

For example, if the employer can afford to pay you $30 an hour, but wants to try to get you for $18 an hour, the range is $18 to $30.

You have every right to try to negotiate the highest salary that the employer is willing to pay you, *within that range.*

Nothing's wrong with the goals of either of you. The employer's goal is to save money, if possible. Your goal is to bring home to your own household the most money that you can, for the work you will be doing.

The Fourth Secret of Salary Negotiation

During Salary Discussion, Never Be the First One to Mention a Salary Figure

Where salary negotiation has been successfully kept offstage for much of the interview process, when it finally does come up, you want the employer to be the first one to mention a figure, if you possibly can.

Why? Nobody knows. But it has been observed over the years that where the goals are opposite, as in this case—you are trying to get the employer to pay the most they can, and the employer is trying to pay the least they can—whoever mentions a salary figure first generally loses. You can speculate from now until the cows come home, as to why this is so. There are a dozen theories. All we really know for sure is that it is true.

Inexperienced employer/interviewers often don't know this strange rule. But experienced ones are very aware of it. That's why they will try to get you to mention a figure first, by asking you some innocent-sounding question, like *"What kind of salary are you looking for?"*

Well, how kind of them to ask me what I want—you may be thinking. No, no, no. Kindness has nothing to do with it. They are hoping you will be the first to mention a figure, because they've learned this lesson from ten thousand interviews in the past.

Accordingly, if they ask you to be the first to name a figure, the simple countermove you should have at the ready is, *"Well, you created this position, so you must have some figure in mind, and I'd be interested in first hearing what that figure is."*

The Fifth Secret of Salary Negotiation

Research the Range That the Employer Likely Has in Mind, and Then Define an Interrelated Range for Yourself, Relative to the Employer's Range

Okay, I admit this is a bit sophisticated, and you may not have the stomach to do this much research. But you ought to at least know how this works. Just in case.

It begins by defining your goal. What you want, in your research, is not just one salary figure. As you may recall, you want *a range*; a range defined by what's the least the employer may offer you, and what's the most the employer may be willing to pay to get you. In any organization that has more than five employees, that range is comparatively easy to figure out. It will be less than what the person who would be above you makes, and more than what the person who would be below you makes. Here are a couple of examples.

If the Person Who Would Be Below You Makes	And the Person Who Would Be Above You Makes	The Range for Your Job Would Be
$75,000	$85,000	$77,000–$83,000
$30,000	$35,500	$32,500–$34,000

One teensy-tiny little problem here: How do you find out the salary of those who would be above and below you? Well, first you have to find out their names or the names of their positions.

If it is a small organization you are going after—one with fifty or fewer employees—finding out this information should be easy. Any employee who works there is likely to know the answer, and you can usually get in touch with one of those employees, or even an ex-employee, through your own personal "bridge-people"—people who know you and also know them. Since up to two-thirds of all new jobs are created by small companies of this size, that's the kind of organization you are likely to be researching, anyway.

On the other hand, if you are going after a larger organization, then you fall back on a familiar life preserver, namely, *every* person you know (family, friend, relative, business, or spiritual acquaintance) and ask them who they know that might know the company in question, and therefore, the information you seek. LinkedIn should prove immensely helpful to you here, in locating such people. If you're not already on it, get on it (www.LinkedIn.com/reg/join).

Maybe this will be easy. Maybe it won't be: it's possible you'll run into an absolute blank wall at a particular organization (everyone who works there is pledged to secrecy, and they have shipped all their ex-employees to Siberia). In that case, seek out information *on their nearest competitor* in the same geographic area. For example, let us say you were trying to find out managerial salaries at Bank X, and that place was proving to be inscrutable about what they pay their managers. You would then turn to Bank Y as your research base, to see if the information is easier to come by there. And if it is, you can assume the two may be basically similar in their pay scales, and that what you learned about Bank Y is probably applicable to Bank X.

Note: In your salary research take note of the fact that most gov-
ernmental agencies have civil service positions paralleling those in
private industry—and government job descriptions and pay ranges are
available to the public. Go to the nearest city, county, regional, state, or
federal civil service office, find the job description nearest the kind of
job you are seeking in private industry, and then ask the starting salary.

When this is all done, if you want to be a true expert at this game,
then you're going to have to do a little bit of math here.

Suppose you guess that the employer's range for the kind of job
you're seeking is $36,500 to $47,200. Before you go in for the interview,
anywhere, you figure out an "asking" range for yourself, that you're
going to use when and if the interview gets to the salary negotiation
part. This asking range is clever, in that it should "hook in" just below
that employer's maximum, and then go up from there. This diagram
shows you how this works:

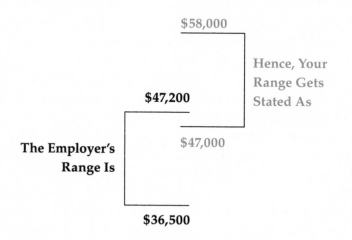

And so, when the employer has stated a figure (probably around their lowest—i.e., $36,500), you will be ready to respond with something along these lines: *"I understand, of course, the constraints under which all organizations are operating these days, but I am confident that my productivity is going to be such that it will justify a salary"*—and here you mention your range, where your bottom figure starts just below the top of their range, and goes up from there—*"in the range of $47,000 to $58,000."*

It will help a lot during this discussion, if you are prepared to show in what ways you will make money or in what ways you will save money for that organization, such as would justify precisely this higher salary you are asking for. Even if they accept your offer at the bottom of your range, you are still near the top figure they're willing to pay.

Yes, it's clever. Yes, it's risky. Yes, it takes some work. But you've got the brains to pull it off. You've got the brains to be good at this salary negotiation game.

What if, after all the trouble you went to, this just doesn't work? At least, at that place. The employer has a ceiling they have to work with, it's below what you're asking, and you are unwilling to lower your definition of what you're worth?

Daniel Porot, job-expert from Switzerland, suggests that if you're dying to work there, but they cannot afford the salary you need and deserve, you might consider offering them part of your time.

If you need, and believe you deserve, say, $50,000 annually, but they can only afford $30,000, you might consider offering them three days a week of your time for that $30,000 (30/50 = 3/5 of a five-day work-week). This leaves you free to take work elsewhere during those other two days. You will of course determine to produce so much work during those three days per week you are there, that they will be ecstatic about this bargain—won't you?

The Sixth Secret of Salary Negotiation

Know How to Bring the Salary Negotiation to a Close; Don't Leave It "Just Hanging"

Salary negotiation with this employer is not finished until you've addressed more than salary. Unless you're an independent contractor, you want to talk about so-called fringe benefits. "Fringes" such as life insurance, health benefits or health plans, vacation or holiday time, and retirement programs typically add anywhere from 15 percent to 28 percent to many workers' salaries. That is to say, if an employee receives a $3,000 salary per week, the fringe benefits are worth another $450 to $840 per week.

So, before you walk into an interview, you should decide what benefits are particularly important to you. And then, after the basic salary discussion is settled, you can go on to ask them what benefits they offer there. If you've given this any thought beforehand, you should have already decided what benefits are most important to you, and be ready to fight for *those.*

And when all this is done, the discussion of the job, the finding out if they like you and if you like them, the salary negotiation, and the concluding discussion of benefits, then you want to get everything they're offering summarized, *in writing.* Believe me you do. In writing, or typed, and *signed.*

Many executives unfortunately "forget" what they told you during the hiring-interview, or even deny they ever said such a thing. It shouldn't happen; but it does. Sometimes they honestly forget what they said.

Other times of course, they're playing a game. Or their successor is, who may disown any *unwritten* promises you claim they made to you at the time of hiring. They may respond with, "*I don't know what caused them to say that to you, but they clearly exceeded their authority, and of course we can't be held to that.*"

I repeat: Get it all in writing. And signed. It's called a letter of agreement—or employment contract. If it is a small employer (ten or fewer employees) they may not know how to draw one up. Just put the search term "sample letter of agreement between employer and employee" into your favorite search engine, and you'll get lots of free examples. I particularly like the one from Inc.com. You or the employer can write this up. Then they can sign it.

You have every right to ask for this. If they simply won't give it to you, *beware.*

Remember, job-hunting always involves luck, to some degree. But with a little bit of luck, a lot of hard work, and determination on your part, the instructions in this book should work for you.

Opportunities to find deeper powers
within ourselves come when life seems
most challenging.

—*Joseph Campbell*

CHAPTER 10

How to Deal with Any Challenges You Have

I know what you're thinking. If you got a job-interview (or interviews), and got turned down, you're thinking that there is some issue (*hidden or obvious*) that is keeping you from getting hired.

Maybe you were thinking this, even before you went in for an interview. (*You turned to this chapter straightaway, didn't you?*)

You're thinking, I'm getting turned down (or *I will be turned down*) because:

I have a physical disability *or*

I have a mental disability *or*

I never graduated from high school *or*

I never graduated from college *or*

I am just graduating *or*

I just graduated two years ago and am still unemployed *or*

I graduated way too long ago *or*

I am too beautiful or handsome *or*

I am too ugly *or*

I am too fat *or*

I am too thin *or*

I am too old *or*

I am too young *or*

I am too near retirement *or*

I have only had one employer in life *or*

I have hopped from job to job all my life *or*

I have been out of the job market too long *or*

I have been in the job market far too long *or*

I am too inexperienced *or*

I have a prison record *or*

I have a psychiatric history *or*

I have not had enough education and am underqualified *or*

I have too much education and am overqualified *or*

I am Latino *or*

I am black *or*

I am Asian *or*

My English is not very good *or*

I speak heavily accented English *or*

I am too much of a specialist *or*

I am too much of a generalist *or*

I am ex-clergy *or*

I am ex-military *or*

I am too assertive *or*

I am too shy *or*

I have only worked for volunteer organizations *or*

I have only worked for small organizations *or*

I have only worked for a large organization *or*

I have only worked for the government *or*

I come from a very different culture or background *or*

I come from another industry *or*

I come from another planet.

If all of this were true, there would be only three weeks in our life when we are employable!

Okay, but let's get one thing straight, from the beginning here: you can't possibly have an issue that will keep all employers from hiring you. You can only have an issue that will keep *some* employers from hiring you. No matter what issue you have, or think you have, it cannot possibly keep you from getting hired anywhere in the world. It can only keep you from getting hired *at some places.*

As I said in chapter 8, there are millions of separate, distinct, unrelated employers out there with very different requirements for hiring. If you know what your *talent* is, I guarantee some employer is looking for *you.* You have to keep going. Some employers out there *do* want you, no matter what the others think. Your job is to find *them.*

It is important to note that while you may suspect a particular issue is keeping you from being hired, you may not be correct. Employers by law are not permitted to discriminate in their hiring process due to:

- Race
- Age
- Religious belief
- Gender (including pregnancy)
- Disability
- Genetic background[1]

Unfortunately, you won't always know if the employer is discriminating against you in one of these protected areas. Discrimination (like prejudice or bias) can be subtle, unconscious, and hidden.

You Cannot Generalize About Employers

I mentioned this, of course, in chapter 1. And here we are back to that same truth. As far as your issue is concerned, you can generalize this much: all employers divide for you into just two tribes—employers

---

1. For complete information about laws regarding equal employment opportunity, start with this site: www.eeoc.gov/eeoc.

who are interested in hiring you for *what you can do*; vs. employers who are bothered by *what you can't do*.

No matter how many times you run into the latter kind, once you discover their attitude, you should just courteously thank them for their time, and ask if they know of any other employers who might be interested in someone with your skills. Then, gently take your leave.

And speaking of courtesy, always remember to write and mail them a thank-you note that very night, no matter how mad or frustrated they may have made you feel. You never know what action might cause an employer to reconsider.

And then keep going, day after day, week after week, month after month, if necessary, until you find the other kind of employer: the one who only looks at what you *can* do, not at what you can't.

Everyone Has Issues

You may wonder how many job-hunters have issues that might hurt their chances of being hired. Well, the answer is: *everyone*. Sometimes our issues are obvious and well known to ourselves and others. Sometimes they're hidden. Remember, you are hired for your skills. And everyone doesn't have every skill.

So when you go job-hunting, if you have an issue, but it doesn't keep you from performing the particular job or career that you are going after, then what's so special about *your* issue, compared with other people's? The answer is *Nothing*.

Unless—*unless*—you are so focused on the idea that you are held back by this issue, and so obsessed with what you *can't* do, that you have forgotten all the things you *can* do.

Unless you're thinking of all the reasons why an employer might not hire you, instead of all the reasons why an employer would be lucky to get you.

Unless you're going about your job-hunt feeling like *a job-beggar*, rather than standing tall to offer yourself as *a helpful resource* for this employer.

What You Can Do, What You Can't

To get your mind off what you *can't* do, and onto what you *can*, take a piece of paper, online or off, and divide it into two columns, viz,

I have this skill:	I don't have this skill:

Then, get a list of transferable skills from somewhere.

a.   You could use the Skills Grid in chapter 5.

b.   Or, you could use the famous List of 246 Skills as Verbs, which you will find on the next page.

c.   ResumeGenius offers what it describes as the longest action-verb list in the universe and breaks the list down by descriptive categories (like "communication") as well as your specific career fields (http://resumegenius.com/longest-action-verb-list-universe).

Whichever list you use, copy as many of the skills as you choose onto that piece of paper, *but* put each skill in the proper column, depending on whether you *can* do the skill, or *cannot*. (*Or not yet, anyway*.) Use additional sheets, if needed.

When you are done with these two columns, *have* and *don't have*, pick out your favorite five things that you *can* do, and *love* to do; and write out some examples of how you actually did *that*, sometime in your past. Your *recent* past, if possible.

A LIST OF 246 SKILLS AS VERBS

achieving
acting
adapting
addressing
administering
advising
analyzing
anticipating
arbitrating
arranging
ascertaining
assembling
assessing
attaining
auditing
budgeting
building
calculating
charting
checking
classifying
coaching
collecting
communicating
compiling
completing
composing
computing
conceptualizing
conducting
conserving
consolidating
constructing
controlling
coordinating
coping
counseling
creating
deciding
defining
delivering
designing
detailing
detecting
determining
developing
devising
diagnosing
digging
directing

discovering
dispensing
displaying
disproving
dissecting
distributing
diverting
dramatizing
drawing
driving
editing
eliminating
empathizing
enforcing
establishing
estimating
evaluating
examining
expanding
experimenting
explaining
expressing
extracting
filing
financing
fixing
following
formulating
founding
gathering
generating
getting
giving
guiding
handling
having
  responsibility
heading
helping
hypothesizing
identifying
illustrating
imagining
implementing
improving
improvising
increasing
influencing
informing
initiating

innovating
inspecting
inspiring
installing
instituting
instructing
integrating
interpreting
interviewing
intuiting
inventing
inventorying
investigating
judging
keeping
leading
learning
lecturing
lifting
listening
logging
maintaining
making
managing
manipulating
mediating
meeting
memorizing
mentoring
modeling
monitoring
motivating
navigating
negotiating
observing
obtaining
offering
operating
ordering
organizing
originating
overseeing
painting
perceiving
performing
persuading
photographing
piloting
planning
playing

predicting
preparing
prescribing
presenting
printing
problem solving
processing
producing
programming
projecting
promoting
proofreading
protecting
providing
publicizing
purchasing
questioning
raising
reading
realizing
reasoning
receiving
recommending
reconciling
recording
recruiting
reducing
referring
rehabilitating
relating
remembering
rendering
repairing
reporting
representing
researching
resolving
responding
restoring
retrieving
reviewing
risking
scheduling
selecting
selling
sensing
separating
serving
setting
setting-up

sewing
shaping
sharing
showing
singing
sketching
solving
sorting
speaking
studying
summarizing
supervising
supplying
symbolizing
synergizing
synthesizing
systematizing
taking instructions
talking
teaching
team-building
telling
tending
testing & proving
training
transcribing
translating
traveling
treating
troubleshooting
tutoring
typing
umpiring
understanding
understudying
undertaking
unifying
uniting
upgrading
using
utilizing
verbalizing
washing
weighing
winning
working
writing

Accommodating Disability

What if you have a *disability* that seems to negate all your dreams? There is something you've always dreamed of doing, but your disability makes it seem impossible.

Well, first of all, make sure you have received the best medical advice and treatments possible. Since your diagnosis, someone may have invented a technology or simple strategy that gets around that disability. You never know. There are some very clever people in the world. Look up your condition on the Internet and see what turns up. Look particularly for any professional association that deals with your disability. Contact them, and ask them what information they have. There may be support systems you haven't discovered yet.

For example, let us say that you are wrestling with decreased vision. Some three million US adults over the age of forty are. But search for "low vision" or "visually impaired" and you will turn up techniques for dealing with this disability. (For example, https://lowvisionfocus.org from the Hadley School for the Blind has free audios and videos—dealing with such themes as how to use the iPhone and iPad to enhance your vision.) Incidentally, for those with poor vision, or long-commute drives, *What Color Is Your Parachute?* exists as an audio book, read by a professional narrator, Mel Foster. It is eleven hours and thirty-two minutes in length, and costs around $15.

An alternative way to accommodate a disability is to search for jobs *similar* to the one you want to do, but can't.

Example: One career counselor was working with a young adult who always dreamed of being a commercial airplane pilot. The killer: His eyesight was too poor to be a pilot. Well, there was a clue as to where to go from there. It was the way our would-be pilot talked about planes. He loved planes.

So the counselor sent him out to the large airport nearby, and told him to list every kind of occupation that he saw or heard about, there at the airport—besides pilot. The next day he showed his list to his counselor. It was very long. When asked if he'd come across any occupation that interested him, he said, "Yes. I love the idea of making the seats that they put inside new airplanes." So, that's the job he pursued. He ended up in the airline industry, even though he couldn't be a pilot.

Potential Employer Judgments or Biases

While federal laws exist to prevent outright discrimination in the workplace, employers are human and will make judgments about candidates. As a job-seeker, part of your role is to be aware of potential negative judgments or biases and address them as needed. Focus on your strengths and skills throughout the process. If an employer turns you down, don't allow that experience to discourage you. It's just one employer. There are more out there, and someone will see you for your strengths and talents.

Here are some potential employer biases:

1. Out of work too long. One employer bias relates to **how long you've been out of work**. We saw this in chapter 1. It is a bias that some employers have, and some employers don't. If you've been out of work a year or more, you will find employers who won't hire you because of it. Too bad! Just keep going until you find employers who don't have that prejudice. It helps to prepare a story that describes your time out of work in a positive light. Focus on the learning, knowledge, or skills you acquired, the volunteer activities you did, the family responsibilities you managed, and so on. For a list of employers who have promised to hire even the long-term unemployed, see http://big.assets.huffington post.com/est_practices_recruiting_longterm_unemployed.pdf.

2. Racial, religious, or sexual identity stereotypes. Despite federal and state laws that protect individuals from discrimination, some employers are prejudiced and it is hard to fight that. "Anti-discrimination laws" won't stop them. They have figured their way around *everything*. They often justify their prejudice with stereotypes that are demonstrably false. Because discrimination is subtle, it can be hard to prove. If you believe discrimination is an issue for you, seek support from affinity or diversity groups who can provide guidance, empathy, and legal recommendations if necessary.

3. Age. The next employer bias that you may run into is **age**. Reason? Millions of baby boomers (*the 76 million people born between 1946 and 1964*) are entering the so-called retirement years. Many of them are not going to find generous pensions waiting when they hit sixty or sixty-five, but are going to have to keep working long after they ever thought they would have to. And how easy will it be to get hired at that age? Guess! But again, your comfort must lie in the fact that this is a bias, not a disadvantage: some employers won't be biased that you are as old as you are, if they see you are still on fire with passion about what you do, not merely marking time between now and then.

   The related employer prejudice that is rearing its ugly head these days concerns **money**. Given all their years of experience, many who are job-hunting over fifty expect a salary befitting all their years of experience and wisdom, only to discover that some employers are prejudiced against paying that much—since they could hire two less experienced workers in their twenties for what it would cost them to hire just one.

   And yet, despite this prejudice, there are still employers out there who *will* hire you, regardless of how old you are, if . . . (and here we have a lot of *"if"s*—all of which lie within your control, thank heaven):

   They will hire you IF you choose to approach a small company and they don't have to put you into a pension plan; and

   They will hire you IF you come with a positive attitude toward your aging. For example, thinking of your current age not in terms of work but in terms of music—particularly a symphony. A symphony, traditionally, has four movements, as they're called. So does Life. There is the first movement, infancy; then the second movement, the time of learning; the long third movement follows, the time of working; and finally, a fourth movement. It is traditionally spoken of in terms of work, hence, we call it *retirement*. It is much better to think of it as the Fourth Movement, a triumphant, powerful ending to the symphony of our life here on Earth; and

They will hire you IF you convey energy, even in this period of your life. Ask any employer what they are looking for, when they interview a job candidate who is fifty years or older, and they will tell you: *energy*. Okay, but where shall we find energy, after fifty? When we were younger, energy came from the *physical* side of our nature. We were "feeling our oats," as they say. We could go all day, and all night. "My, where do you get all your energy?" our grandmother would ask us. We were a dynamo of *physical* energy. But after fifty, physical energy may be harder to come by, despite workouts, exercise, and marathons. Increasingly, our energy must spring not from our muscles but from our excitement about Life; there are inevitably *some* employers dying to have that excitement in their organization; and

They will hire you IF you have done some life/work planning, and you know alternative ways to describe who you are and what you can do, because you did the homework on Who You Are, in chapter 5; and

They will hire you IF you *keep going* on interviews until you encounter an employer or two who isn't biased by your age.

What do I mean by *keep going*? Well, here is one successful job-hunter's actual records (the "process" she is referring to, is Daniel Porot's PIE Method, described at the end of this chapter):

> *Here are the figures you wanted: In the course of my surveying, September through November, I was referred to 120+ people. Of these I contacted 84 and actually met with 50. I met most people at their offices, a few for lunch, a couple for dinner, and one for breakfast! The process worked so well for me, I am really excited about my new prospects.*

Job-hunting success, regardless of your age, often requires this kind of persistence, keeping at it, keeping at it, keeping at it, working at your job-hunt far longer and far harder than the average job-hunter would ever dream of doing, because you know you will be valuable to any organization that is able to see you clearly, without prejudice.

4. Education. Employers may have two biases here: they may consider you undereducated, that is, lacking in knowledge or skills

needed for the position, or overeducated, that is, having too much knowledge, skills, or experience.

In the latter case, they are likely concerned that you will be bored, expect a larger salary than they are prepared to pay, or want to be promoted too quickly. They might assume that you are seeking a particular position simply as a way to get into an organization, and you will become dissatisfied if you have to stay in it for any length of time. If this is the case, you will want to have a clear explanation of why you are seeking this position. Perhaps you rose to a position that required more of you in terms of hours or responsibilities. It's not unusual for great line workers to be promoted to management roles only to learn they miss the work they used to do, or don't like their new management duties. In that case you have an excellent story to tell.

On the other hand, if they consider you undereducated, this could be a literal fact (such as lacking a required degree or licensure) or a bias ("We only hire people with college degrees"). This is an increasingly common issue: many employers list a college degree as a basic requirement regardless of the position. It can exclude individuals who worked their way up in an organization that acknowledged their skills, not their degree. To overcome such bias, you must be very clear about the skills you possess for this position and provide proof that you can perform them as well as someone with a degree. Having a portfolio or other demonstration of your skills can be particularly helpful here. You should express a desire to learn and to build skills as needed. You might also inquire whether the employer sponsors on-the-job training or pays for additional education. You might be surprised to learn that is part of the benefit package. But regardless of future learning opportunities, you must strongly demonstrate your ability to perform the duties of the position and your ability to hit the ground running when you are employed.

5. Returning veterans. Next employer bias: hiring **returning vets**. According to a recent survey, 41 percent of returning vets do not feel their military skills and training are respected by employers. Well, let's face it: some—but only "some"—employers *are* biased against

hiring returning vets. They've seen one too many headlines about PTSD, even though four out of five returning vets do *not* have *post-traumatic stress disorder*. Fortunately, there are other employers who know this, and actually prefer hiring returning vets.

6. Ex-offenders.Next employer bias: hiring **ex-offenders**. Ex-offenders face particular challenges in the hiring process due to the increasing use of background and credit checks. It is extremely important that you use as many connections, networks, or agencies to assist you in this process.

There are a number of resources that can help. For example, Mark Drevno has written a book for ex-offenders called *Jails to Jobs: Seven Steps to Becoming Employed* (2014). Mark will send readers of *Parachute* an electronic version of his book **for free**, if they email him at info@jailstojobs.org requesting it, and mention that they are a reader of *Parachute*. He also runs a public charity called Jails to Jobs, which has a website called (you guessed it) www.jailstojobs.org, which gives step-by-step help with finding employment. There Mark has a Tattoo Removal Directory, which is helpful for anyone who feels their tattoos are keeping them from getting a job, and want them removed. Mark also has a new book, *Tattoo Removal: Establishing a Free or Low-Cost Community-Based Program*. There are 282 such programs in 43 states, already. Anyone who wants to start a community program can secure a free electronic version of this book, by emailing Mark and mentioning they saw this mentioned in *Parachute*.

There is also a free 67-page workbook that you can print out from your computer. It is called the *STEP AHEAD Workbook*, and was produced with funding from the Minnesota Department of Corrections. Currently, it is sponsored by Minnesota State Colleges and Universities: https://careerwise.minnstate.edu/exoffenders/workbook.html.

The Department of Labor's CareerOneStop site offers guidance and support for ex-offenders, including videos and a downloadable pdf of state resources, including where to find training and job-listings: www.careeronestop.org/ExOffender/default.aspx.

HelpforFelons.org offers state-by-state information about jobs, financial support including food stamps and housing, temp agencies, etc: https://helpforfelons.org/reentry-programs-ex-offenders-state.

The National Conference of State Legislatures also offers information for employers and former offenders at their site: www.ncsl.org/research/civil-and-criminal-justice/ex-offender-employment-opportunities43.aspx.

7. Former patients of psychiatric hospitals. According to the National Alliance on Mental Illness, 18.5 percent of US adults experience mental illness in a given year. That doesn't necessarily mean that they were hospitalized, but it does mean they had serious problems.[2] And probably overcame them. Again, focus on your strengths and skills. The only questions an employer need ask are, "What skills are needed to do this job, and does this person have them?" *and* "Does this person get along well with other people?" You do not need to disclose a disability (including mental illness) unless you need a specific accommodation. While you search for your next employer, look at their Human Resources webpage and check out any wellness programs they offer to employees. Be aware of situations that might trigger symptoms and avoid jobs that will increase their likelihood.

8. Others. There is hardly a group you can name that does not face bias from *some* employers. That's because employers are human beings, glorious in their individuality and lamentable in their humannesss, including their prejudices. Employers vary greatly. There are employers good and kind, and employers who aren't. Personally, I draw comfort from all the employers I run into who are a credit to the human race. Here is a letter I got from a successful job-hunter[3] recently:

> *As we went along in the interview, some of the things the employer told me were, "I'm very flexible with schedules. I want to put people in activities that I know they'll be the best in, but that means that some weeks you're scheduled for three evening shifts. If that's ever a problem, I really want you to tell me, because I can fix it. I'm also a firm believer that you*

---

2. "Mental Health by the Numbers," National Alliance on Mental Illness, www.nami.org/learn-more/mental-health-by-the-numbers.
3. Kayla DeVitto.

*need to be at your absolute best before you can pour into people
here. That means, if you get really stressed out, I want you to
tell me. Just yesterday one of our employees came to me and
said, 'I'm so overwhelmed right now!' So I sat down with her
and we moved some stuff around. Now, that also means that
we are extremely team-oriented. If someone cannot take a shift
because something is going on at home, everyone needs to be
willing to take that up sometimes. But, you always know that
everyone here is willing to do the same for you. Also, when
we're stressed we seem to resort to silliness." I knew immediately that this was the place for me. . . .*

The Last Issue: Shyness

During the whole job-hunt, what's going to torpedo you most? What
issue is king? Well, shyness is near the top of the list. Call it anything else
if you want to—low self-esteem, fear, anxiety, nervousness, sweating—
but shyness it is, and shyness it remains. Often, we, the unemployed, who
may be absolute experts at connecting and communicating with face-
less people on the Internet—through computer games, apps, Facebook,
LinkedIn, Twitter, Instagram, and other social media—suddenly turn
to jelly when we have to go face-to-face with people.

Shy. A lot of us would never think to use that word to describe ourselves. But surveys have found that as many as 75 percent of us have
been painfully shy at some point in our lives. Many of us still are. (*This
always comes as a great surprise to my European friends, because they picture
Americans as assertive, aggressive, and similar words. And sure, some of us
are; but that's not who most of us are, especially when we're out of work, and
have go sit across the desk from employers, face-to-face. I myself have been
painfully shy, much of my life. But no one ever guesses.*)

So, what to do if we are shy and feel utterly unequipped to deal with
all the social interaction we're going to have to do during our job-hunt?
There is an answer, and a method that works. First, a bit of history.

John Crystal, whose groundbreaking work as a career counselor
provided much of the basis for the Parachute Approach, often ran into

this problem. He suggested that the way anyone cures themselves of shyness is through enthusiasm. If you're talking with someone, for example, and you are enthusiastic about the topic under discussion, you will forget that you are shy, in your excitement. Everything depends on what you're talking about, and how you feel about that topic.

So, he said, if you're shy, only go after a job you feel really enthusiastic about. Seek information only about a curiosity that you feel enthusiastic about the prospect of learning the answer to. And so on. And so forth.

John followed this up by inventing a practical three-stage plan of action, to cure job-hunters of shyness. Those who have followed John's sage advice in this regard have had a success rate of 86 percent in overcoming their shyness and fears, and finding a job.

Daniel Porot subsequently took John's system and organized it. He observed that John was really recommending three types of interviews, as I noted in chapter 8:

- Interviews for employment.

- But preceded, necessarily, by interviewing just for information, which—among other things—is a warm-up for employment interviews.

- And this was preceded by practice interviewing, which—among other things—is a warm-up for information interviews.

Each type of interview prepares for the next; and there you have it: a three-stage plan, for overcoming shyness.

Daniel, who has been Europe's premiere job-hunting expert for decades, organized this into an attractive and well-thought-out chart and gave it its now famous name: "the PIE Method," which has helped thousands of job-hunters and career-changers all around the world with their shyness and with their job-hunt.[4]

---

4. Daniel has summarized his system in a book published here in the US in 1996: it is called *The PIE Method for Career Success: A Unique Way to Find Your Ideal Job*, published by JIST Works, Inc. It is now basically out of print but can be found used on Amazon.com, BarnesandNoble.com, or Alibris.com for as little as $5.65 plus shipping. Daniel has a *wonderful* website at www.porot.com/en.

Why is it called "PIE"?

P   is for the warm-up phase. John Crystal named this warm-up
     "The Practice Field Survey." Daniel Porot calls it P for pleasure.

I   is for "Informational Interviewing."

E   is for the employment interview with the-person-who-has-
     the-power-to-hire-you.

How do you use this P for practice to get comfortable about going
out and talking to people one-on-one?

This is achieved by choosing a topic—any topic, however silly or
trivial—that is a pleasure for you to talk about with your friends
or family. To avoid anxiety, it should not be connected to any present or
future careers that you are considering. Rather, the kinds of topics that
work best, for this exercise, are:

- a hobby you love, such as skiing, bridge playing, exercise, computers, etc.

- any leisure-time enthusiasm of yours, such as a movie you just
  saw that you liked a lot

- a longtime curiosity, such as how do they predict the weather,
  or what police officers do

- an aspect of the town or city you live in, such as a new shopping
  mall that just opened

- an issue you feel strongly about, such as the homeless, AIDS
  sufferers, ecology, peace, health, returning veterans, etc.

There is only one condition about choosing a topic: it should be
something you love to talk about with other people; a subject you know
nothing about, but you feel a great deal of enthusiasm for, is far prefer-
able to something you know an awful lot about, but it puts you to sleep.

Having identified your enthusiasm, you then need to go talk to
someone who is as enthusiastic about this thing as you are. For best
results with your later job-hunt, this should be someone you don't
already know. Ask around among your friends and family, *Who do you
know that loves to talk about this?* It's relatively easy to find the kind of
person you're looking for.

You love to talk about skiing? Try a ski-clothes store, or a skiing instructor. You love to talk about writing? Try a professor who teaches English on a nearby college campus. You love to talk about physical exercise? Try a trainer, or someone who does physical therapy.

Once you've identified someone you think shares your enthusiasm, you then go talk with them.

When you are face-to-face with your fellow enthusiast, the first thing you must do is relieve their understandable anxiety. Everyone has had someone visit them who has stayed too long, who has worn out their welcome. If your fellow enthusiast is worried about you staying too long, they'll be so preoccupied with this fear that they won't hear a word you are saying.

So, when you first meet them, ask for only ten minutes of their time. Period. Stop. Exclamation point. And watch your time like a hawk, using your watch or smartphone timer, as I explained in chapter 8.

Okay, you're there. What to talk about? Well, a topic may have its own unique set of questions. For example, I love movies and TV, so if I met someone who shared this interest, my first question would be, "What movies or shows have you seen lately?" Or, "What do you think of *Game of Thrones*?" Or, "Who's your favorite actress?" And so on.

If it's a topic you love, and often talk about, you'll know what kinds of questions you begin with. But, if no questions come to mind, your fallback position is the following ones, which have proved to be good conversation starters for thousands of job-hunters and career-changers before you, no matter what their topic or interest.

Addressed to the person you're doing the Practice Interviewing with:

- How did you get involved with/become interested in this? (*"This"* is the hobby, curiosity, aspect, issue, or enthusiasm that you are so interested in.)
- What do you like the most about it?
- What do you like the least about it?
- Who else would you suggest I go talk to who shares this interest?
- Can I use your name?

Initial:	Pleasure **P**	Information **I**	Employment **E**
Kind of Interview	Practice Field Survey	Informational Interviewing or Research	Employment Interview or Hiring-Interview
Purpose	To Get Used to Talking with People to Enjoy It; to "Penetrate Networks"	To Find Out If You'd Like a Job, Before You Go Trying to Get It	To Get Hired for the Work You Have Decided You Would Most Like to Do
How You Go to the Interview	You Can Take Somebody with You	By Yourself or You Can Take Somebody with You	By Yourself
Who You Talk To	Anyone Who Shares Your Enthusiasm About a (for You) Non-Job-Related Subject	A Worker Who Is Doing the Actual Work You Are Thinking About Doing	An Employer Who Has the Power to Hire You for the Job You Have Decided You Most Would Like to Do
How Long a Time You Ask For	Ten Minutes (and DON'T run over—asking to see them at 11:45 a.m. may help keep you honest, since most employers have lunch appointments at noon)	Ditto	Ditto (or nineteen minutes; but notice the time, and keep your word)
What You Ask Them	Any Curiosity You Have About Your Shared Interest or Enthusiasm	Any Questions You Have About This Job or This Kind of Work	You Tell Them What It Is You Like About Their Organization and What Kind of Work You Are Looking For

Initial:	Pleasure **P**	Information **I**	Employment **E**
What You Ask Them (*continued*)	If Nothing Occurs to You, Ask: **1.** How did you start, with this hobby, interest, etc.? **2.** What excites or interests you the most about it? **3.** What do you find is the thing you like least about it? **4.** Who else do you know who shares this interest, hobby, or enthusiasm, or could tell me more about my curiosity? **a.** Can I go and see them? **b.** May I mention that it was you who suggested I see them? **c.** May I say that you recommended them? Get their name and address.	If Nothing Occurs to You, Ask: **1.** How did you get interested in this work and how did you get hired? **2.** What excites or interests you the most about it? **3.** What do you find is the thing you like the least about it? **4.** What kinds of challenges or problems do you have to deal with in this job? **5.** What skills do you need in order to meet those challenges or problems? **6.** Who else do you know of who does this kind of work, or similar work but with this difference_____? Get their name and address.	You Tell Them: **1.** The kinds of challenges you like to deal with. **2.** What skills you have to deal with those challenges. **3.** What experience you have had in dealing with those challenges in the past.
Afterward: That Same Night	SEND A THANK-YOU NOTE.	SEND A THANK-YOU NOTE.	SEND A THANK-YOU NOTE.

- May I tell them it was you who recommended that I talk with them?

- *Then, choosing one person from the list of several names they may have given you, you say,* "Well, I think I will begin by going to talk to this person. Would you be willing to call ahead for me, so they will know who I am when I go over there?"

Incidentally, it's perfectly okay for you to take someone with you during this Practice Interviewing—preferably someone who is more outgoing than you feel you are. And on the first few interviews, let them take the lead in the conversation, while you watch to see how they do it.

Once it is *your turn* to conduct these Practice Interviews, it will usually be easy for you to figure out what to talk about.

Alone or with someone, keep at this Practice Interviewing until you feel very much at ease in talking with people and asking them questions about things you are curious about.

In all of this, as you're trying to conquer shyness, *fun* is the key. If you're having fun, you're doing it right. That depends, of course, on how enthusiastic you are about what you're exploring.

If you're not having fun, you need to keep at it, until you are. It may take seeing four people. It may take ten. Or twenty. You'll know. Once you're comfortable with Practice Interviewing, you'll be ready to move on to the next step, Informational Interviewing, which I discussed in chapter 6.

In Conclusion:
Self-Esteem Versus Egotism

As most of us know, the proper attitude toward ourselves is called "good self-esteem." But self-esteem is an art. An art of *balance*. A balance between thinking too little of ourselves, and thinking too much of ourselves.

The name for thinking too much of ourselves is "egotism." We have all run into that, at some point in our lives, so we know what it looks like. Some of us have even caught a passing glimpse of it in the mirror.

In our culture and others, we are taught to recoil from this in horror. We even have mythologies warning us against it; the story of Narcissus comes to mind. Poor guy! (*See https://en.wikipedia.org/wiki/ Narcissus_(mythology) if you are unfamiliar with the myth.*)

In order to avoid egotism, a lot of us go way overboard in the other direction. We shrink from ever declaring that we have any virtue, any excellency, any special gifts, lest we be accused of boasting. And so we fall into that opposite pit from egotism, namely, ingratitude. We appear ungrateful for the gifts that life, the universe, God—you name it—has already given us.

So, how do we adopt the proper attitude toward our gifts—speaking of them honestly, humbly, gratefully—without sounding egotistical?

Just this: The more you see your own gifts clearly, the more you must pay attention to the gifts that others have.

The more sensitive you become to how unique you are, the more you must become sensitive to how unique those around you are.

The more you pay attention to yourself, the more you must pay attention to others.

The more you ponder the mystery of You, the more you must ponder the mystery of all those you encounter, every loved one, every friend, every acquaintance, every stranger.

People from other cultures will tell you about *"the tall poppy" theory of life*, with its implication that you shouldn't stand taller than others in your field. That has a lot of truth to it. You can become equal to others not by lowering yourself but by raising them.

Pay attention to others. What are the favorite skills of your best friend or mate? Do you know? Are you sure? Have you asked them what they think they are? Have you complimented them on these skills, during the past week? Start now!

Just remember, it's no sin to praise yourself as long as that heightens your awareness of what there is to praise in others.

I was told many years ago by my grandmother who raised me: If somebody puts you on a road and you don't feel comfortable on it and you look ahead and you don't like the destination, and you look behind and you don't want to return to that place, step off the road.

—*Maya Angelou*

CHAPTER 11

The Five Ways to Choose/Change Careers

The First Way to Choose/Change Careers:
THE INTERNET

The first idea that occurs to people seeking guidance on how to choose or change careers, these days, is the Internet. Naturally, there is lots of advice there, but more specifically there is O*NET OnLine, which I mentioned in chapter 5. It is a digital, online treasure house of information, and up-to-date information at that, about careers.

Go to the site (www.onetonline.org/find or www.onetonline.org/search) and you will see. Suggested careers (or occupations) are grouped or classified by any or all of the following: industries in great demand; green economies; largest number of openings anticipated; STEM disciplines (that would be Science, Technology, Engineering, and Math); amount of preparation or training required; O*NET-SOC codes; Military Occupation Classification (equivalencies); abilities required; occupational knowledge required; interests, skill sets, work values, and work activities required; values you want at work; tasks and duties involved; tools, technology, machines, equipment, and software used; and so on.

Once you find an occupation you want to know more about, they have a specially developed Content Model (www.onetcenter.org/content.html) that can run ten to twelve pages of printouts for each occupation. Maintained by the US government's Department of Labor, it is very thorough, but at the same time it only covers about nine hundred occupational titles, not the thousands of occupations in existence.

This decision to just cover nine hundred or so, leaves a lot of careers, occupations, and jobs *uncovered and unmentioned*.[1] Still, you may find a lot of very helpful stuff there.

The Second Way to Choose/Change Careers:
TESTS

They're technically not "tests." Their real name is instruments, or assessments. But we'll use the popular name for them here.

I'm not sure how well they'll help you choose a new career, but you will find them everywhere: in books, on the Internet, in the offices of guidance counselors, or vocational psychologists, career coaches, etc. And *sometimes* this turns out to be exactly the kind of guidance, the kind of insight, the kind of direction, that career-choosers or changers are looking for.

But why only *sometimes*? Why doesn't this search for *a magic bullet* always work? Aha! Good question! Since I've watched these tests literally for decades, I can share with you my:

Six Learnings About Testing

1. You are absolutely unique. There is no person in the world like you. It follows from this that no test can measure YOU; it can only describe the family to which you belong.

   Tests tend to divide the population into what we might call groups, tribes, or families—made up of all those people who answered the test the same way. After you've taken any test,

---

1. Limited funds are cited by O*NET as a large part of the reason for this decision.

don't ever say to yourself, "This must be who I am." (No, no, this must be who your family am.)

I grew up in the Bolles family (surprise!) and they were all very "left-brained." I was a maverick in that family. I was right-brained. Fortunately, my father was an immensely loving man, who found this endearing. When I told him the convoluted way by which I went about figuring out something, he would respond with a hearty affectionate laugh, and a big hug, as he said "Dick, I will never understand you." Tests are about families, not individuals. The results of any test are descriptors—not of you, but of your family—i.e., all those who answered the test the same way you did. The SAI family. Or the blue family. Or the INTJ family. Or whatever. The results are an accurate description of that family of people, in general; but are they descriptors of you? Depends on whether or not you are a maverick in that family, the same way I was in mine. These family characteristics may or may not be true in every respect to you. You may be exactly like that group, or you may be different in important ways.

2. **Don't try to figure out ahead of time how you want the test to come out. Stay loose and open to new ideas.**

It's easy to develop an emotional investment that the test should come out a certain way. I remember a job-hunting workshop where I asked everyone to list the factors they liked about any place where they had ever lived, and then prioritize those factors, to get the name of a new place to live. We had this immensely lovable woman from Texas in the workshop, and when we all got back together after a "break" I asked her how she was doing. With a glint in her eye she said, "I'm prioritizing, and I'm gonna keep on prioritizin', until it comes out: Texas!" That was amusing, as she intended it to be; it's not so amusing when you try to make the test results come out a certain way. If you're gonna take tests, you need to be open to new ideas. If you find yourself always trying to outguess the test, so it will confirm you on a path you've already decided upon, then testing is not for you.

3. **In taking a test, you should just be looking for clues, hunches, or suggestions, rather than for a definitive answer that says "this is what you must choose to do with your life."**

And bear in mind that an online test isn't likely to be as insightful as one administered by an experienced psychologist or counselor, who may see things that you can't. But keep saying this mantra to yourself, as you read or hear the test results: "Clues. Clues, I'm only looking for clues."

4. Take several tests and not just one. Just one test can easily send you down the wrong path.

Quite frankly, tests are notoriously flawed, unscientific, and inaccurate. Sometimes tests are more like parlor games than anything else. Basing your future on tests' outcomes is like putting your trust in the man behind the curtain in *The Wizard of Oz*.

5. In good career planning, you're trying, in the first instance, to broaden your horizons, and only later narrow your options down; you are not trying to narrow them down from the outset.

Bad career planning looks like this illustration on the right.

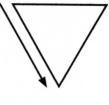

Most computerized tests embody the idea of starting with a wide range of options, and narrowing them down. So, each time you answer a question, you narrow down the number of options. For example, if you say, "I don't like to work outdoors," immediately all outdoor jobs are eliminated from your consideration, etc., etc.

A model of good career planning looks like this illustration (right), instead.

Good career-choice or career-planning postpones the "narrowing down," until it has first broadened your horizons, and expanded the number of options you are thinking about. For example, you're in the newspaper business; but have you ever thought of teaching, or drawing, or doing fashion? You first expand your mental horizons, to see all the possibilities, and only then do you start to narrow them down to the particular two or three that interest you the most.

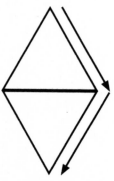

So, what's a good test? All together now: A test that broadens to show you new possibilities for your life.

And, what's a bad test? Again, all together: A test that narrows the possibilities for your life. Often this is the result of a counselor's interpretation of a test, or rather misinterpretation.

Interest-based career tests can only reflect what you know about yourself at the time you take the test, and can't predict what skills or talents you might have or want to use. They are meant to be interpreted broadly, yet people almost always interpret their results literally. One psychology professor who has had an outstanding career in research, writing, and teaching took a career test in college that pointed him toward accounting. He looked at the accounting curriculum but found it dry and boring. He later realized that the test was probably reflecting the fact that he liked math and his father was an accountant. Accounting was simply a field he was familiar with, not really a career interest. Creative types often get results such as "florist" on career tests even if they have no interest in plants; one computer-based test became notorious for recommending that social types who "like people" become funeral directors, much to the dismay of some. If the test isn't interpreted carefully by a skilled counselor, you are likely to be led astray. A career test can be ultimately helpful in shaping your ideas, but do not expect it will tell you what to do.

6. Testing will always have "mixed reviews."

On the one hand, you can run into successful men and women who will tell you they took this or that test twenty years ago, and it made all the difference in their career direction and ultimate success. On the other hand, there are the horror stories.

If you like tests, help yourself. There are lots of them on the Internet. Counselors can also give them to you, for a fee; if you want one, shop around. If you want to know where to start, you might try these tests, which are the ones I personally like the best:

> *Dr. Martin Seligman's assessment website, Authentic Happiness.* This site provides a variety of assessments related to work, including the Values-In-Action (VIA)

Survey of Character Strengths and the Work-Life Questionnaire, at www.authentichappiness.sas.upenn .edu/testcenter. They are all free, but you need to create a password.

Dr. John Holland's Self-Directed Search. We saw this already in chapter 5 with the People petal (page 46), but in case you don't recall, this is at www.self-directed-search.com and costs $9.95 to take online.

eParachute's JUMP Application. This is the creation of my own team. It is a three-step process: Discover, Create, and Explore. It can be found at www.eParachute.com/para20, and costs $4.99 for a year's subscription.

The University of Missouri's Career Interests Game, which can be found at http://career.missouri.edu/career-interest-game. This is based on a shortened version of the Self-Directed Search, namely, my "Party Exercise." Well redesigned here.

If you want further suggestions, you can type "career tests" or "personality tests" into Google, and see what turns up. You'll find lots and lots of stuff. Just be careful that you aren't charged for the tests, unless you want to be.

The Third Way to Choose/Change Careers:
USING THE FLOWER EXERCISE

This pathway to choosing or changing your career is not very popular—compared, say, to the Internet, because it requires a lot more time of you, and a lot more work. I described it back in chapters 4, 5, and 6 (*in case you're skipping around in this book, and haven't been there yet*). It is a careful, thorough, step-by-step process, for ensuring that you are choosing a career that fits you like a glove: a dream career, or dream job, your mission in life, as it is often called. It is not for the faint-hearted or the lazy. But if the other ways to change careers don't turn up any careers that look interesting to you, you may end up being very grateful that there is this way. I get letters like this all the time:

> I have already benefited greatly from the Flower Exercise. I found hope in having a second alternative after doing the homework. . . . The series of life-changing activities in this book has definitely helped me to better understand who I am, to further appreciate my talents, and to utilize the resources I have readily available.

So, just in case you haven't looked at chapters 4, 5, and 6 yet, let me quickly rehearse here the steps involved in this way of choosing a new career:

1. You do the Flower Exercise (in chapter 5), which gives you the basic building blocks of Who You Are, so you can match a career to You.

2. Then you put together on one piece of paper your five favorite transferable skills, and your three favorite fields of knowledge, and start informational interviewing (refer to chapter 6) so as to find the names of careers that fit those building blocks (or "petals").

3. Along the way, you see if you can figure out how to combine your three favorite fields into one career, so as to make yourself unique.

4. Then you "try on" the jobs to see if they fit You, by talking to actual workers in the kind of career or careers you have tentatively picked out.

5. Then you find out what kinds of organizations in the geographical area that interests you (where you are already?) have such jobs.

6. Then you find out the names of actual organizations that interest you, where you could do your most effective work.

7. And, finally, you learn about those places before you walk in, or secure an appointment to talk to them about working there, whether or not they have a known vacancy at that moment.

The essence of what you're doing here is this: look at your past, break that experience down into its most basic "atoms" (namely, skills), then build a new career for the future from your favorite "atoms," retracing your steps from the bottom up, in the exact opposite direction. This is illustrated in the model on the following page.

THE SYSTEMATIC BREAKDOWN AND BUILDING UP TO DEFINE A CAREER THAT FITS YOU

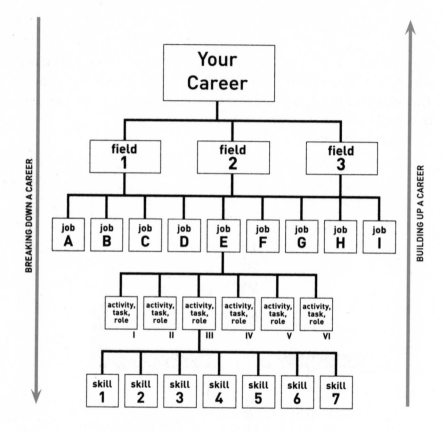

The Fourth Way to Choose/Change Careers:
CHANGING A CAREER IN TWO STEPS

This is not so much a way to identify a new career, as a way to move into that career, once you have figured out where you want to go next. This is a plan that has worked very well for many career-changers: changing careers in two steps, not one.

And how exactly do you do that?

THREE TYPES OF CAREER-CHANGE, VISUALIZED

A

Accountant

Television

DIFFICULT PATH (ONE STEP)

C

Reporter

Television

B

Accountant

Medicine

D

Reporter

Medicine

⇨ More Feasible Path #1 (two steps)
⬛➤ More Feasible Path #2 (two steps)

Well, let's start with a definition: a job is *a job-title* in a *field*.

That means, a job has two parts: *title* and *field*. *Title* is really a symbol for *what you do. Field* is *where you do it*, or *what you do it with*.

A dramatic career-change typically involves trying to change both at the same time. It's what's called *Difficult Path* in the diagram on page 241. The problem with trying to take this difficult path is that you can't claim any prior experience. But if you do it in two steps, ah! That's different.

Let's say you are presently an accountant working for a television network, and you want to make a career-change. You want to become a reporter on new medical developments.

If you try the Difficult Path on the previous page, if you go out into the job market as the first—accountant in the television industry—and you try to jump to a new career as the second—reporter in medicine— well, that's a pretty large jump. Of course, sometimes you can pull that off, with a bit of luck and a huge number of links on LinkedIn, friends on Facebook, or followers on Twitter.

But what if?

What if that doesn't work? Then you're likely to run into the following scenario:

Interviewer: *"So, I see you want to be a reporter. Were you ever a reporter before?"* Your answer: *No.*

Interviewer: *"And I see you want to be in the medical field. Were you ever in the medical field before?"* Your answer: *No.*

End of story. You are toast.

On the other hand, if you were to change only one of these *at a time*—field or job-title—you could always claim prior experience.

In the diagram on the previous page, let's say you move from A to B to D, over a period of three years, and in two steps.

Interviewer during your first move (a change just in your field): *"Were you ever in this kind of work before?"* Your answer: *"Yes, I've been an accountant for x number of years."*

Interviewer during your second move (a change now in your job-title): *"Were you ever in this kind of work before?"* Your answer: *"Yes, I've been in medicine for x number of years."*

Another example: Let's say in that diagram, you make a different set of two moves over a period of three years: you move from A to C to D.

Interviewer during your first move (a change just in your job-title): *"Were you ever in this kind of work before?"* Your answer: *"Yes, I've been in television for x number of years."*

Interviewer during your second move (a change just in your field): "Have you ever done this kind of work before?" Your answer: *"Yes, I've been a reporter for x number of years."*

By doing career-change in two steps, each time you make a move you are able to legitimately claim that you've had prior *experience.*

Needless to say, your likelihood of getting hired each time has just increased tremendously.

The Fifth Way to Choose/Change Careers:
FINDING OUT WHAT THE JOB MARKET WILL NEED

With a run of just plain bad luck, you may have used all four previous ways of finding or changing careers, but nothing worked. You're stuck. Your needs or wishes are dying on the vine.

Well, then be glad there is this fifth way of changing careers. It is not based on *your* needs or wishes, but on projections about the coming needs and wishes of the job market. It starts at the opposite end: not what *you* want, but what *the market* wants.

Technically called "Projections," they are also called *Hot Jobs,* though I'd take that with a grain of salt, if I were you.

There are dozens of such lists (just Google *hot jobs*) but take what you read, wherever you read it, not with just a grain of salt, but with a *barrel.*[2] "Projections" is just a nice word for "guesses." The way that *some* of these writers decide what constitutes a "hot job" would make your hair stand on end. I know; I've talked with them. Sometimes, they just choose a title because it sounds new, strange, or exotic. For example, the most common occupation in the US is retail salesperson, but would you know that, from this list of *"hot jobs"*? This is from *CBS News:*[3]

---

2. Put "10 Toughest Jobs to Fill" into your favorite search engine. You will turn up such articles as www.careercast.com/jobs-rated/toughest-jobs-to-fill-2018.
3. "9 Best Jobs in America for 2018," *CBS Moneywatch,* www.cbsnews.com/media/9-best-jobs-in-america-for-2018.

1. Data Scientist

2. Development & Operations (DevOps) Engineer

3. Marketing Manager

4. Occupational Therapist

5. Human Resources (HR) Manager

6. Electrical Engineer

7. Strategy Manager

8. Mobile Developer

9. Product Manager

The US government gets into this projections game—though on a more sophisticated level—with their *Occupational Outlook Handbook 2018–2019*, online at www.bls.gov/ooh. Here you can browse careers/ occupations by occupational group, number of new jobs projected to be available, faster-than-average job growth projected, level of education or training required, median pay, etc. Oh, and it has a lovely feature called "similar occupations." That's great if for any reason you don't qualify for some job that otherwise really fascinates you. Bottom line: While it can sound like the smartest option—to pick a career that's "hot"—it can backfire on you later.

Conclusion:
EIGHT CAUTIONS ABOUT CHOOSING/CHANGING CAREERS

Whenever you have to choose or change a career, here are eight cautions to keep in mind. (Many of these you're already aware of, I'm sure; this is just a reminder.)

1. Go for *any* career that seems fascinating or even interesting to you. But *first* talk to people who are already doing that work, to find out if the career or job is as great as it seems at first impression. Ask them *What do you like best about this work? What do you like least about this work? And, how did you get into this work?* This

last question can give you important clues about how you could get into this line of work or career, yourself. Ask them how they perceive their career: what are its component parts. **Every person may see their vocation in a different light. Don't assume that the way the person you are interviewing defines it, is the way you must also. Beneath any job-title, there is often lots of room for you to maneuver and define that job in a way that uniquely suits you, your gifts, and your creativity.** One architect, for example, may perceive his or her vocation in a different way from another architect. When Frei Otto received the Pritzker Prize posthumously in March of 2015, it was said of him, *"He . . . embraced a definition of architect to include researcher, inventor, form-finder, engineer, builder, teacher, collaborator, environmentalist, humanist, and creator of memorable . . . spaces." He was inspired by "natural phenomena—from birds' skulls to soap bubbles and spiders' webs."*[4]

2. In moving from one career to another, make sure that you preserve constancy in your life as well as change, during the transition. In other words, don't change *everything*. Remember the words of Archimedes about his mythical long lever: *Give me a fulcrum and a place to stand, and with a lever I will move the Earth.*[5] You need a firm place to stand, when you are moving your life around you, and that place is provided by the things that stay constant about you: your character, your faith, your values, your gifts or immutable skills.

3. If you can, you'll do better to start with yourself and what *you* want, rather than with the job market, and what's "hot." The difference is "enthusiasm" and "passion." Yours. You're much more attractive to employers when you're *on fire*. Maybe times are just too tough where you are, to start with your vision of what you want to do with your life, for now, anyway; but *try*.

4. The best *work*, the best career, for you, the one that makes you happiest and most fulfilled, is going to be one that uses your

---

4. Robin Pogrebin, "Pritzker Prize for Frei Otto, German Architect, Is Announced After His Death," *New York Times*, March 10, 2015.
5. Archimedes (ca. 235 BCE), Greek inventor, mathematician, and physicist. His saying is here loosely paraphrased.

favorite transferable skills, in your *favorite* subjects, fields, or special knowledges, in a job that offers you your *preferred* people-environments, your *preferred* working conditions, with your *preferred* salary or other rewards, working toward your *preferred* goals and values. This requires thorough inventory of who you are. Detailed instructions are to be found back in chapter 5.

5. The more time and thought you can give to the choosing of a new career, the better your choice is going to be. There is a penalty for seeking "quick and dirty" fixes.

6. If you are young, or relatively young, it's okay to make a mistake in your choice. You'll have time to correct a bad decision. Most of us will have at least five to seven *careers* during our lifetime, and ten or more *jobs*.

7. Choosing and then finding employment in a new career that you really fancy should feel like a fun task, as much as possible. The more fun you're having, the more this points to the likelihood that you're doing it right. To make it more fun, take a large piece of white paper, and then with some colored pencils or pens draw a picture of your ideal life: where you live, who's with you, what you do, what your dwelling looks like, what your ideal vacation looks like, etc. Don't let *reality* get in the way. Pretend a magic wand has been waved over your life, and it gives you everything you think your ideal life would be. Now, *of course* you're going to tell me you can't draw. Okay, then make symbols for things, or create little "doodads," with labels—anything so that you can *see* all together on one page your vision of your ideal life—however haltingly expressed.

The power of this exercise sometimes amazes me. Reason? By avoiding words and using pictures or symbols as much as possible, it bypasses the left side of the brain ("the safekeeping self," as George Prince calls it) and speaks directly to the right side of your brain ("the experimental self"), whose job is to engineer change. Do fun things like this, as you're exploring a new life for yourself.

8. One final word of caution here: if you're just graduating from high school, don't go get a college degree in some career field just because you think that this will guarantee you a job! It will not.

I wish you could see my emails, filled with bitter letters from people who believed this myth, went and got a degree in a field that looked just great, thought it would be a snap to find a job, but are still unemployed two years later. Good times or bad. They are bitter (often), angry (always), and disappointed in a society that they feel lied to them. Law graduates have been particularly in the news in recent years, suing their law school for falsifying employment figures for graduates.

To avoid this costly mistake, what you must do is take the choosing of a career into your own hands, with the help of this book, and then explore the career you've chosen down to the last inch, find out if you love it, and *then* go get your degree. Not because it guarantees a job, but because you feel passion, enthusiasm, and energy with this choice. You feel you have found the kind of life that other people only dream of.

I do not think there is any thrill
That can go through the human heart
Like that felt by the inventor
As he sees some creation of the brain
Unfolding to success. . . .
Such emotions make a man forget
Food, sleep, friends, love, everything.
        —*Nikola Tesla*

CHAPTER 12

How to Start Your Own Business

If your job-hunt isn't going well, the idea may occur to you in some moment of desperation: maybe I should stop trying to find jobs where I work for someone else. I should start my own business.

Some people have always wished they didn't have to work for someone else, but could be their own boss. According to some surveys, up to 80 percent of all workers toy with this idea at some point in their lives.[1] People dream. Maybe your dream is: I want to create a website where I can teach people how to "go green," and help preserve the environment. Or maybe your dream is: I want to sell jewelry. Or maybe: I want to start my own security service. Or maybe it is: I want to run my own bake shop, where I can sell my own homemade bread and pies. Or: run a bed-and-breakfast place. Or: grow lavender, and sell soap and perfume made from it. Or: be a consultant to people who need my expertise, gathered in the business world over many years. Or: sell real estate. Stuff like that.

Or maybe you don't have a dream. All you know is you don't want to work for someone else; you want to be your own boss. And you're open to any and all suggestions.

---

1. And each year, 10 percent of all workers actually do start their own business.

Is It as Difficult as We Are
So Often Told?

Sometimes taking this step is easy. Sometimes it is super difficult. Let's consider a couple of real case histories.

Case History #1. Alan was trained as a physical therapist and had no difficulty finding employment at local hospitals. But he didn't like being indoors all the time; he longed for a way to work outside. He considered his assets: he was a skilled photographer, a good furniture refinisher, and he loved thrift shops and flea markets. He also liked working with his hands. He particularly liked a certain period of furniture and quickly taught himself to become an expert. He learned how much fans of that furniture would pay for pieces from that period. He began scouring local thrift shops, flea markets, estate sales, and the Internet looking for pieces that were for sale at a price below their true worth. He bought the pieces, took them to his garage, which he had converted to a workshop, and refinished them so they looked beautiful. He then took attractive photos of them, and posted the photos on eBay, Etsy, NextDoor, and other sites. He became known for his expertise, and people soon bought up anything he would post online. He kept a list of his repeat customers, often sending them a notice of a new product before publicly announcing it. He is making a great profit from his work—and he is outdoors most of the time.

Case History #2. Beth was a stay-at-home parent and former librarian who liked to keep her research skills fresh by volunteering at a local library. She enjoyed helping the patrons find resources for their various projects. When her mother became seriously ill, Beth no longer had time to volunteer, but watching an episode of the TV show *Finding Your Roots* inspired her to start a new project: researching her mother's family tree. She set up accounts with several genealogy sites and quickly found the process of uncovering family information fascinating. She created an extensive and attractive "family tree scrapbook" with legal records, photos, newspaper clippings, and other items she found online, tracing her mother's family back to the 1700s. She left the scrapbook in her mother's room at the medical facility and a few days later one of the nurses approached her and inquired about the scrapbook. The nurse wanted to know if she would create a similar project for her mother and father. Word spread, and Beth had a new part-time "job" she could blend in with her family responsibilities. She purchased some ancestry software, joined the National Genealogical Society, and started taking online courses in genealogy. She hopes to become a certified genealogist at some point and is marketing her business through presentations at her library and elsewhere. She likes that she can control the pace and timing of her work, and that she will be able to grow her business when her family responsibilities are reduced.

Case History #3. Maria worked in a corporate human resources office for ten years, interviewing candidates for jobs, managing benefit packages, and ensuring that all the paperwork in the hiring process was properly managed and recorded. She found that her energy would rise when she was interviewing candidates for opportunities in the company; her energy fell when she filled out all the forms and paperwork connected with the hiring process. Her company offered training courses and when she found one on career coaching, she signed up. Throughout the course, she found herself thinking, "I could do this," but she was reluctant to give up her income and benefits. So she started small: she created a website and offered coaching sessions on Saturday mornings. She ran a few coaching groups at her church, and from those groups she started working with just a client or two. In the meantime, she created a name for her new business and wrote a guide to resume writing, which she offered for free to anyone who gave her their email address through her website. She started a blog on her website and began accepting speaking opportunities in her community. As she developed her business, she decided to focus exclusively on helping clients craft their "marketing package" for the job-search. When she started getting more clients than she could handle, she raised her rates, thinking that would discourage people. But it didn't, and with the new higher rates she was receiving she could seriously consider leaving her full-time job. After two years, she took the plunge and now works with clients from all over the world, helping them shape their marketing packages, including their resumes and online presence. She doesn't make the same income she did in her corporate job, but she loves the freedom and flexibility, and because she doesn't have to go to an office every day, she is saving money on gas mileage, professional clothing, lunches, and child care.

These are real-life stories; I only changed the names to protect their privacy.

You will notice, right away, some things that are common to these case histories:

a. These people didn't need a whole lot of money to launch their own business.

b. They did have to do research, sometimes plenty of it, to make it work.

c. All three of them used the Internet to make their product, service, or expertise known.

d. None of them went down the traditional paths that people used to go down, when considering self-employment, such as buying a franchise, or being sucked in by one of those well-advertised "work-at-home" projects that used to sound appetizing to the unwary. "Being self-employed" wears quite a different face these days, compared to what it used to.

So, now you're reading this chapter, and you're weighing the idea of going out on your own, starting your own business, being your own boss. Where do you start?

When You Have No Idea What Business You Want to Go Into

Let's assume you want to be your own boss, but you have no idea what kind of business you want to have. How do you start? There are four steps that any thorough, intelligent person should faithfully follow: Write. Read. Explore. Get Feedback.

WRITE

1. Begin with chapter 5 in this book: Don't just read it. *Do it!* As I repeat throughout this book, Who precedes What. First get a clearer picture of Who you are, before you try to decide What you want to do. **Ultimately, *what* you decide to do should flow from *who* you**

are. When done, look at your whole Flower Diagram and see if any or all of the petals give you an idea for your own business.

2. Get out a piece of blank paper, and jot down any ideas. Use this same piece of paper for any ideas that come to you, as you do the rest of these steps. You want it all on one page. (Something to do with the right side of your brain, and intuition.)

3. Then write your resume, if you haven't already, answering all the questions you will find in chapter 7 under the heading A Starter Kit for Writing Your Resume (page 147). When done, read it over, and see if anything there gives you an idea for a business of your own. It may be that you have been doing it for years—but in the employ of someone else. But now, you're thinking about doing this kind of work for yourself, whether it be as an independent accountant, massage therapist, business consultant, repair person, dance instructor, home decorator, home care nurse, craftsperson, or producer or seller of some kind of product or service. If so, add your great idea on that piece of paper.

4. If nothing inspires you, try Daniel Pink's prescription:[2]

   a. Make a list of five things you are good at.

   b. Then make a second list of five things you love to do.

   c. Then make a third list of where the first two lists overlap.

   d. Read that list. Ask yourself, "Will anyone pay me to do these things?"

5. If you're dying to be your own boss, but still have no idea what business to go into, try this: go to O*NET (www.onetonline.org). Click on Find Occupations, then, underneath it, click on Career Cluster. Look at that list and see if any cluster appeals to you. Jot it down on that piece of paper. Then go back to the home page and under Advanced Search, click on Browse by O*NET Data. You will see there are ten subheadings beneath that title: Abilities, Interests, Knowledge, Skills, Work Activities, Work Context, Work Styles, Work Values, Skills Search, and Tools and Technology. Click on each of those ten, in turn, and jot down anything that proves to be attractive or interesting, again, on that piece of paper.

2. *Free Agent Nation* (Business Plus, 2002), www.danpink.com/books/free-agent-nation.

READ

Hopefully, from all this thinking, and tasks, you will have some ideas. It will be nice if you see the possibilities of three different business ventures. But if there's one of the three that you would really die to do, and you feel passionate about it, then explore that one first. Second. And third!

Now, what you want to do next is read up on all the virtues and perils of running your own business. Look before you leap! The Internet has tons of stuff about this. For example:

Free Agent Nation

www.workforce.com/articles/dan-pink-interview-free-agent-nation-evolves

Daniel Pink, before he became famous for such books as *Drive* and *To Sell Is Human*, was the first to call attention to how many people were refusing to work for any employer. He defined them as free agents. His classic book was *Free Agent Nation*. His basic thesis: Self-employment has become a broader concept than it was in another age. The concept now includes not only those who own their own business but also free agents—independent contractors who work for several clients; temps and contract employees who work each day through temporary agencies; limited-time-frame workers who work only for a set time, as on a project, then move on to another company; consultants; and so on. This is a fascinating article to help you decide if you want to be a "free agent."

Small Business Administration

www.sba.gov

The SBA is a federal program that was established to help start, manage, and grow small businesses. Lots of useful articles and advice are online here.

Business Owner's Toolkit

www.bizfilings.com/toolkit

Yikes, there is a lot of information here for the small business owner. Everything about your business: starting, planning, financing, marketing, hiring, managing, getting government contracts, taxes—all that stuff, including any forms you will need to fill out.

The Business Owners' Idea Café

www.businessownersideacafe.com/starting_business/index.php

Great, fun site for the small business owner. Lots of practical advice, and they have a Facebook site as well.

Nolo's Business, LLCs & Corporations

www.nolo.com/legal-encyclopedia/business-llcs-corporations

Lots of practical nitty-gritty stuff here: laws, forms, contracts, and resources needed if you start your own business.

Home Businesses

www.ahbbo.com/archives.html

To help you make your own home business succeed, this is a great site, with lots of information for you. There are hundreds of articles here. Just be careful: "home business" opportunities are filled with scams. Always do your research first: start with the Better Business Bureau's scam tracker (www.bbb.org/scamtracker/us) and use Google to further investigate before you invest any money.

EXPLORE

Let's hope that now you have some idea for starting your own business. But you know that a lot of start-ups, online and off, don't make it. You want to avoid this happening to you. You want to interview others who have started the same kind of business, so you don't make the same mistakes they did. Your exploring, then, should have three steps to it, summarized by this simple formula:

$$A - B = C$$

To explain:

You must find out what skills, knowledge, or experience it takes to make this kind of business idea work, by interviewing several business owners. This is List "A."

Then you need to make a list of the skills, knowledge, or experience that you have. This is List "B." Then by subtracting "B" from "A," you will arrive at a list of skills, etc., that are required for success in such a business, but that you don't have. And you must then go out and hire or co-opt a friend or mate or volunteer who has those skills you are lacking (at the moment, anyway). This is List "C."

I will explain these three steps in a little more detail:

You prepare for these lists by first writing out in as much detail as you can just exactly what kind of business you are thinking about starting. Do you want to be a freelance writer, or a craftsperson, or a consultant, independent screenwriter, copywriter, digital artist, song-writer, photographer, illustrator, interior designer, videographer, film-maker, counselor, therapist, plumber, electrician, agent, soap maker, bicycle repairer, public speaker, or what?

Then you interview people already doing the kind of work you'd like to do. You should approach this exploration, having found at least three names. Find them through your favorite Internet search engine, or from LinkedIn, Yelp, the Chambers of Commerce, or various smart-phone apps. When you talk to them, you explain that you're exploring the possibility of starting your own business, similar to theirs, and would they mind sharing something of their own history. You ask them what skills, knowledge, or experience they think are necessary to making this kind of business successful.

These days, everyone's preference is to do such interviewing by email. I think this is a big mistake. Face-to-face is to be preferred, in every case. Try businesspeople in a city that's an hour's drive away. They are not as likely to see you as a potential competitor, unless you're going to compete with each other head-to-head on the Internet. You want them first of all to tell you something of the history of their busi-ness, how they got started, what kinds of challenges they encountered, what kinds of mistakes. Face-to-face they may tell you more about the challenges they ran into, the obstacles and pitfalls they encountered, than they ever would in an email; and you want this information, believe me you do, so that you can avoid making the same missteps if you decide to start a similar business. (No need for you to step on the same land mines that they did.)

You also want them to help you compile a list of the necessary skills, knowledge, and experience they think are essential for the type of business they're doing, and you're thinking of doing.

When you have a list you're satisfied with, give this list a name. Call it "A."

Back home you sit down and inventory your own skills, knowledge, and experience, by doing the inventory of who you are described in chapter 5, the Flower Exercise. Give this list a name, also. Call it "B."

Having done this, subtract "B" from "A." This gives you another new list, which you should name "C." "C" is by definition a list of the skills or knowledge that you don't have, but must find—either by taking courses yourself, or by hiring someone with those skills, or by getting a friend or family member (who has those skills) to volunteer to help you for a while.

For example, if your investigation revealed that it takes good accounting practices in order to turn a profit, and you don't know a thing about accounting, you now know enough to go out and hire a part-time accountant immediately—or, if you absolutely have no money, maybe you can talk an accountant friend of yours into giving you some volunteer time, for a while.

I can illustrate this whole process with a case history. Our job-hunter is a woman who has been making harps for some employer, but now is thinking about going into business for herself, not only making harps at home, but also designing harps, with the aid of a computer. After interviewing several home-based harp makers and harp designers, and finishing her own self-assessment, her chart of $A - B = C$ came out looking like the example on page 259.

If she decides she does indeed want to try her hand at becoming an independent harp maker and harp designer, she now knows what she needs but lacks: computer programming, knowledge of the principles of electronics, and accounting. In other words, List C. These she must either go to school to acquire for herself, or enlist from some friends of hers in those fields, on a volunteer basis, or go out and hire, part-time. It should be always possible—with a little blood, sweat, and imagination—to find out what $A - B = C$ is, for any business you're dreaming of doing.

GET FEEDBACK

So, are you cut out for this sort of thing? Only you can answer that, in your innermost thoughts. But you can get some help.

Take seriously the feedback you received when speaking to other business owners. Don't gloss over negative observations you received: examine them and decide if they apply to you.

If you have a spouse or partner, tell them what you're up to, find out what their opinion is, explore whether this is going to require sacrifices from them (not just you), and how they feel about that. If your life is shared with them, and vice versa, you have no right to make this decision unilaterally, all by yourself. They should be part of the whole journey, not just at the end when your mind is already made up. You have a responsibility to make them full partners in any decision you're facing. Love demands it!

If after all this feedback, you decide you still want to create your own job by starting this kind of business, go ahead and try—no matter what your well-meaning but cautious friends or family may say. They love you, they're concerned for you, and you should thank them for that; but come on, you only have one life here on this Earth, and that life is yours to say how it will be spent, or not spent. Parents, children, well-meaning friends, etc., can give loving advice, but in the end they get no vote. Only you and your partner do.

Just remember, it takes a lot of guts to try ANYTHING new (to you) in today's slowly recovering economy. It's easier, however, if you keep these things in mind:

1. There is always some risk in trying something new. Your goal, I hope, is not to avoid risk—there is no way to do that—but to make sure ahead of time that the risks are manageable.

2. As we have seen, you find this out before you start, by first talking to others who have already done what you are thinking of doing; then you evaluate whether or not you still want to go ahead and try it.

3. Have a plan B, laid out, before you start, as to what you will do if it doesn't work out; i.e., know where you are going to go next. Don't wait, puh-leaze! Write it out, now: This is what I'm going to do, if this doesn't work out.

A - B = C

Skills and Knowledge Needed to Run This Kind of Business Successfully	Skills and Knowledge That I Have	Skills and Knowledge Needed, Which I Don't Have, So I'm Going to Go Out and Hire Someone Who Has Them
Precision-working with tools and instruments	Precision-working with tools and instruments	
Planning and directing an entire project	Planning and directing an entire project	
Programming computers, inventing programs that solve physical problems		Programming computers, inventing programs that solve physical problems
Problem solving: evaluating why a particular design or process isn't working	Problem solving: evaluating why a particular design or process isn't working	
Being self-motivated, resourceful, patient, persevering, accurate, methodical, and thorough	Being self-motivated, resourceful, patient, persevering, accurate, methodical, and thorough	
Thorough knowledge of: 　Principles of electronics	*Thorough knowledge of:*	*Thorough knowledge of:* 　Principles of electronics
Physics of strings	Physics of strings	
Principles of vibration	Principles of vibration	
Properties of woods	Properties of woods	
Accounting		Accounting

THE ORANGE PAGES

APPENDIX A

Finding Your Mission in Life

There are those who think that belief in God is just some fairy tale that humankind invented, to fortify themselves against the darkness. Naturally, therefore, they think that anyone who says they believe in God these days is demonstrably feebleminded, or a pathetic child who has never grown up intellectually.

Given this view, they are horrified to find a section on faith or religion in a job-hunting book. They have written to me, and said so.

Well, here it is, anyway.

That's because the percentage of the world's population that says they don't believe there is a God averages less than 18 percent (it varies from country to country: here in the US the figure is 11 percent, while in Canada that figure is 19 to 30 percent). Still, that leaves us with an overwhelming percentage of the US population (89 percent) believing in God.[1] And my more than ten million readers are a pretty typical cross section of this country.

A comprehensive demographic study of more than 230 countries and territories conducted by the Pew Research Center's Forum on Religion & Public Life estimates that there are 6.1 billion religiously affiliated adults and children around the globe, representing 84 percent of the 2015 world population of 7.3 billion.

---

1. See the Gallup poll, published 6/29/16, at www.gallup.com/poll/193271/americans-believe-god.aspx.

That demographic study—based on analysis of more than 2,500 censuses, surveys, and population registers—found there are 2.3 billion Christians (31 percent of the world's population), 1.8 billion Muslims (24 percent), 1.1 billion Hindus (15 percent), nearly 500 million Buddhists (7 percent), and 14.6 million Jews (0.2 percent) as of 2015. (The most recent year for which we have figures.)

This book is used by ten million readers in twenty-six countries. So, leaving out a section that 84 percent of my readers worldwide might be interested in, and helped by, in order to please just 16 percent of my readers, seems to me insane.

Indeed, according to the Pew Research Center, more than 75 percent of the world's population lives in areas with severe religious restrictions. That's restrictions against Muslims, Jews, Christians, and other religions. According to the United States Department of State, Christians in more than sixty countries face persecution from their governments or surrounding neighbors simply because of their belief in Jesus Christ.

"Christians . . . have now experienced the full impact of the world's hostility and indifference. We are staggered and alarmed by the extent of it, and dumfounded by its partial success. Numerically we are drastically reduced, proportionately to the enormously increased population, and we shall probably continue in that way; perhaps with even greater numerical reductions. . . . No doubt we survive as a minority but by no means as a pitiful or contemptible minority. We die daily because of our own weakness and unworthiness, yet we live, nevertheless because God is with us. . . . Modern man relies on nothing that will not some day be taken away from him. Those who are utterly committed to the Christian faith rely in the last resort on nothing that could possibly be taken away. That is why the Church, contrary to all appearances, is stronger than the world. And that is why it is the duty of Christians to be sympathetic, compassionate, and merciful in their dealings with their estranged brethren."[2]

I do not want to add to that feeling by keeping silent. Faith is welcome in this book.

---

2. *The Church To-day and To-morrow: The Prospect for Post-Christianity* by Julian Victor Langmead Casserley (1909–1978). (London: SPCK, 1965), pp. 102, 113f.

As I started writing this section, I toyed at first with the idea of following what might be described as an "all-paths approach" to religion: trying to stay as general and nonspecific as I could. But, after much thought, I decided not to try that. This, because I have read many other writers who tried, and I felt the approach failed miserably. An "all-paths" approach to religion ends up being a "no-paths" approach, just as a woman or man who tries to please everyone ends up pleasing no one. It is the old story of the "universal" vs. the "particular."

Those of us who do career counseling could predict, ahead of time, that trying to stay universal is not likely to be helpful, in writing about faith. We know well from our own field that truly helpful career counseling depends upon defining the particularity or uniqueness of each person we try to help. No employer wants to know what you have in common with everyone else. He or she wants to know what makes you unique and individual. As I have argued throughout this book, the inventory of your uniqueness or *particularity* is crucial if you are ever to find meaningful work.

This particularity invades *everything* a person does; it is not suddenly "jettisonable" when he or she turns to matters of faith. Therefore, when I or anyone else writes about faith, I believe we must write out of our own particularity—which *starts,* in my case, with the fact that I write, and think, and breathe as a Christian—as you might expect from the fact that I was an ordained Episcopalian minister for many years. Understandably, then, this chapter speaks from a Christian perspective. I want you to be aware of that, at the outset. Balanced against this is the fact that I have always been acutely sensitive to the fact that this is a pluralistic society in which we live, and that I in particular owe a great deal to my readers who have religious convictions quite different from my own. It has turned out that the people who work or have worked here in my office with me, over the years, have been predominantly of other faiths.

Furthermore, *Parachute*'s more than ten million readers have included not only Christians of every variety and persuasion, Christian Scientists, Jews, Hindus, Buddhists, and adherents of Islam, but also believers in "new age" religions, secularists, humanists, agnostics, atheists, and many others. I have therefore tried to be very courteous toward the feelings of all my readers, *while at the same time* counting on them to translate my Christian thought-forms into their own. This ability to thus translate is the indispensable sine qua non of anyone who wants to communicate helpfully with others in this pluralistic society of ours.

In the Judeo-Christian tradition from which I come, one of the indignant biblical questions was, "Has God forgotten to be gracious?" The answer was a clear "No." I think it is important *for all of us* also to seek the same goal. I have therefore labored to make this chapter gracious as well as thought provoking.

Turning Point

For many of us, the job-hunt offers a chance to make some fundamental changes in our whole life. It marks a turning point in how we live our life.

It gives us a chance to ponder and reflect, to extend our mental horizons, to go deeper into the subsoil of our soul.

It gives us a chance to wrestle with the question, "Why am I here on Earth?" We don't want to feel that we are just another grain of sand lying on the beach called humanity, unnumbered and lost in the billions of other human beings.

We want to do more than plod through life, going to work, coming home from work. We want to find that special joy "that no one can take from us," which comes from having a sense of Mission in our life.

We want to feel we were put here on Earth for some special purpose, to do some unique work that only we can accomplish.

We want to know what our Mission is.

The Meaning of the Word *Mission*

When used with respect to our life and work, *Mission* has always been a religious concept, from beginning to end. It is defined by *Webster's* as "a continuing task or responsibility that one is destined or fitted to do or specially called upon to undertake," and historically has had two major synonyms: *Calling* and *Vocation*. These, of course, are the same word in two different languages, English and Latin. Both imply God.

To be given a Calling or Vocation implies *Someone who calls*. To have a Destiny implies *Someone who determined the destination for us*. Thus, the concept of Mission lands us inevitably in the lap of God, before we have hardly begun.

I emphasize this, because there is an increasing trend in our culture to try to speak about religious subjects without reference to God. This is true of "spirituality," "soul," and "Mission," in particular. More and more books talk about Mission as though it were simply "a purpose you choose for your own life, by identifying your enthusiasms."

This attempt to obliterate all reference to God from the originally religious concept of Mission is particularly ironic because the proposed substitute word—enthusiasms—is derived from two Greek words, *en theos*, and means "God in us."

In the midst of this increasingly secular culture, we find an oasis that—along with athletics—is very hospitable toward belief in God. That oasis is *job-hunting*. Most of the leaders who have evolved creative job-hunting ideas were—from the beginning—people who believed firmly in God, and said so: Sidney Fine, Bernard Haldane, John Crystal, Arthur and Marie Kirn, Arthur Miller, Tom and Ellie Jackson, Ralph Matson, and of course myself.

I mentioned at the beginning of this appendix that 89 percent of us in the US believe in God. According to the Gallup Organization, 90 percent of us pray, 88 percent of us believe God loves us, and 33 percent of us report that we have had a life-changing religious experience.

However, it is not clear that we have made much connection between our belief in God and our work. Often our spiritual beliefs and our attitude toward our work live in separate mental ghettos, within our mind.

A dialogue between these two *is* opened up inside our head, and heart, when we are out of work. Unemployment, particularly in this brutal economy, gives us a chance to contemplate why we are here on Earth, and what our Calling, Vocation, or Mission is, uniquely, for each of us.

Unemployment becomes *life transition*, when we can't find a job doing the same work we've always done. Since we have to rethink one thing, many of us elect to rethink *everything*.

Something awakens within us. Call it *yearning*. Call it *hope*. We come to realize the dream we dreamed has never died. And we go back to get it. We decide to resume our search . . . for the life we know within our heart that we were meant to live.

Now we have a chance to marry our work and our religious beliefs, to talk about Calling, and Vocation, and Mission in life—to think out why we are here, and what plans God has for us.

That's why a period of unemployment can absolutely change our life.

The Secret to Finding Your Mission in Life: Taking It in Stages

I will explain the steps toward finding your Mission in life that I have learned in all my years on Earth. Just remember two things. First, I speak from a lifelong Christian perspective, and trust you to translate this into your own thought-forms.

Second, I know that these steps are not the only Way. Many people have discovered their Mission by taking other paths. And you may, too. But hopefully what I have to say may shed some light upon whatever path you take.

I have learned that if you want to figure out what your Mission in life is, it will likely take some time. It is not a *problem* to be solved in a day and a night. It is a *learning process* that has steps to it, much like the process by which we all learned to eat. As a baby, we did not tackle adult food right off. As we all recall, there were three stages: first there had to be the mother's milk or bottle, then strained baby foods, and finally—after teeth and time—the stuff that grown-ups chew. Three stages—and the two earlier stages were not to be disparaged. It was all eating, just different forms of eating—appropriate to our development at the time. But each stage had to be mastered, in turn, before the next could be approached.

There are usually three stages also to learning what your Mission in life is, and the two earlier stages are likewise not to be disparaged. It is all "Mission"—just different forms of Mission, appropriate to your development at the time. But each stage has to be mastered, in turn, before the next can be approached.

Of course, there is a sense in which you never master any of these stages, but are always growing in understanding and mastery of them, throughout your whole life here on Earth.

As it has been impressed on me by observing many people over the years (admittedly through *Christian spectacles*), it appears that the three parts to your Mission here on Earth can be defined generally as follows:

1. *Your first Mission here on Earth* is one that you share with the rest of the human race, but it is no less your individual Mission for the fact that it is shared, and it is, **to seek to stand hour by hour in the conscious presence of God, the One from whom your Mission is derived.** *The Missioner before the Mission,* is the rule. In religious language, your Mission here is *to know God, and enjoy Him forever, and to see His hand in all His works.*

2. Once you have begun doing that in an earnest way, *your second Mission here on Earth* is also one that you share with the rest of the human race, but it is no less your individual Mission for the fact that it is shared, and that is, **to do what you can, moment by moment, day by day, step by step, to make this world a better place, following the leading and guidance of God's Spirit within you and around you.**

3. Once you have begun doing that in a serious way, *your third Mission here on Earth* is one that is uniquely yours, and that is

   a. **to exercise the Talent that you particularly came to Earth to use—your greatest gift, which you most delight to use,**

   b. **in the place(s) or setting(s) that God has caused to appeal to you the most,**

   c. **and for those purposes that God most needs to have done in the world.**

When fleshed out, and spelled out, I think you will find that there you have the definition of your Mission in life. Or, to put it another way, these are the three Missions that you have in life.

The Two Rhythms of the Dance of Mission: Unlearning, Learning, Unlearning, Learning

The distinctive characteristic of these three stages is that in each we are forced to *let go* of some fundamental assumptions that our culture has taught us about the nature of Mission. In other words, throughout this quest and at each stage we find ourselves engaged not merely in a process of *Learning,* we are also engaged in a process of *Un*learning. Thus, we can restate the three Learnings, in terms of what we also need to *un*learn at each stage:

- We need in the first stage to *un*learn the idea that our Mission is primarily to keep busy *doing* something (here on Earth), and learn instead that our Mission is first of all to keep busy *being* something (here on Earth). In Christian language (and others as well), we might say that we were sent here to learn how *to be* sons of God, and daughters of God, before anything else. *"Our Father, who art in heaven. . . ."*

- In the second stage, "Being" issues into "Doing." At this stage, we need to *un*learn the idea that everything about our Mission must be *unique* to us, and learn instead that some parts of our Mission here on Earth are *shared* by all human beings; e.g., we were all sent here to bring more gratitude, more kindness, more forgiveness, and more love into the world. We share this Mission because the task is too large to be accomplished by just one individual.

- We need in the third stage to *un*learn the idea that the part of our Mission that is truly unique, and most truly ours, is something Our Creator just *orders* us to do, without any agreement from our spirit, mind, and heart. (On the other hand, neither is it something that each of us chooses and then merely asks God to bless.) We need to learn that God so honors our free will, that He has ordained that our unique Mission be something that we have some part in choosing.

In this third stage we need also to *un*learn the idea that our unique Mission must consist of some achievement for all the world to see—and learn instead that as the stone does not always know what ripples it has caused in the pond whose surface it impacts, so neither we nor those who watch our life will always know *what we have achieved* by our life and by our Mission. *It may be* that by the grace of God we helped bring about a profound change for the better in the lives of other souls around us, but it also may be that this takes place beyond our sight, or after we have gone on. And we may never know what we have accomplished, until we see Him face-to-face after this life is past.

Most finally, we need to *un*learn the idea that what we have accomplished is our doing, and ours alone. It is God's Spirit breathing in us and through us that helps us do whatever we do, and so the singular first-person pronoun is never appropriate, but only the plural. Not "*I* accomplished this" but "*We* accomplished this, God and I, working together. . . ."

That should give you a general overview. But I would like to add some random comments on my part about each of these three Missions of ours here on Earth.

Some Random Comments About Your First Mission in Life

Your first Mission here on Earth is one that you share with the rest of the human race, but it is no less your individual Mission for the fact that it is shared: and that is, **to seek to stand hour by hour in the conscious presence of God, the One from whom your Mission is derived.** The Missioner before the Mission, is the rule. In religious language, your Mission is: To know God, and enjoy Him forever, and to see His hand in all His works.

Comment 1:
How We Might Think of God

Each of us has to go about this primary Mission according to the tenets of our own particular religion. But I will speak what I know within the context of my own particular faith, and you may perhaps translate and apply it to yours. I will speak as a Christian, who believes (passionately) that Christ is the Way and the Truth and the Life. But I also believe, with St. Peter, "that God shows no partiality, but in every nation anyone who fears Him and does what is right is acceptable to Him" (Acts 10:34–35).

Now, Jesus claimed many unique things about Himself and His Mission; but He also spoke of Himself as the great prototype for us all. He called Himself "the Son of Man," and He said, "I assure you that the man who believes in me will do the same things that I have done, yes, and he will do even greater things than these . . ." (John 14:12).

Emboldened by His identification of us with His Life and His Mission, we might want to remember how He spoke about His Life here on Earth. He put it in this context: **"I came from the Father and have come into the world; again, I am leaving the world and going to the Father"** (John 16:28).

If there is a sense in which this is, in even the faintest way, true also of our lives (and I shall say in a moment in what sense I think it is true), then instead of calling our great Creator "God" or "Father" right off, we might begin our approach to the subject of religion by referring to the One Who gave us our Mission and sent us to this planet not as "God" or "Father" but—*just to help our thinking*—as **"The One From Whom We Came and The One To Whom We Shall Return,"** when this life is done.

If our life here on Earth is to be at all like Christ's, then this is a true way to think about the One Who gave us our Mission. We are not some kind of eternal, preexistent *being*. We are creatures, who once did not exist, and then came into Being, and continue to have our Being, only at the will of our great Creator. But as creatures we are both body and soul; although we know our body was created in our mother's womb, our soul's origin is a great mystery. Where it came from, at what moment the Lord created it, is something we cannot know. It is not unreasonable to suppose, however, that the great God created our *soul* before it entered our body, and in that sense we did indeed stand before God before we were born; and He is indeed **"The One From Whom We Came and The One To Whom We Shall Return."**

Therefore, before we go searching for "what work was I sent here to do?" we need to establish—or in a truer sense *reestablish*—contact with **"The One From Whom We Came and The One To Whom We Shall Return."** Without this reaching out of the creature to the great Creator, without this reaching out of *the creature with a Mission* to *the One Who Gave Us That Mission*, the question, *"What is my Mission in life?"* is void and null. The *what* is rooted in the *Who;* absent the Personal, one cannot meaningfully discuss The Thing. It is like an adult who cries, "I want to get married," without giving any consideration to *who* it is they want to marry.

Comment 2:
How We Might Think of Religion or Faith

In light of this larger view of our creatureliness, we can see that *religion* or *faith* is not a question of whether or not we choose to (*as it is so commonly put*) "have a relationship with God." Looking at our life in a larger context than just our life here on Earth, it becomes apparent that some sort of relationship with God is a given for us, about which we have absolutely no choice. God and we **were** and **are** related, during the time of our soul's existence before our birth and in the time of our soul's continued existence after our death. The only choice we have is what to do about **The Time in Between**, i.e., what we want the nature of our relationship with God to be during our time here on Earth and how that will affect the *nature* of the relationship, then, after death.

One of the corollaries of all this is that by the very act of being born into a human body, it is inevitable that we undergo a kind of *amnesia*—an amnesia that typically embraces not only our nine months in the womb, our baby years, and almost one-third of each day (sleeping), but, more important, any memory of our origin or our destiny. We wander on Earth as an amnesia victim. To seek after Faith, therefore, is to seek to climb back out of that amnesia. Religion or Faith is **the hard reclaiming of knowledge we once knew as a certainty.**

Comment 3:
The First Obstacle to Executing This Mission

This first Mission of ours here on Earth is not the easiest of Missions, simply because it is the first. Indeed, in many ways, it is the most difficult. All we can see is that our life here on Earth is a very physical life. We eat, we drink, we sleep, we long to be held, and to hold. We inherit a physical body, with very physical appetites, we walk on the physical earth, and we acquire physical possessions. It is the most alluring of temptations, *in our amnesia*, to come up with just a *Physical* interpretation of this life: to think that the Universe is merely interested in the survival of species. Given this interpretation, the story of our individual life could be simply told: we are born, grow up, procreate, and die.

But we are ever recalled to do what we came here to do: that without rejecting the joy of the Physicalness of this life, such as the love of the blue sky and the green grass, we are to reach out beyond all this to recall and recover a *Spiritual* interpretation of our life. *Beyond* the physical and *within* the physicalness of this life, to detect a Spirit and a Person from beyond this Earth who is with us and in us—the very real and loving and awesome Presence of the great Creator from whom we came—and the One to whom we once again shall go.

Comment 4:
The Second Obstacle to Executing This Mission

It is one of the conditions of our earthly amnesia and our creatureliness that, sadly enough, some very *human* and very *rebellious* part of us *likes* the idea of living in a world where we can be our own god—and therefore loves the purely Physical interpretation of life, and finds it *anguish* to relinquish it. Traditional Christian vocabulary calls this "sin" and has a lot to say about the difficulty it poses for this first part of our Mission. All who live a thoughtful life know that it is true: our greatest enemy in carrying out this first Mission of ours is indeed *our own* heart and our own rebellion.

Comment 5:
Further Thoughts About What Makes Us
Special and Unique

As I said earlier, many of us come to this issue of our Mission in life, because we want to feel that we are unique. And what we mean by that is that we hope to discover some "specialness" intrinsic to us, which is our birthright, and which no one can take from us. What we, however, discover from a thorough exploration of this topic, is that we are indeed special—but only because God thinks us so. Our specialness and uniqueness reside in Him, and His love, rather than in anything intrinsic to our own *being*. The proper appreciation of this distinction causes our feet to carry us in the end not to the City called Pride, but to the Temple called Gratitude.

What is religion? Religion is the service of God out of grateful love for what God has done for us. The Christian religion, more particularly, is the service of God out of grateful love for what God has done for us in Christ.
—PHILLIPS BROOKS, author of *O Little Town of Bethlehem*

Comment 6:
The Unconscious Doing
of the Work We Came to Do

You may have *already* wrestled with this first part of your Mission here on Earth. You may not have called it that. You may have called it simply "learning to believe in God." But if you ask what your Mission is in life, this one was and is the precondition of all else that you came here to do. Absent this Mission, it is folly to talk about the rest. So, if you have been seeking faith, or seeking to strengthen your faith, you have—willy-nilly—already been about *the doing of the Mission you were given*. Born into **This Time in Between**, you have found His hand again, and reclasped it. You are therefore ready to go on with His Spirit to tackle together what you came here to do—the other parts of your Mission.

Some Random Comments About Your Second Mission in Life

Your second Mission here on Earth is also one that you share with the rest of the human race, but it is no less your individual Mission for the fact that it is shared, and that is, **to do what you can moment by moment, day by day, step by step, to make this world a better place—following the leading and guidance of God's Spirit within you and around you.**

Comment 1:
The Uncomfortableness of One Step at a Time

Imagine yourself out walking in your neighborhood one night, and you find yourself surrounded by such a dense fog that you have lost your bearings and cannot find your way. Suddenly, a friend appears out of the fog, and asks you to put your hand in theirs, and they will lead you home. And you, not being able to tell where you are going, trustingly follow them, even though you can only see one step at a time. Eventually, you arrive safely home, filled with gratitude. But as you reflect upon the experience the next day, you realize how unsettling it was to have to keep walking when you could see only one step at a time, even though you had guidance you knew you could trust.

Now I have asked you to imagine all of this, because this is the essence of the second Mission to which *you* are called—and *I* am called—in this life. It is all very different than we had imagined. When the question, *"What is your Mission in life?"* is first broached, and we have put our hand in God's, as it were, we imagine that we will be taken up to *some mountaintop*, from which we can see far into the distance. And that we will hear a voice in our ear, saying, "Look, look, see that distant city? That is the goal of your Mission; that is where everything is leading, every step of your way."

But instead of the mountaintop, we find ourselves in *the valley*— wandering often in a fog. And the voice in our ear says something quite different from what we thought we would hear. It says, "Your Mission is to take one step at a time, even when you don't yet see where it all is leading, or what the Grand Plan is, or what your overall Mission in life is. Trust Me; I will lead you."

Comment 2:
The Nature of This Step-by-Step Mission

As I said, in every situation you find yourself, you have been sent here to do whatever you can—moment by moment—that will bring more gratitude, more kindness, more forgiveness, more honesty, and more love into this world.

There are dozens of such moments every day. Moments when you stand—as it were—at a spiritual crossroads, with two ways lying before you. Such moments are typically called **"moments of decision."** It does not matter what the frame or content of each particular decision is. It all devolves, in the end, into just two roads before you, *every time*. **One** will lead to *less* gratitude, *less* kindness, *less* forgiveness, *less* honesty, or *less* love in the world. **The other** will lead to *more* gratitude, *more* kindness, *more* forgiveness, *more* honesty, or *more* love in the world. Your Mission, each moment, is to seek to choose the latter spiritual road, rather than the former, *every time*.

Comment 3:
Some Examples of This Step-by-Step Mission

I will give a few examples, so that the nature of this part of your Mission may be unmistakably clear.

You are out on the freeway in your car. Someone has gotten into the wrong lane, to the right of *your* lane, and needs to move over into the lane you are in. You *see* their need to cut in, ahead of you. **Decision time.** In your mind's eye you see two spiritual roads lying before you: the one leading to less kindness in the world (you speed up, to shut this driver out, and don't let them move over), the other leading to more kindness in the world (you let the driver cut in). **Since you know this is part of your Mission, part of the reason why you came to Earth, your calling is clear. You know which road to take, which decision to make.**

You are hard at work at your desk, when suddenly an interruption comes. The phone rings, or someone is at the door. They need something from you, a question of some of your time and attention. **Decision time.** In your mind's eye you see two spiritual roads lying before you: the one leading to less love in the world (you tell them you're just too busy to be bothered), the other leading to more love in the world (you put aside your work, decide that God may have sent this person to you, and say, "Yes, what can I do to help you?"). **Since you know this is part of your Mission, part of the reason why you came to Earth, your calling is clear. You know which road to take, which decision to make.**

Your mate does something that hurts your feelings. **Decision time.** In your mind's eye you see two spiritual roads lying before you: the one leading to less forgiveness in the world (you institute an icy silence between the two of you, and think of how you can punish them or otherwise get even), the other leading to more forgiveness in the world (you go over and take them in your arms, speak the truth about your hurt feelings, and assure them of your love). **Since you know this is part of your Mission, part of the reason why you came to Earth, your calling is clear. You know which road to take, which decision to make.**

You have not behaved at your most noble recently. And now you are face-to-face with someone who asks you a question about what happened. **Decision time.** In your mind's eye you see two spiritual roads lying before you: the one leading to less honesty in the world (you lie about what happened, or what you were feeling, because you fear losing their respect or their love), the other leading to more honesty in the world (you tell the truth, together with how you feel about it, in retrospect). **Since you know this is part of your Mission, part of the reason why you came to Earth, your calling is clear. You know which road to take, which decision to make.**

Comment 4:
The Spectacle That Makes the Angels Laugh

It is necessary to explain this part of our Mission in some detail, because so many times you will see people wringing their hands and saying, *"I want to know what my Mission in life is,"* all the while they are cutting people off on the highway, refusing to give time to people, punishing their mate for having hurt their feelings, and lying about what they did. And it will seem to you that the angels must laugh to see this spectacle. *For these people wringing their hands*, their Mission was right there, on the freeway, in the interruption, in the hurt, and at the confrontation.

Comment 5:
The Valley Versus the Mountaintop

At some point in your life your Mission may involve some grand *mountaintop experience*, where you say to yourself, "This, this, is why I came into the world. I know it. I know it." *But until then*, your Mission is here in *the valley*, and the fog, and the little callings moment by moment, day by day. More to the point, it is likely you cannot ever get to your mountaintop Mission unless you have first exercised your stewardship faithfully in the valley.

It is an ancient principle, to which Jesus alluded often, that if you don't use the information the Universe has already given you, you cannot expect it will give you any more. If you aren't being faithful in small things, how can you expect to be given charge over larger things? (Luke 16:10–12, 19:11–24). If you aren't trying to bring more gratitude, kindness, forgiveness, honesty, and love into the world each day, you can hardly expect that you will be entrusted with the Mission to help bring peace into the world or anything else large and important. If we do not live out our day-by-day Mission in the valley, we cannot expect we are yet ready for a larger *mountaintop* Mission.

Comment 6:
The Importance of Not Thinking of
This Mission as "Just a Training Camp"

The valley is not just a kind of "training camp." There is in your imagination even now an invisible *spiritual* mountaintop to which you may go, if you wish to see where all this is leading. And what will you see there, in the imagination of your heart, but the goal toward which all this is pointed: **that Earth might be more like heaven. That human life might be more like God's**. That is the large achievement toward which all our day-by-day Missions *in the valley* are moving. This is a *large* order, but it is accomplished by faithful attention to the doing of our great Creator's will in little things as well as in large. It is much like the building of the pyramids in Egypt, which was accomplished by the dragging of a lot of individual pieces of stone by a lot of individual men.

The valley, the fog, the going step-by-step, is no mere training camp. The goal is real, however large. **"Thy Kingdom come, Thy will be done, on Earth, as it is in heaven."**

Some Random Comments About Your Third Mission in Life

Your third Mission here on Earth is one that is uniquely yours, and that is:

a. to exercise the Talent that you particularly came to Earth to use—your greatest gift that you most delight to use,

b. in those place(s) or setting(s) that God has caused to appeal to you the most,

c. and for those purposes that God most needs to have done in the world.

Comment 1: Our Mission Is Already Written, "in Our Members"

It is customary in trying to identify this part of our Mission, to advise that we should ask God, in prayer, to speak to us—and tell us plainly what our Mission is. We look for a voice in the air, a thought in our head, a dream in the night, a sign in the events of the day, to reveal this thing that is otherwise (*it is said*) completely hidden. Sometimes, from just such answered prayer, people do indeed discover what their Mission is, beyond all doubt and uncertainty.

But having to wait for the voice of God to reveal what our Mission is, is not the truest picture of our situation. St. Paul, in Romans, speaks of a law "written in our members"—and this phrase has a telling application to the question of how God reveals to each of us our unique Mission in life. Read again the definition of our third Mission (above) and you will see: The clear implication of the definition is that God has **already** revealed His will to us concerning our vocation and Mission, by causing it to be **"written in our members."** We are to begin deciphering our unique Mission by studying our Talents and skills, and more particularly which ones (or one) we most rejoice to use.

God actually has written His will *twice* in our members: *first in the Talents* that He lodged there, and second *in His guidance of our heart*, as to which Talent gives us the greatest pleasure from its exercise (**it is usually the one that, when we use it, causes us to lose all sense of time**).

Even as the anthropologist can examine ancient inscriptions, and divine from them the daily life of a long-lost people, so we by examining **our Talents** and **our heart** can *more often than we dream* divine the Will of the Living God. For true it is, our Mission is not something He will reveal; it is something He **has already** revealed. It is not to be found written in the sky; it is to be found written in our members.

Comment 2:
Career Counseling—We Need You

Arguably, our first two Missions in life could be learned from religion alone—without any reference whatsoever to career counseling, the subject of this book. Why, then, should career counseling claim that this question about our Mission in life is its proper concern, *in any way?*

It is when we come to this third Mission, which hinges so crucially on the question of our Talents, skills, and gifts, that we see the answer. If you've read the body of this book, before turning to this section, then you know without my even saying it, how much the identification of Talents, gifts, or skills is the province of career counseling. Its expertise, indeed its *raison d'être*, lies precisely in the identification, classification, and (forgive me) "prioritization" of Talents, skills, and gifts. To put the matter quite simply, career counseling knows how to do this better than any other discipline—**including** traditional religion. This is not a defect of religion, but the fulfillment of something Jesus promised: "When the Spirit of truth comes, He will guide you into all truth" (John 16:13). Career counseling is part (we may hope) of that promised late-coming truth. It can therefore be of inestimable help to the pilgrim who is trying to figure out what their greatest, and most enjoyable, Talent is, as a step toward identifying their unique Mission in life.

If career counseling needs religion as its helpmate in the first two stages of identifying our Mission in life, then religion repays the compliment by clearly needing career counseling as its helpmate here in the third stage.

And this place where you are in your life right now—facing the job-hunt and all its anxiety—is the perfect time to seek the union within your own mind and heart of both career counseling (as in the pages of this book) and your faith in God.

Comment 3:
How Our Mission Got Chosen—
A Scenario for the Romantic

It is a mystery that we cannot fathom, in this life at least, as to why one of us has this Talent, and the other one has that; why God chose to give one gift—and Mission—to one person, and a different gift—and Mission—to another. Since we do not know, and in some degree cannot know, we are certainly left free to speculate, and imagine.

We may imagine that before we came to Earth, our souls, *our Breath, our Light*, stood before the great Creator and volunteered for this Mission. And God and we, together, chose what that Mission would be and what particular gifts would be needed, which He then agreed to give us, after our birth. Thus, our Mission was not a command given preemptorily by an unloving Creator to a reluctant slave without a vote, but was a task jointly designed by us both, in which as fast as the great Creator said, "I wish" our hearts responded, **"Oh, yes."** As mentioned in an earlier comment, it may be helpful to think of the condition of our becoming human as that we became amnesiac about any consciousness our soul had before birth—and therefore amnesiac about the nature or manner in which our Mission was designed.

Our searching for our Mission now is therefore a searching to recover the memory of something we ourselves had a part in designing.

I am admittedly a hopeless romantic, so of course I like this picture. If you also are a hopeless romantic, you may like it, too. There's also the chance that it just may be true. We will not know until we see Him face-to-face.

Comment 4:
Mission as Intersection

There are all different kinds of voices calling you to all different kinds of work, and the problem is to find out which is the voice of God rather than that of society, say, or the superego, or self-interest. By and large a good rule for finding out is this: The kind of work God usually calls you to is the kind of work (a) that you need most to do and (b) the world most needs to have done. If you really get a kick out of your work, you've presumably met requirement *a*, but if your work is writing TV deodorant commercials, the chances are you've missed requirement *b*. On the other hand, if your work is being a doctor in a leper colony, you have probably met *b*, but if most of the time you're bored and depressed by it, the chances are you haven't only bypassed *a* but probably aren't helping your patients much either. Neither the hair shirt nor the soft birth will do. **The place God calls you to is the place where your deep gladness and the world's deep hunger meet.**

—FRED BUECHNER, *Wishful Thinking—A Theological ABC*

Excerpted from *Wishful Thinking—A Theological ABC* by Frederick Buechner, revised edition published by HarperOne. Copyright © 1973, 1993 by Frederick Buechner.

Comment 5:
Examples of Mission as Intersection

Your unique and individual Mission will most likely turn out to be a mission of Love, acted out in one or all of three arenas: either in the Kingdom of the Mind, whose goal is to bring more Truth into the world; or in the Kingdom of the Heart, whose goal is to bring more Beauty into the world; or in the Kingdom of the Will, whose goal is to bring more Perfection into the world, through Service.

Here are some examples:

"My mission is, out of the rich reservoir of love that God seems to have given me, to nurture and show love to others— most particularly to those who are suffering from incurable diseases."

"My mission is to draw maps for people to show them how to get to God."

"My mission is to create the purest foods I can, to help people's bodies not get in the way of their spiritual growth."

"My mission is to make the finest harps I can so that people can hear the voice of God in the wind."

"My mission is to make people laugh, so that the travail of this earthly life doesn't seem quite so hard to them."

"My mission is to help people know the truth, in love, about what is happening out in the world, so that there will be more honesty in the world."

"My mission is to weep with those who weep, so that in my arms they may feel themselves in the arms of that Eternal Love that sent me and that created them."

"My mission is to create beautiful gardens, so that in the lilies of the field people may behold the Beauty of God and be reminded of the Beauty of Holiness."

Comment 6:
Life as Long as Your Mission Requires

Knowing that you came to Earth for a reason, and knowing what that Mission is, throws an entirely different light upon your life from now on. You are, generally speaking, delivered from any further fear about how long you have to live. You may settle it in your heart that you are here until God chooses to think that you have accomplished your Mission, or until God has a greater Mission for you in another Realm. You need to be a good steward of what He has given you, while you are here; but you do not need to be an anxious steward or stewardess.

You need to attend to your health, *but you do not need to constantly worry about it*. You need to meditate on your death, *but you do not need to be constantly preoccupied with it*. To paraphrase the glorious words of G. K. Chesterton: **"We now have a strong desire for living combined with a strange carelessness about dying. We desire life like water and yet are ready to drink death like wine."** We know that we are here to do what we came to do, and we need not worry about anything else.

Comment 7:
Using Internet Resources

There is a website that deals with news, etc., about all faiths, which you may want to look at: www.beliefnet.com.

Then there is a Jesuit site that leads you in a daily meditation for ten minutes or more (in more than twenty languages with a visual, but otherwise no sound or distraction): http://sacredspace.ie.

There is also a site that gives you a daily podcast of church bells, music, Scripture reading, and meditations or homily, with no visuals, but with sound, and an audio MP3 file that can be sent to your phone, computer, etc.: www.pray-as-you-go.org.

There is a site dedicated to helping you keep a divine consciousness 24/7, by helping you link up to other people of faith, through prayer circles, sharing of personal stories of faith, etc., aimed especially, but not exclusively, toward young adults. Its ultimate message: you are not alone: www.24-7prayer.com/communities.

Last, there is a site dedicated to helping you find a spiritual counselor (or "spiritual director"), as well as retreat centers, in the Christian, Islamic, Buddhist, Jewish, or Interfaith faiths: www.sdiworld.org.

Final Comment:
A Job-Hunt Done Well

If you approach your job-hunt as an opportunity to work on this issue as well as the issue of how you will keep body and soul together, then hopefully your job-hunt will end with your being able to say "Life has deep meaning to me now. I have discovered more than my ideal job; I have found my Mission, and the reason why I am here on Earth."

APPENDIX B

A Guide to Dealing with Your Feelings While Out of Work

Unemployment can take a terrible toll upon the human spirit. In a study of more than six thousand job-hunters, interviewed every week for up to twenty-four weeks, it was found that

> *many workers become discouraged the longer they are unemployed.*
> *In particular, the unemployed express feeling more sad the longer*
> *they are unemployed, and sadness rises more quickly with*
> *unemployment duration during episodes of job search. In addi-*
> *tion, reported life satisfaction is lower for the same individual*
> *following days in which comparatively more time was devoted to*
> *job search. . . . These findings suggest that the psychological cost*
> *of job search rises the longer someone is unemployed. . . . One*
> *reason why job search assistance may have been found to consis-*
> *tently speed individuals' return to work in past studies is that*
> *it may help the unemployed to overcome feelings of anxiety and*
> *sadness that are associated with job search.*[1]

---

1. Alan B. Krueger and Andreas Mueller, "Job Search, Emotional Well-Being and Job Finding in a Period of Mass Unemployment: Evidence from High-Frequency Longitudinal Data," *Brookings Papers on Economic Activity*, March 8, 2011.

I know the truth of this from my own experience. I have been fired twice in my life. I remember how it felt each time I got the lousy news. I walked out of the building dazed, as though I had just emerged from a really bad train wreck. The sun was shining brightly, not a cloud in the sky; and, since it was lunch hour, as it happened, the streets were filled with laughing happy people, who apparently had not a care in the world.

I remember thinking, "The world has just caved—my world at least. How can all these people act as though nothing has happened?"

And I remember the feelings. The overwhelming feelings, that only intensified in the weeks after that. Describe my state however you want—feeling sad, being in a funk, feeling despair, feeling hopeless, feeling like things "will always be this way," or feeling depressed—it doesn't matter. I was terribly unhappy. Unemployment was rocking my soul to its foundations. I needed to know what to do about my feelings.

I have since learned that my experience was not the least unusual. Many of us, if not most of us, when we are out of work for a long time feel weary and depressed.[2] Our greatest desire is to get rid of these depressed feelings. After talking to thousands of job-hunters, I think there are:

Ten Things We Can Do
to Deal with Our Feelings,
When We Are Unemployed

1. We can catch up on our sleep, even if it means we have to take naps during the day because our attempt to sleep at nighttime is, at the moment, a disaster. We tend to feel depressed if we are short on our sleep, or our body is otherwise run-down.

---

2. Serious clinical depression often has a lifelong history, and requires treatment, particularly when a person is feeling endangering impulses, such as suicide. In such a case, you should seek competent psychological or psychiatric help. (For immediate help, this minute, call 1-800-273-8255 or go online to www.suicidepreventionlifeline.org. There are counselors 24/7 at both places who deal with anyone, including the military or veterans, in trouble.)

There are two states that can be easily confused:

First of all, the world never looks bright or happy to us when we are very short on sleep.

Second, the world never looks bright or happy to us when we are feeling depressed.

It is therefore easy to confuse the two feeling-states. Over the years, I have seen many job-hunters who first thought they were really depressed over their situation later discover they were really depressed just because they were so tired. Or a bit of both. Anyway, sleep or nap, we often turn into happier, more upbeat people, just by catching up on our sleep. This can make us feel better—sometimes much better.

2. There are other things that we can do to keep ourselves more physically fit while unemployed. Job-hunters have told me they found it important to:

  • get regular exercise, involving a daily walk;

  • drink plenty of water each day (this seems silly, but I found out we tend to skip the water, and get dehydrated, when we're out of work);

  • eliminate sugar as much as possible from the diet;

  • take supplementary vitamins daily (no matter how many doctors and nutritionists try to tell us that we already get enough from our daily food);

  • eat balanced meals (not just pig out on junk food in front of the telly);

  • and all that other stuff that our mothers always told us to do.

3. We can do something about the physical space around us. Our surroundings often mirror how we feel about ourselves. If our physical environment looks like a disaster area, that in itself can make us depressed. When we are unemployed, we can vow we will live simpler—something that maybe we've wanted to do for a long time. We can begin by taking care that each time we handle a thing, we take it all the way to its new destination; we don't just drop it on the counter, thinking that we will deal with it later. We can take care that when we take our clothes off at night, we

don't just drop them on the floor, but hang them up or put them in a laundry hamper. And that, when we finish eating, we put the dishes where they are going to be washed, and put our food back in the refrigerator. And we can determine that when we do such things as get a screwdriver out, to fix a screw that's dropped out of something, we take the screwdriver all the way back to the toolbox or wherever its final destination is. And so on.

When we determine to always put our things away in a timely fashion, neatness will start to appear in our physical environment; this can help lift our spirits immensely, as our physical space mirrors an upbeat life.

4. We can get outdoors daily and take a good walk. Hiding in our cave (figuratively speaking) will only make us feel more *down*. Seeing green trees (in season), sunlight, mountains, flowers, people, will do our heart good, each day.

5. We can focus on other people and their problems—not just our own. If our unemployment is dragging on and on, and we're starting to have a lot of time on our hands, we can find someplace in town that is dealing with people worse off than we are, and go volunteer there. I'm talking food banks, hospitals, housing aid, anything dealing with kids—especially deprived kids, or kids with tremendous disabilities—that sort of thing. We can do a search on Google, put in the name of our town or city plus the name of the problem we want to help with, and see what turns up. If we determine to help someone else in need while we're unemployed, we won't feel so discarded by society.

And speaking of other people, we can renew our acquaintance with old friends. We can explore the friendships we already have, not because they are useful in our job-hunt but just because they are valuable human beings. Theologian Phillips Brooks used to say there are two kinds of exploration: one involves going out to explore new country; the other involves digging down more deeply into the country we already occupy. Do both, when you're feeling *down*.

6. We can go on fun mini-adventures. Often there are portions of our surroundings that we have never explored, but a tourist

would "hit" on the very first day they were there. I lived in New York City for a long time; never once went up in the Empire State Building. I lived in San Francisco for years; never once went out to the Zoo. You get the point. If I lived in either of these cities today, and was unemployed for any length of time, I would set out to visit places I'd never seen. We can stop obsessing about how much we lost from our past, and turn our face toward the future. There are new worlds to conquer, after all.

7. We can deal with our feelings by expanding our mental horizons, and learning something new. We can go read up on subjects that have always interested us, but we've never had enough time to explore. While we're unemployed, we have the time. Visit your local public library for books, CDs, DVDs, and online resources. If we can't think of any subject, there's always the human mind. The mind, after all, is what is trying hard to figure out what we should do next. The more we understand it, the better we can heal. If you're looking for suggestions, I'd read anything by Martin Seligman. There's *Learned Optimism: How to Change Your Mind and Your Life*, which, as one reviewer commented, "vaulted me out of my funk." It has excellent chapters on dealing with depression. Or there's Seligman's 2012 book, *Flourish: A Visionary New Understanding of Happiness and Well-Being*. Psychologist David Burns's excellent book, *Feeling Good: The New Mood Therapy*, has been clinically proven to improve both depression and anxiety. If you want to delve into improving your memory, there's Joshua Foer's *Moonwalking with Einstein: The Art and Science of Remembering Everything*. And, last but not least, if you want to learn more about how one mind influences another mind, there is Robert B. Cialdini's *Influence: The Psychology of Persuasion*. All these authors have extensive videos on YouTube.

Speaking of videos, there are a million *free* videos online, where you can learn just about anything. In addition to videos, there are videocasts, webcasts, podcasts, and every other kind of *-cast*. You can type the word *webcast*, plus the subject in which you are interested, into your favorite browser, like Google, and then pick through whatever turns up. There are also, of course, books. From online bookstores, there are tons of eBooks available, running around ten bucks, or a little more. You can also enroll in low-cost online classes through Udemy (www.udemy.com).

8. We can talk, talk, talk with our loved ones, or a close friend, about all the feelings we have. It's amazing how giving voice to thoughts and feelings, particularly when we don't much care for those thoughts and those feelings, causes them to lose their power over us. So we should do it, because otherwise stuff bottled up inside us tends to fester and grow. We don't want that. We must just take care that we don't pick *the town gossip* to confide in, nor a friend or loved one who just can't keep their mouth shut. You know who they are.

9. We can pound a punching bag or even some pillows, to get some of the angry energy out of us. It's astonishing how many of the unemployed have told me this actually helps them get rid of some of their anger. And this helps lift our depression as well. Sometimes feeling *down*, and feeling *angry* seem almost to be two different sides of the same coin. If we don't have a gym in our life we can build one at home, simply by putting a pile of pillows on top of our bed, and then pounding the pillows repeatedly, as hard as we can—without breaking anything in our hands, wrists, or arms. This often really helps. We are strange creatures.

10. We can make a list each day of the things that make us grateful, glad, or even happy, day by day. There is a habit of mind that is deadly while we're out of work, and that is spending too much of our day, every day, brooding about what is wrong in our lives: what is wrong with people, what is wrong with our situation, what is wrong with anything and everything. By listing three things we are thankful for, we teach ourselves to focus on what precious gifts we still have at the end of the day, whether they be intelligence, health, or love.

If we want to get over being depressed, it is crucial that we give up endless complaint, it is crucial that we come to forgiveness for any past wrongs done to us, it is crucial that we, as Baltasar Gracián put it, "Get used to the failings of our friends, family, and acquaintances." We are all human. We are all capable of turning our face toward the future, rather than toward the past.

A Guide to Choosing a Career Coach or Counselor

All readers of this book divide into two families, or groups. The first group are those who find the book is all they need, particularly if they do the exercises in chapter 5 successfully, on their own.

The second group are those who find they need a little bit of extra help. Either they bog down in their effort to complete the whole book, or they start the exercises in chapter 5 and then get stuck, at some point. So they want some additional help.

If You Decide You Need One

Fortunately, there are a lot of people out there, anxious to help you with your job-hunt or career-change, in case this book isn't sufficient by itself. They go by various names: career coach, career counselor, career development specialist, you name it. They're willing to help you for a fee—because this is how they make their living. That fee will usually equal the fee charged by other types of counselors in town, say, a good psychologist. That will range from about $40 an hour in rural areas, on up to . . . *you don't want to know*. The fee may be charged by the hour (recommended) or as one large lump sum up front (definitely not recommended). And most towns or cities of any size have free or almost-free help, too, even though it's likely to be in a group and not face-to-face with an individual counselor.

Now, about those coaches or counselors who charge to help you. There are some simply excellent ones out there. In fact, I wish I could say that *everyone* who hangs out a sign in this business could be completely recommended. But—alas! and alack!—they can't all be. This career-coaching or career-counseling field is largely unregulated. And even where there is some kind of certification, resulting in their being able to put a lot of degree-soundin' initials after their name, that doesn't really tell you much. It means a lot *to them* of course; in many cases, they purchased those initials with their blood, sweat, and tears. (*Although a few, sad to say, got the initials after their name by mail order or after one long weekend of training. Tsk, tsk. But, oh well, no different I suppose from a lot of other professions. Some people are always looking for shortcuts.*)

I used to try to explain what all those initials meant. There is a veritable alphabet soup of them, with new ones born every year. But no more; I've learned, from more than forty years of experience in this field, that 99.4 percent of all job-hunters and career-changers don't care a fig about these initials. All they want to know is, *Do you know how to help me find a job?* Or, more specifically, *Do you know how to help me find my dream job—one that matches the gifts, skills, and experience that I have, one that makes me excited to get up in the morning, and excited to go to bed at night, knowing I helped make this Earth a little better place to be in? If so, I'll hire you. If not, I'll fire you.*

How to Lose Your Money

So, *bye-bye initials!* Let us start, instead, with this basic truth. *All coaches and counselors divide basically into three groups:*

a. those who are honest, compassionate, and caring, and know what they're doing;

b. those who are honest but don't know what they're doing; and

c. those who are dishonest, and merely want your money—large amounts, in a lump sum, and up front. These are often so-called executive counseling firms—*some* executive counseling firms—rather than individual counselors.

In other words, you've got compassionate, caring people in the same field with scam artists. Your job, if you want help and don't want to waste your money, is to learn how to distinguish the one from the other.

It would help, of course, if someone could just give you a list of those who are firmly in the first category—honest and know what they're doing. But unfortunately, no one (including me) has such a list, or ever has had. You've got to do your own homework or research here, and your own interviewing, in your chosen geographical area. *And if you're too lazy to take the time and trouble to do this research, you will deserve what you get.*

Why is it that *you* and only *you* can do this particular research? Well, let's say a friend tells you to go see so-and-so. He's a wonderful coach or counselor, but unhappily when you meet him he reminds you of your Uncle Harry, whom you detest. Bummer! But, no one except you knows that you've always disliked your Uncle Harry.

> That's why no one else can do this research for you—because the real question is not "Who is best?" but "Who is best for you?" Those last two words demand that it be you who "makes the call."

A special word, here, to those considering paying any firm that focuses on executives or people who make or would like to make a high salary. (This warning is regarding *firms*, not *individual* counselors.) If you are an executive, you are considered a fair target for any scam the mind can imagine. New ones appear every year. I have consulted with the Federal Trade Commission in Washington, and States Attorneys General over the years, where they have described the scams to me in detail. I have collected news items, done individual interviews with those who got "taken," and I wish I could tell you about individual firms, but that's not my job. Do your own research. If you are considering signing up with any such firm, Google them first: you will come across timely research about *any* firm. Example: http://corcodilos.com/blog/3219/theladders-how-the-scam-works-2. If you are too lazy to do this research, and subsequently get "taken," let me share the words a Scotsman once said to me, when I got "taken": *"I'm sorry ya lost yer money, but ya dinna do your homework."*

Now, for all my other readers: your dilemma is between categories *a* and *b* on page 291. How do you find an honest counselor *who knows what they're doing,* and can give you a little bit of help, if you bog down in using this book, most especially with chapter 5?

The first bright idea that will occur to you might be something along the lines of, "Well, I'll just see who Bolles recommends." Sorry, no such luck. I rarely if ever recommend anyone. Some of the coaches or counselors listed on my website try to claim that their very listing here constitutes a recommendation from me. Oh, come on! They're there because they asked to be. I ask a few questions, but I don't have time to do any thorough research on them. The online sampler is more akin to the Yellow Pages than it is to *Consumer Reports.* Let me repeat this—as I have for forty years now—and repeat it very loudly:

> The listing of a career counselor or coach on my website does NOT constitute an endorsement or recommendation by me. Never has meant that. Never will. (Any counselor or coach listed here who claims that it does—either in their ads, or brochures, or publicity—gets permanently removed from the site the following year after I find out about it, and without warning.) This is not "a hall of fame"; it is just a *Sampler* of names of those *who have* asked *to be listed, who have answered some reasonable questions, and who have some familiarity with the Parachute process.*

Consider the listings as just a starting point for your search. You must check them out. You must do your own homework. You must do your own research.

A Guide to Choosing a
Good Career Coach

So, how do you go about this research toward the goal of finding a good career coach or counselor, if you decide you need more help than this book can give you? Well, you start by collecting three names of career coaches or counselors in your geographical area.

How do you find those names? Several ways.

First, you can get names from your friends: ask if any of them have ever used a career coach or counselor. And if so, did they like 'em? And if so, what is that coach's or counselor's name? And how do you get in touch with them, so you can ask them some questions before deciding whether you want to sign up with them, or not?

The good news here, of course, is the Internet. You can discover career coaches, counselors, and psychologists through an online search. They don't even have to be in your local area—many conduct their individual and group sessions through Skype or on the phone. You can check Yelp (www.yelp.com) listings for reviews; just remember that not all reviews will be accurate (just like a friend's recommendation) for you. You can also Google their name to see what shows up—everything from their LinkedIn account (they should have one!) to other rating sites. Finally, you can check with licensing or certification boards to verify credentials.

Once you have three names, it's time to go do some comparison shopping. You want to talk with all three of them and decide which of the three (if any) you want to hook up with.

What will this initial interview cost you, with each coach or counselor? The answer to that is easy: when first setting up an appointment, *ask*. You do have the right to inquire ahead of time how much they are going to have to charge you for the exploratory interview.

Some—a few—will charge you nothing for the initial interview. One of the brightest counselors I know says this: *I don't like to charge for the first interview because I want to be free to tell them I can't help them, if for some reason we just don't hit it off.*

However, do not expect that most coaches or counselors can afford to give you this exploratory interview for nothing! If they did that, and got a lot of requests like yours, they would never make a living.

If this is not an individual counselor, but *a firm* trying to sell you a "pay-me-first" package *up front*, I guarantee they will give you the initial interview for free. They plan to use that "intake" interview (as they call it) to sell you a much more expensive program. They will even ask you to bring your spouse or partner along. (If they can't persuade one of you, maybe they can persuade the other.)

The Questions to Ask

When you are face-to-face or on the phone with the coach or counselor, you ask each of them the same questions, listed on the form below. (Keep a little pad, notebook, or smartphone with you, so you can write down their answers.)

After completing the conversations, look over your notes that evening, and compare those places. A chart like this, drawn in your notebook, may help:

MY SEARCH FOR A GOOD CAREER COUNSELOR

Questions I Will Ask Them	Answer from Counselor #1	Answer from Counselor #2	Answer from Counselor #3
1. What is your program?			
2. Who will be counseling? And how long has this person been counseling?			
3. What training/ education/ certification does this person have?			
4. What is your success rate?			
5. What is the cost of your services?			
6. Is there a contract up front? If so, may I see it please, and take it home with me?			

You need to decide (a) whether you want **none** of the three, or (b) **one** of the three (and if so, which one).

Remember, you don't have to choose *any* of the three coaches, if you didn't really care for any of them. If that is the case, go choose three more names from your Internet search or wherever, dust off the notebook, and go out again. It may take a few more hours to find what you want. **But the wallet, the purse, the job-hunt, and the life you save will be your own**.

As you look over your notes, you will soon realize there is no definitive way for you to determine a career coach's intentions. It's something you'll have to *smell out*, as you go along. But here are some clues.

Bad Vibes, On Up to Really Bad Vibes

If they give you the feeling that everything will be done for you, by them (*including interpretation of tests, and decision making about what this means you should do, or where you should do it*)—rather than asserting that you are going to have to do almost all the work, with their basically being your coach,

(Give them 15 bad points)

You want to learn how to do this for yourself; you're going to be job-hunting again, you know. That's the nature of our world today. Job-hunting is a repetitive activity in human life.

If you don't like the counselor, period!

(Give them 150 bad points)

I don't care what their expertise is, if you don't like them, you're going to have a rough time getting what you want. I guarantee it. Rapport is everything.

If you ask how long this particular counselor has been doing this, and they get huffy or give a double-barreled answer, such as, "I've had eighteen years' experience in the business and career counseling world,"

(Give them 20 bad points)

What that may mean is: seventeen and a half years as a fertilizer salesman, and one half year doing career counseling. Persist: "How long have you been with this firm, and how long have you been doing formal career coaching or counseling, as you are here?" You don't want someone who's brand-new to advising job-hunters. They may call this "their practice," but what they mean is that they are practicing . . . on you.

If they try to answer the question of their experience by pointing to their degrees or credentials,

(Give them 3 bad points)

Degrees or credentials tell you they've passed certain tests of their qualifications, but often these tests bear more on their expertise at career assessment than on their knowledge of creative job-hunting.

If, when you ask about that firm's success rate, they say they have never had a client who failed to find a job, no matter what,

(Give them 500 bad points)

They're lying. I have studied career counseling programs for more than forty years, have attended many, have studied records at state and federal offices, and have hardly ever seen a program that placed more than 86 percent of their clients, tops, in their best years. And it goes downhill from there. A prominent executive counseling firm was reported by the Attorney General's Office of New York State to have placed only 38 out of 550 clients (a 93 percent failure rate). On the other hand, if they make it clear that they have had a good success rate, but if you fail to work hard at the whole process, then there is no guarantee you are going to find a job, give them three stars.

If any counselor shows you letters from ecstatically happy former clients, but when you ask to talk to some of those clients, you get stonewalled,

(Give them 200 bad points)

Here is a job-hunter's letter about his experience with an executive counseling firm he was considering:

> *I asked to speak to a former client or clients. You would have thought I asked to speak to Elvis. The counselor stammered and stuttered and gave me a million excuses why I couldn't talk to some of these "satisfied" former clients. None of the excuses sounded legitimate to me. We went back and forth for about thirty minutes. Finally, he excused himself and went to speak to his boss, the owner. The next thing I knew I was called into the owner's office for a more "personal" sales pitch. We spoke for about forty-five minutes as he tried to convince me to use his service. When I told him I was not ready to sign up, he became angry and asked my counselor why I had been put before "the committee" if I wasn't ready to commit? The counselor claimed*

*I had given a verbal commitment at our last meeting. The owner
then turned to me and said I seemed to have a problem making a
decision and that he did not want to do business with me. I was
shocked. They had turned the whole story around to make it look
like it was my fault. I felt humiliated. In retrospect, the whole
process felt like dealing with a used car salesman. They used
pressure tactics and intimidation to try to get what they wanted.
As you have probably gathered, more than anything else this
experience made me angry.*

If you are dealing with a career counseling firm, and you ask what
is the cost of their services, and they reply that it is a lump sum that
must all be paid "up front" before you start or shortly after you start,
all at once or in rapid installments,

(Give them 300 bad points)

*We're talking about firms here, not the average individual counselor or
coach. The basic problem with firms is that both "the good guys" and "the
crooks" do this. The good guys operate on the theory that if you give them
a large sum up front, you will then be really committed to the program. The
crooks operate on the theory that if you give them a large sum up front, they
don't have to give you anything back, except endless excuses and subterfuge,
after a certain date (quickly reached).*

And the trouble is that there is absolutely no way for you to distinguish crook from good guy, at first impression; they only reveal their
true nature after they've got all your money. And by that time, you have
no legal way to get it back, no matter what they verbally promised.[1]

*Let me repeat: With firms that make you sign a contract and pay basically
up front, there is no way to distinguish the good guys from the crooks. The
only safe counseling is one with no contract, and you just pay for each hour,
as you use it.*

---

1. Sometimes the written contract—there is *always* a written contract, when you are dealing with
the bad guys, and they will probably ask your partner to sign it, too—will claim to provide for
an almost complete refund, at any time, until you reach a cutoff date in the program, which
the contract specifies. Unfortunately, fraudulent firms bend over backward to be extra nice,
extra available, and extra helpful to you, from the time you first walk in, until that cutoff point
is reached. Therefore, when the cutoff point for getting a refund has passed, you let it pass
because you are very satisfied with their past services, and believe there will be many more
weeks of the same. Only, there aren't. At fraudulent firms, once the cutoff point is passed,
the career counselor suddenly becomes virtually impossible for you to get ahold of. Call after
call will not be returned. You will say to yourself, "What happened?" Well, what happened, my
friend, is that you paid up in full, they have all the money they're ever going to get out of you,
and now, they want to move on.

I have tried for years to think of some way around this dilemma, to be fair to the good guys, but there just is none. So if you decide to pay up front, be sure it is money you can afford to lose.

If Money Is a Problem for You:
Hourly Coaching

Most career coaches or counselors charge by the hour. You pay only for each hour as you use it, according to their set rate. Each time you keep an appointment, you pay them at the end of that hour for their help, according to that rate. Period. Finis. You never owe them any money (unless you made an appointment and failed to keep it). You can stop seeing them at any time, if you feel you are not getting the help you wish. The fee varies *greatly*. It can range from $75 an hour on up to $350 an hour and beyond. It often keeps pace with the fees of psychiatrists or psychologists in that neck of the woods. Counselors in cities tend to charge more than counselors out in the country.

That fee is for *individual time* with the career coach or counselor. If you can't afford that fee, ask whether they also run groups. If they do, the fee will be much less. And, in one of those delightful ironies of life, since you get a chance to listen to problems that other job-hunters in your group are having, the group will often give you more help than an individual session with a counselor would have. Not always; but often. It's always ironic when *cheaper* and *more helpful* go hand in hand.

If the career counselor in question does offer groups, there should (again) never be a contract. The charge should be payable at the end of each session, and you should be able to drop out at any time, without further cost, if you decide you are not getting the help you want.

There are some career counselors who run free (or almost free) job-hunting workshops through local churches, synagogues, chambers of commerce, community colleges, adult education programs, and the like, as their community service or *pro bono* work (as it is technically called). I have had reports of workshops from a number of places in the US and Canada. They exist in other parts of the world as well. If money is a problem for you, in getting help with your job-hunt, ask around to see if workshops exist in your community. Your chamber of commerce will know, or your church or synagogue.

If Your Location Is a Problem for You: Distance-Coaching or -Counseling

The assumption, from the beginning, was that career counseling would always take place face-to-face. Both of you, counselor and job-hunter, together in the same room. Just like career counseling's close relatives: marriage counseling, or even AA.

Of course, a job-hunter might—on occasion—phone his or her counselor the day before an interview, to get some last-minute tips or to answer some questions that a prospective interviewer might ask, *tomorrow*.

What is different, today, is that in some cases, career counseling is being conducted exclusively over the phone or through Skype from start to finish. Some counselors now report that they haven't laid eyes on more than 90 percent of their clients, and wouldn't know them if they bumped into them on a street corner. I call this "distance-coaching or -counseling." This increasing availability of "distance-counseling" is good news, and bad news.

Why good news? You can be anywhere in the world, but as long as you have the Internet on your desk or in your hand, you can still connect with the best distance-counseling there is.

And the bad news? Well, just because a counselor or coach does distance-counseling doesn't mean they are really good at doing it. Some are superb; but some are not. So, you're still going to have to research any *distance-counselor* very carefully.

It is altogether too easy for a counselor to get sloppy doing distance-counseling—for example, browsing the newspapers while you are telling some long personal story, etc., to which they are giving only the briefest attention. (Of course, the increasingly wider use of video calling programs such as Skype may cure that!)

You must always remember that distance-counseling, attractive as it is for many, as necessary as it will be for some, definitely has limits.

To the caveman, the technology that enables all this to happen in this twenty-first century would be jaw-droppingly awesome. But, good career counseling or coaching *is not just about technology*. What is truly awesome, in the end, is our power to help each other on this Earth. And how much that power resides, not in techniques or technology—though these things are important—but in each of us just being a good human being. And a *loving* human being.

THE FINAL WORD

Notes from the Author

The focus of this book is not on me. It's on You. You are the heroes and heroines of this book. You are the ones who struggle to make life work, who tell me of your victories (and defeats). You are the inventive ones. You are the ones who tell me solutions to job-hunting or career-changing problems that puzzle me.

I know that this book demands a lot of every reader, just as life demands a lot of all of us, and I am amazed at how many of the more than ten million people who have bought this book (in one of its annual editions) are willing to sit down and do the hard work of the Self-Inventory in chapters 4 and 5.

It takes more than one person to create a book. My particular thanks go to Lisa Westmoreland and Marci M. Bolles. Lisa is an executive editor at Ten Speed Press and has helped greatly with the form and updating of this edition. And Marci has helped greatly with the typing of this manuscript.

My gratitude also to George Young for his help with updating my veterans handout.

This is a book about jobs, but more important it is a book about life and hope. I have learned that the secret of living is not to set as our goal a happy life, nor even a successful life (as the world measures "success"), but a victorious life, meeting the obstacles and challenges that life naturally throws into our path, and by grit, determination, and Grace, overcoming them all. And lucky those who find love on their journey. I quote from what a woman dying of ALS once said: "Throughout all this I have learned that the *only* thing that matters is love. When you live in love, everything else just falls into place." May you find such love in your life. I have, with my wonderful wife, Marci.

But there are others, too. Were it not for this book, and social media sites such as Facebook, I would never have met you, never have known so many valiant and courageous souls, as you have faced and faced down so many difficulties that might have defeated me. I don't just appreciate my readers; I admire my readers. You are such an inspiration to me.

I am a grateful man, and this is the place, each year, where I recite my litany of love and gratitude, for all the people in my life, past and present.

First of all, I am enchanted by every moment of my life that I get to spend with such a wondrous woman as my wife, Marci. I treasure her love, brains, wit, and caring. For example, back in 2014, I badly injured my back, while vacationing (*and tossing heavy luggage around*) over in Paris and the UK. Always in excellent health (until then), my recovery has been slow but steady. Marci (*coincidentally a licensed nurse*) has created the most loving, beautiful healing environment all around me, for which I shall ever be grateful. I'm grateful, too, for Marci's grown children from a previous marriage, Janice (Marcel) and Adlai (Aimee), and their kids, Logan and Aiden. They are wonderful to me.

I am grateful beyond measure for the family that brought me into this world. I had a really wonderful Mom and Dad, and I loved the brother I grew up with (famous reporter/martyr Don Bolles), and my one sister (Ann).

I am so grateful for my children—Stephen, Mark, Gary, and Sharon—and my grandchildren—all ten of them. We lost Mark in 2012 to a massive cerebral hemorrhage, at age fifty-eight. I wept over that, a lot. He lived with me for six out of the last twelve years of his life, and was the author of our book *Job-Hunting Online*. He was a treasure.

I am so grateful for my three remaining children and their families, plus their most-loving mother, my first wife, Jan, who shares in all our family gatherings.

As for friends—what would any of us do without our friends?— I want to express my gratitude for my dearest friend (*besides Marci*), Daniel Porot of Geneva, Switzerland—we taught together for two weeks every summer, for nineteen years; also for Dave Swanson, plus my international friends, Brian McIvor of Ireland; John Webb and Madeleine Leitner of Germany; Yves Lermusi, of Checkster fame, who came from Belgium; Pete Hawkins of Liverpool, England; Debra Angel MacDougall of Scotland; Byung Ju Cho of South Korea; Tom O'Neil of New Zealand; and, in this country, the late Howard Figler, beloved friend and coauthor of our manual for career counselors; Marty Nemko; Joel Garfinkle; Dick Knowdell; Rich Feller; Dick Gaither; Warren Farrell; Chuck Young; Susan Joyce; and the folks over at Ten Speed Press in Emeryville, California.

Of course, with the passage of time, friends do die. I think it is important to remember them, with deep gratitude for their lives well-lived. I still think of Howard Figler, whom we lost in February 2015. He was the coauthor with me of *The Career Counselor's Handbook* (second edition, 2007). He and I had years of fun writing together. We also lost Judi Grutter, expert on testing and assessments. She died in December of 2014. Prior to that, we lost Jay Conrad Levinson in October of 2013. He was the popular author of many books in the *Guerrilla Marketing* series. And prior to him, we lost my longtime publisher, Phil Wood, in December, 2010. He was my publisher from the day I first wrote *Parachute*; he was a dear man, and I owe him more than I can ever say for helping *Parachute* find its audience, and for letting me have great control over the annual editions. *Parachute* would never have sold more than ten million copies, as it has, if it were not for him.

I much appreciate the staff over at Ten Speed, whom I know best there, including Aaron Wehner (Publisher), Lisa Westmoreland (Executive Editor and *my* best editor *ever*), Ashley Pierce, Mari Gill, Chris Barnes, and George Young. And again, my special thanks to my readers for buying my books, trusting my counsel, and following your dream.

In concluding my litany of gratitude, I must be sure to include our Creator. It is not fashionable these days to talk about one's faith, but I'm going to do it anyway. I am very quiet about my faith; it's just . . . there. But I want to quietly acknowledge that it is the source of whatever grace, wisdom, or compassion I have ever found, or shared with others. I have all my life been a committed Christian, a devoted follower of Jesus Christ, and an Episcopalian/Anglican. (I was an ordained priest in that Church for fifty years.) I thank my Creator every night for such a life, such a wonderful mission, as He has given me: to help millions of people make their lives really count for something, as we all go spinning through space, here on Spaceship Earth.

A Grammar and Language Note

I want to explain four points of grammar, in this book of mine: pronouns, commas and colons, italics, and spelling. My unorthodox use of them invariably offends unemployed English teachers so much that instead of finishing the book, they immediately write to apply for a job as my editor.

Let me explain. Throughout this book, I often use the apparently plural pronouns "they," "them," and "their" after singular antecedents—such as, "You must approach someone for a job and tell them what you can do." This sounds strange and even wrong to those who know English well. To be sure, we all know there is another pronoun—"you"—that may be either singular or plural, but few of us realize that the pronouns "they," "them," and "their" were also once treated as both plural and singular in the English language. This changed, at a time in English history when agreement in number became more important than agreement as to gender. Today, however, our priorities have shifted once again. Now, the distinguishing of gender is considered by many to be more important than agreement in number.

The common artifices used for this new priority, such as "s/he," or "he and she," are—to my mind—tortured and inelegant. Casey Miller and Kate Swift, in their classic *The Handbook of Nonsexist Writing* agree, and argue that it is time to bring back the earlier usage of "they," "them," and "their" as both singular and plural—just as "you" is/are. They further argue that this return to the earlier historical usage has already become quite common out on the street—witness a typical sign by the ocean that reads, "Anyone using this beach after 5 p.m. does so at their own risk." I have followed Casey and Kate's wise recommendations in all of this.

As for my commas and colons, they are deliberately used according to my own rules—rather than according to the rules of historic grammar (which I did learn—I hastily add, to reassure my old Harvard professors, who despaired of me weekly, during English class). In spite of those rules, I follow my own, which are: to write conversationally, and put in a comma or colon wherever I would normally stop for a breath, were I speaking the same line.

The same conversational rule applies to my use of italics. This book is a conversation: I'm sitting down with you to tell you what I know. Conversations have rhythms. You emphasize a word here, you speak a word softly there. There are pauses. The speed of one sentence sometimes changes from the previous. All of this is difficult to reproduce in print, if all the text looks equal. So I use italics, I use dashes, I use parentheses, I use color, etc., to reproduce in print—as much as I can—the rhythms of natural speech.

Finally, I guess some of my spelling (and capitalization) is weird. (You say "weird"; I say "playful.") Fortunately, since this is my own book, I get to play by my own peculiar inclinations and playfulness; I'm just grateful that ten million readers have gone along. Nothing delights a child (at heart) more, than being found at play.

—Dick Bolles

PS Over the last forty years, a few critics have complained that this book is too complicated in its vocabulary and grammar for anyone except a college graduate. Two readers, however, have written me with a different view.

The first one, from England, said there is an index that analyzes a book to tell you what grade in school you must have finished, in order to be able to understand it. My book's index, he said, turned out to be 6.1, which means you need only have finished sixth grade in a US school in order to understand it.

Here in the US, a college instructor came up with a similar finding. He phoned me to tell me that my book was rejected by the authorities as a proposed text for the college course he was teaching, because (they said) the book's language/grammar was not up to college level. "What level was it?" I asked. "Well," he replied, "when they analyzed it, it turned out to be written on an eighth-grade level."

Sixth or eighth grade—that seems just about right to me. Why make job-hunting complicated, when it can be expressed so simply even a child could understand it?

About the Author

DICK BOLLES—more formally known as Richard Nelson Bolles—led the career development field for more than four decades. He was featured in *Time*, the *New York Times*, *BusinessWeek*, *Fortune*, *Money*, *Fast Company*, the *Economist*, and *Publishers Weekly*, and appeared on the *Today* show, CNN, CBS, ABC, PBS, and other popular media. Bolles keynoted hundreds of conferences, including the American Society for Training & Development and the National Career Development Association. A member of Mensa, the Society for Human Resource Management, and the National Resume Writers Association, he was considered "the most recognized job-hunting authority on the planet" (*San Francisco Chronicle*) and "America's top career expert" (*AARP*).

Time magazine chose *What Color Is Your Parachute?* as one of the hundred best nonfiction books written since 1923. The Library of Congress chose it as one of twenty-five books down through history that have shaped people's lives. It appeared on the *New York Times* bestseller list for more than five years. The book has sold ten million copies, to date, and has been translated into twenty languages and used in twenty-six countries.

Bolles was trained in chemical engineering at Massachusetts Institute of Technology, and earned a bachelor's degree cum laude in physics from Harvard University, a master's in sacred theology from General Theological (Episcopal) Seminary in New York City, and three honorary doctorates. He passed away in 2017 at age ninety after a lifetime of service to job-hunters across the world.

Website: www.jobhuntersbible.com
Online tools: www.eparachute.com

Index

Additional Helpful Resources

A slender guide to writing a winning resume and cover letter that will help you land interviews, by Richard N. Bolles.

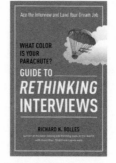

A slender guide to help you ace the interview and land your dream job, by Richard N. Bolles.

Richard N. Bolles presents advice tailored for high schoolers, by Carol Christen, a *Parachute* expert and teenage specialist.

Internet job-search tips from Mark Emery Bolles and Richard N. Bolles.

A complete guide for practicing or aspiring career counselors, by Howard Figler and Richard N. Bolles.

Richard N. Bolles presents retirement advice from John E. Nelson, *Parachute* expert and aging specialist.

A fill-in edition of the famous Flower Exercise by Richard N. Bolles.

A quick guide for when time is of the essence, by Richard N. Bolles.

Visit eParachute.com and JobHuntersBible.com

Available from TEN SPEED PRESS
wherever books are sold.
www.tenspeed.com